Leadership Accountability in a Globalizing World

Leadership Accountability in a Globalizing World

Christopher Williams
Centre for International Education and Research (CIER)
University of Birmingham, UK

First published 2006 by
PALGRAVE MACMILLAN
Houndmills, Basingstoke, Hampshire RG21 6XS and
175 Fifth Avenue, New York, N.Y. 10010
Companies and representatives throughout the world.

PALGRAVE MACMILLAN is the global academic imprint of the Palgrave Macmillan division of St. Martin's Press, LLC and of Palgrave Macmillan Ltd. Macmillan® is a registered trademark in the United States, United Kingdom and other countries. Palgrave is a registered trademark in the European Union and other countries.

ISBN-13: 978–1–4039–8696–2
ISBN-10: 1–4039–8696–7

This book is printed on paper suitable for recycling and made from fully managed and sustained forest sources.

A catalogue record for this book is available from the British Library.

Library of Congress Cataloging-in-Publication Data
Williams, Christopher, 1952 Sept. 6–
    Leadership accountability in a globalizing world / Christopher Williams.
      p. cm.
    Includes bibliographical references and index.
    ISBN 1–4039–8696–7 (cloth)
     1. Globalization – Political aspects. 2. Political leadership. I. Title.
JZ1318.W547 2006
327.1—dc22   2005045601

10 9 8 7 6 5 4 3 2 1
15 14 13 12 11 10 09 08 07 06

Printed and bound in Great Britain by
Antony Rowe Ltd, Chippenham and Eastbourne

Contents

5 Prognoses: Changing Relationships   178

6 Conclusion: The Accountability Webs   220

List of Figures

List of Photos

Group I: An era of leadership accountability

1 Headings *in absentia*
2 The anti-corruption 'accountability webs'
3 Global feuding
4 Prime Minister Junichiro Koizumi
5 Changing loyalties
6 Comparative accountability

Group II: Changing power relations

UN 50th anniversary meeting of the General Assembly, 1995

7 Prime Minister PV Narasimha Rao of India
8 President Pasteur Bizimungu of Rwanda
9 President Jean-Bertrand Aristide of Haiti
10 President Jacques Chirac of France
11 Prime Minister Benazir Bhutto of Pakistan
12 Vice-President Taha Marouf of Iraq

UN General Assembly, 1999

13 Alberto Fujimori, President of the Republic of Peru
14 Mohammad Nawaz Sharif, Prime Minister of Pakistan
15 Frederick Chiluba, President of the Republic of Zambia
16 William Jefferson Clinton, President of the United States of America

List of Abbreviations

ADB	Asian Development Bank
AIDS	Acquired immunodeficiency syndrome
AU	African Union
BBC	British Broadcasting Corporation
BCCI	Bank of Credit and Commerce International
BPI	Bribe Payers Index (TI)
CEO	Chief executive officer
CIA	Central Intelligence Agency
CPI	Corruption Perceptions Index (TI)
DIS	Defence Intelligence Staff (UK)
EC	European Commission
ECJ	European Court of Justice
Eta	*Euskadi ta askatasuna* (Basque Homeland and Freedom)
EU	European Union
FAO	Food and Agriculture Organization
GM	Genetically modified
GLRI	Global Leadership Responsibility Index
GNP	Gross national product
GNP	Grand National Party (Korea)
HRW	Human Rights Watch
ICC	International Criminal Court
ICJ	International Court of Justice
ICRC	International Committee of the Red Cross
ICT	Information and communications technology
IISS	International Institute for Strategic Studies
ILO	International Labour Organization
IMF	International Monetary Fund
IPCC	International Panel on Climate Change
ISG	Iraq Survey Group
JIC	Joint Intelligence Committee (UK)
LSE	London School of Economic and Social Sciences
NAB	National Accountability Bureau (Pakistan)
NATO	North Atlantic Treaty Organization
NGO	Non-governmental organization
OECD	Organisation for Economic Co-operation and Development
PLO	Palestinian Liberation Organization

PPT	Permanent People's Tribunal
RUF	Revolutionary United Front (Sierra Leone)
SCR	Security Council Resolution
TI	Transparency International
TNCs	Transnational companies
TUC	Trades Union Congress
UK	United Kingdom
UNEP	United Nations Environment Programme
US	United States of America
VCAP	UN Declaration of Basic Principles of Justice for Victims of Crime and Abuse of Power
VOA	Voice of America
WHO	World Health Organization
WMDs	Weapons of mass destruction
WTO	World Trade Organization

Introduction

> It is dangerous to be right when those in power are wrong.
>
> Voltaire (1694–1778)

One aspect of globalization has received surprisingly little analytical attention – the globalization of leadership accountability. Interest is evident within the media and civil society and among a few of the more astute political and commercial leaders, but generally the significance of the personalization of up-system challenges has not been fully recognized. The evidence presented in *Leadership accountability in a globalizing world* shows that there is a growing realization that political violence, corruption and environmental harm are caused by powerful individuals who can be identified and challenged. And there is similar 'second track' movement across the world challenging local power elites in the public services, workplace, and religious organizations. In previous eras, leaders were unassailable, but now they are being made to answer for their actions, like anyone else. The globalization of personal accountability is catching up with the globalization of personal power.

In ancient Greece, leaders who declared war were morally required to lead their troops into battle. Hindu *dharma* put everyone beneath the law, including kings, as did Magna Carta. But beyond a few traditions of this nature, leaders have not been inclined to see themselves accountable as individuals. They are either above the law as sovereign[1] – *rex non potest peccare* (the king can do no wrong) or they have immunity just because they are leaders – immunity *rationae materiae*. Alternatively, they are mere representatives of a state or organization which, they believe, carries the responsibility for any wrongdoings. Writing in 1915, historian R. Michels was not optimistic about change:

> Historical evolution mocks all the prophylactic measures that have been adopted for the prevention of oligarchy. If laws are passed to control the dominion of the leaders, it is the laws which gradually weaken, and not the leaders.[2]

But Michels was talking about the era of 'great men' leadership. *Leadership accountability in a globalizing world* argues that the situation is now evolving. This view stems from the development of a proposed 'Code for Global Leadership' at the United Nations University Leadership Academy in 2001,[3] which brought together the ethics and norms that are now being applied to challenge and question powerful individuals. This new book explains a significant era in world history when leaders are becoming more accountable to their populations, to the international community, and to themselves.

The first purpose of the book is to provide the basis for developments within leadership training and education. Future leaders, at all levels, will need to recognize the dynamics of global accountability and learn how to respond. They will need to be persuaded that there are now new and personalized forms of up-system accountability emerging. There is certainly need for concern. A Gallup survey for the World Economic Forum in 2004 found that 52 per cent of those polled believed that political leaders 'behave unethically' and 63 per cent think they are 'dishonest'.[4] Serving and potential leaders need to understand how to avoid 'cumulative lock-in' which can trap them in self-destructive downward spirals of deceit and improper conduct, and the nature and power of contemporary 'social impetus' that may challenge their actions. More broadly, they need to consider the inevitable consequence of leadership that is seen as unaccountable or improper, the loss of moral authority. Leadership training usually focuses on technical matters – 'doing things right'. The purpose of understanding accountability is the ethical side – 'doing the right things'.[5]

The second purpose of the book is the other side of the same coin – to provide the bases for legitimate global civil society movements. The aim is not only to facilitate effective and appropriate action, but also to encourage action that is itself morally defensible and accountable. In the future, civil society organizations and leaders should not be predator and prey. They should be addressing a common problem – the abuse of power by 'any person in any place, anywhere, at any time'.[6] The aim of the book is not to fuel wars for or against accountability. It is to evolve global leadership accountability into a global public good.

The chapters in this book address the obvious questions. What has happened so far, and what is happening now? Why is it happening? How is it happening? What are the likely future outcomes? The first chapter considers the three basic sectors of accountability at the present time – political violence, corruption and environmental security – and the significance of immunity. Increasingly, 'dormant precedents' are being applied and extended internationally within and across these sectors. The chapter also proposes that a concept used during the UK House of Lords hearing concerning General Pinochet – the 'public order of the international community' – might provide a broad framework for future developments. Chapter 2 looks especially at the phenomenon of global feuding – 'regime change' and 'retributive accountability' – and events surrounding the attacks of 11 September 2001 provide a case study. The prevailing perception of US and British leaders involved in the invasion of Iraq was that they practised deceit, and this seemed an inevitable consequence of the 'cumulative lock-in' that trapped them into an increasingly problematic situation. One paradoxical outcome is that history may view the 'terrorists' who employ 'instruments of mass effect' as more progressive because their means of retributive accountability caused less harm than those of the national leaders – they moved towards 'de-linking war from violence'.

Chapter 3 proposes an explanation for the current strength of the accountability movement. It addresses the question of why there is now such a concern about the conduct of 'distant others' by 'disinterested others'. The answer is presented in the form of a 'social impetus–trends theory' which builds on the idea of 'cumulative lock-in' and links aspects of leadership, evolutionary and global information theories. This proposes that contemporary social impetus will create a new and forceful global dynamic that will challenge leaders at all levels, particularly those whose decisions appear to be belief-based. Chapter 4 considers the role of global civil society, and how the new accountability non-governmental organizations (NGOs) use social strategies and sanctions to personalize protest. They are constructing challenges on a case-by-case basis, and reflecting the multiple loyalties of the actors. But the chapter concludes on a cautionary note about the danger of creating scapegoats and collateral damage, and the need for 'smart accountability'.

Chapter 5 considers future developments and the probable changes in power relationships between leaders and those they have traditionally seen as followers. What are the issues that will concern the accountability movement in the near future, and who is identifying them? Journalists and historians are closing the 'time gap' through which despots often evade identification. Deceit will remain central in the future, as it has in the past, but it seems probable that laws will evolve to address 'causing harm by deceiving a population'. The discussion then considers the possible shifts in relative moral authority between nations – might the East take on the moral authority claimed by the West for the past half-century? It also proposes a Global Leadership Responsibility Index to track future change, and this seems to present American leadership in a very poor light, below China, Japan and South Korea. Then on an institutional level, what are the probable influences of the accountability movement on democratic processes? It seems likely that 'direct democratic accountability' will be seen as more important than voting systems, particularly within emergent forms of global governance. The conclusions summarize how the world community is constructing 'accountability webs' that may not be knowingly linked but which share common aims and are therefore mutually reinforcing. It also provides a vision of how a global senior citizenry may become a significant part of leadership accountability in the future.

An Era of Leadership Accountability

The Nuremberg and Tokyo war crimes trials marked the start of an era of leadership accountability, which has addressed abuses of power for political violence, corruption, and environmental victimization. Because these three sectors have not been viewed together, the significance of this global trend has not been fully appreciated. If the tradition of 'one law for the rich and another law for the poor' is redressed, the legitimacy of justice systems generally will be greatly enhanced.

1

Hearings *in absentia* – Sam Hinga Norman at the Special Court for Sierra Leone

Sam Hinga Norman was one of the first defendants to appear at the Special Court for Sierra Leone, but he refused to attend further and the trial continued without him. Because of the unwillingness of powerful people to appear in court, trials *in absentia* are likely to gain legitimacy. The European Court of Human Rights and the International Criminal Tribunal for Rwanda (Arusha) have also upheld this principle (Chapter 1).

Photo by permission of the Sierra Leone Special Court, press room.

The anti-corruption 'accountability webs'

Cooperation between the OECD, the International Chamber of Commerce (ICC) and Transparency International (TI) is an example of how 'accountability webs' are created between governmental, commercial and civil society organizations (Chapters 1, 4 and 6). The OECD's Bribery Convention (1999) has been paralleled by the ICC's Commission on Anti-Corruption, TI's Corruption Perceptions Index and the UN Convention against Corruption.

Left to right: **Donald J. Johnston**, OECD Secretary-General, **Caroline Newton**, International Chamber of Commerce (ICC), **François Vincke**, President, Anti-Corruption Commission, ICC, **Fritz Heimann**, Director, Transparency International.

Photo © OECD

Global feuding – the bombed United Nations headquarters in Baghdad

On 19 August 2003, an effective and popular UN leader, Sergio Viera de Mello, and other UN staff were killed in this attack. Those responsible did not seem to acknowledge the distinction between the US and the UN, just as the US had not acknowledged the distinction between the Iraqi population and the al-Qaida operatives responsible for the 9/11 attacks. Traditional feuding has a retributive 'eye-for-an-eye' logic and operates within rational codes, but the rationale of global feuding is often distorted by all parties (Chapter 2).

UN Photo UNE 3749

Prime Minister Junichiro Koizumi

In 2004, a Japanese court found Prime Minister Junichiro Koizumi's visits to the Yasukuni shrine unconstitutional. This resulted from a case brought by 211 private citizens who were relatives of war victims. It is unprecedented for the Japanese public to bring a prime minister to account in this way. Koizumi did not make a customary visit to the shrine on the 60th anniversary of the end of the Second World War, in 2005.

UN photo 91882/Joshua Kristal

5
Changing loyalties

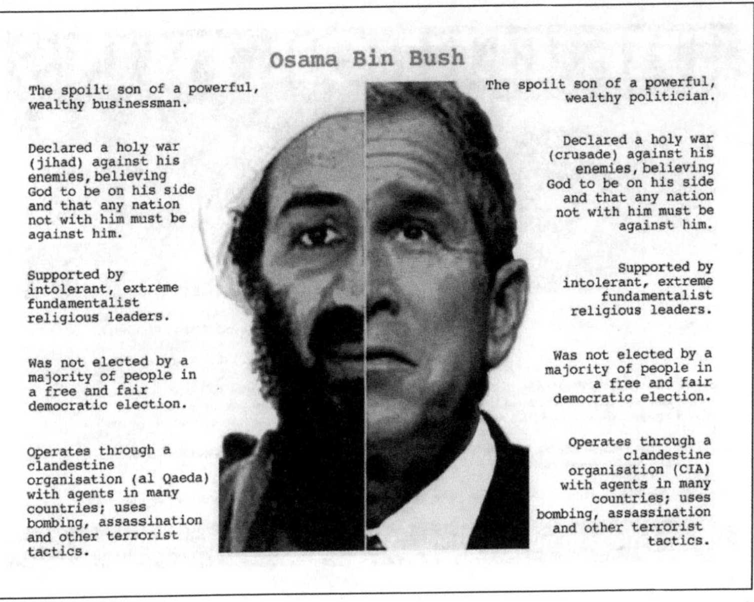

Accountability challenges are now being made on a case-by-case basis about specific conduct, and reflect multiple, not traditional, loyalties. The leaders involved in the events surrounding 9/11 were all trying to hold each other to account, and were all challenged. This was denied by political leaders, but the paradox was not missed by civil society organizations such as Gathered Images, which produced this postcard (Chapters 1, 2 and 4).

Postcard reproduced by permission of Gathered Images – www.gatheredimages.com

Comparative accountability

Future historians may conclude that the 'instruments of mass effect' used by current 'terrorists' were more progressive than the military violence used by state leaders, because this fitted a trend of 'de-linking war and violence' (Chapters 1 and 2). Comparisons are being made between the 3,000 American deaths on 9/11 and the 100,000 who may have died as a result of retaliatory action in Iraq, and with responses to other abuses of power including environmental victimization. The International Campaign for Justice in Bhopal used this image to campaign outside the Indian High Commission in London, in 2002.

Picture credit: http://www.bhopal.net

1
An Era of Accountability

> It seems more natural in a globally framed world than it did in
> a statist world to posit accountability of leaders as an essential
> attribute of a more globalised world order.
>
> Richard Falk[1]

The start of the twenty-first century marked a period of significant questioning of leadership practice and privilege from the international community, civil society and leaders themselves. This has been most apparent in three sectors – political violence, political and economic corruption, and environmental security – but there has also been a significant 'second track' movement, for instance within public services and the workplace. The question of immunity and extradition is relevant across these three sectors and the role of civil society organizations, discussed in Chapter 4, has been central. This is distinct from related concerns. It is not issue-based accountability, for example about poverty or ecological degradation. It is not the down-system accountability of subordinates by superiors within a line-management system. Nor is it purely about political judgement and decision-making. The focus is now about specific wrongdoing for which specific powerful individuals are being brought to account by their peers and populations – personalized up-system leadership accountability.

The change has been noted in many ways. For example, in the UK, Peter Hain, then minister of state at the UK Foreign Office, identified the trend in 2001 when he talked of a new 'globalisation of responsibility'.[2] An opposition counterpart, Lord Howell of Guildford, claimed, 'While in the past, political leaders could get away with [bad] behaviour, we have now moved into a revolutionary new world … Voters want service and ongoing accountability, not dictation and top down arrogance'.[3] From a journalist's perspective Ed Vulliamy, known for his reporting of the conflicts in Central and Southern Europe, chose the word 'reckoning'.[4] Fergal Keane talks of 'something very profound [that] will register among the greatest achievements in the history of humanity' – events 'have forced the world to accept that leaders should be made account-able for the orders they give'.[5] During the 2002 BBC Reith Lectures, philosopher Onora O'Neill talked of 'a revolution in accountability' affecting the public services.[6] As a member of the UN High Level Panel on Threats, Challenges and Change, former Australian foreign minister Gareth Evans mentioned in 2005 the need for a 'serious impunity exer-cise' against violent leaders in Sudan.[7] It is not just that such phrases have been given substance by the very many instances and wide variety of leadership accountability in a short space of time. There were three other striking features. Many of the reports also embody a 'first' of some sort, there has been an astonishing domino effect and, judging by the advanced age of many of those being challenged, accountability processes can no longer simply be timed out by powerful people.

Political violence

> We must make clear to the Germans that the wrong for which their leaders are on trial is not that they lost the war, but that they started it. And we must not allow ourselves to be drawn into a trial of the causes of war, for our position is that no grievances or policies will justify resort to aggressive war. It is renounced and condemned as an instrument of policy.
>
> Supreme Court Justice Robert H. Jackson, USA Senior
> Representative at the 1945 Nuremberg War Crimes
> Trials, and Chief Prosecutor[8]

Following the Second World War, the Nuremberg and Tokyo war crimes trials provided the foundations for an international ethos within which leaders were to be made more accountable to their peers and their pub-lic for political violence. They affirmed the early Geneva Conventions and other proto-international law such as the Lieber Code of 1863,[9] and reflected conclusions such as this from the Carnegie inquiry into the Causes and Conduct of the Balkan Wars in 1912–13 (note the date) which concluded:

> The real culprits ... are not, we repeat, the Balkan peoples ... The true culprits are those who mislead public opinion and take advantage of

the people's ignorance to raise disquieting rumours … inciting their country and consequently other countries into enmity. The real culprits are those who by interest or inclination, declaring constantly that war is inevitable, end by making it so, asserting that they are powerless to prevent it. The real culprits are those who sacrifice the general interest to their own personal interest.[10]

Geoffrey Robertson's *Crimes against humanity* provides a comprehensive discussion of subsequent developments. The main criticism of the Second World War trials was that they amounted to victors' justice. They ignored American and British *prima facie* war crimes such as the fire-bombing of Dresden, and of Japanese cities in which nearly two million civilians died. And there was no chance to question the use of A-bombs which were exploded over Hiroshima and Nagasaki. Although less publicized, North Korea also took firm action against its power elites who had collaborated with Japan during the war. Judicial process may also have been questionable, but the notion that power does not mitigate wrongdoing was similar. It was probably only the Cold War that prevented the impetus of these innovations bringing about a proper international criminal court much earlier. Not least was the problem that many despots were created and supported by the US during this time, including General Pinochet, Saddam Hussein and many of Africa's regimes.

Despite this delay, there were three latent but lasting outcomes from these post-war initiatives. The first was that the new ethic went beyond the idea that holders of high office were to be equally accountable and created a new norm – the abuse of power and trust could now make leaders *more* culpable than others. The second implication stems paradoxically from the fact that the trials were one-sided. Because of this, the new standards set for leadership accountability were ground-breaking and unambiguous. Had the trials been set up to try US, British and other allied crimes, it is unlikely that the standards would have been so progressive. The tribunals created 'dormant precedents' that would resurface after the end of the Cold War. The third and less obvious outcome was that 'the West', in the form of American and British leaders, could claim moral authority on an international level. This was furthered through influence within the new UN, and became an assumed right in the minds of many Western leaders. After the invasion of Iraq, George Bush claimed in 2004: 'America has a responsibility to take a lead in the world, to help people be free.'[11] British prime minister Tony Blair asserted, 'This is literally a fight between the forces of good and the forces of evil.'[12] The possibility that there is now a potential shift in global moral authority away from the Western nations, because of the dynamics of global leadership accountability, is one of the main conclusions from this book.

The contemporary international tribunals

> Specific individuals bear the major share of the responsibility, and it is they, not the group as a whole, who need to be held to account, through fair and meticulously detailed presentation and evaluation of evidence, precisely so that the next time round no one will be able to claim that all the Serbs did this, or all the Croats or all the Tutsis – so that people are able to see how it is specific individuals who are continually endeavouring to manipulate them in that fashion.
>
> Justice Richard Goldstone, South African
> Chief Prosecutor, Arusha Tribunal[13]

The eventual *ad hoc* war tribunals concerning Yugoslavia in The Hague,[14] Rwanda in Arusha and the treaty-based Special Court for Sierra Leone reinstated this post-Second World War ethos. In August 2001, after twenty years' delay, the Cambodian Constitutional Council approved the creation of 'Extraordinary Chambers for the investigation and prosecution of senior Khmer Rouge leaders and others implicated in the atrocities committed between 1975–79', with local and international judges.[15] Also in August 2002, the East Timor war crimes court, operating under UN administration, started work. The Iraq Tribunal was presented to the world as being in the same tradition but it was different in significant ways, as described in the next chapter. But these forums have not created entirely new laws. Acts such as murder, rape, assault and incitement have been criminal in almost every country for centuries. The innovation is that the statutes and structures of the forums can address the nature of these crimes when perpetrated on a massive scale by powerful people. They take account, for example, of chains of command, misuse of public media and power over agents.[16]

Alternative international strategies have reinforced the endeavours of the formal courts and included international sanctions, aid conditionality, suspending relations or quarantining a post, country confinement, travel bans and exile. Sometimes these approaches caused more harm to populations than to despots, but soon the international community was creating 'smart sanctions' that targeted their prey more cleverly.[17]

> ... most of the sanctioned countries are authoritarian regimes that don't give a damn about what the people think ... The whole notion of sanctions affecting the people in order to affect the leadership is invalidated. So, we must make a distinction between generalized sanctions that affect the people more than the leadership and targeted sanctions that affect the leadership more than the people ... sanctions must be efficient ... they must affect the conduct of those who took the decisions which led to condemnation by the international community, not the conduct of those who had no part in it ... *targeting the leadership is crucial, because the leaders do not care about the fate of their own people.*
>
> Juan Somavia, Director General, ILO[18]

The idea of providing remedy to victims was less problematic and reflected little-known standards in the UN Victims of Crime and Abuse of Power Declaration (1985) which requires that 'the victim should receive restitution from the state whose officials or agents were responsible for the harm inflicted'.[19] The European Convention on Human Rights also expects that those who have suffered in relation to a contravention of the Convention 'shall have an effective remedy before a national authority notwithstanding that the violation has been committed by persons acting in official capacity'.[20] The International Covenant is similar.[21]

These initiatives framed the creation of the permanent International Criminal Court (ICC) in April 2002, when the number of states ratifying the treaty reached 60. Under the new US president, George Bush, America then withdrew its support, although the agreement had been signed under President Bill Clinton. This was in contrast to the enthusiastic US engagement with the *ad hoc* tribunals, which included using the threat of withdrawing aid to Yugoslavia to get compliance with court orders. And from a historical perspective, the withdrawal was also in contrast with the fact that the US had to persuade Winston Churchill to set up the Nuremberg court instead of engaging in summary executions of Nazi leaders. The US then blocked aid to 35 countries that had refused to give US personnel immunity from prosecution at the ICC. The chief prosecutor of the Hague Tribunal, Judge Richard Goldstone, commented that the US decision was 'pettiness' as it was 'not going to affect in any way the establishment of the International Criminal Court'.[22] The US found itself in the company of other countries that had not signed – including China,

Yemen, India, Pakistan, Indonesia, Iraq and Turkey – and those that did not ratify – such as Iran, Israel and Russia. One year after its inception in July 2002, 500 cases from 66 countries had been put before the court, although for technical reasons many of these could not be heard. By 2005, the Security Council had asked the court to consider human rights abuses in Dafur, Sudan, the first such decision by the council, and 55 political and other leaders were investigated. This event created an interesting double standard. The US government wanted to respond to the problems in Dafur, yet it did not support the ICC, but it did not veto the Security Council resolution calling for ICC action. By October the ICC had issued its first arrest warrants, for leaders of the Lord's Resistance Army in Uganda.

> The adoption of the [ICC] Statute was a giant step towards universalising the fight against impunity to include every country, every leader, and every militia guilty of crimes against our common humanity.
>
> Kofi Annan, Secretary General of the
> United Nations, 1999[23]
>
> This is about globalized justice … We are going to fill the impunity gap.
> Bruno Cathala, the French judge with responsibility
> for the ICC, at its inception[24]

The *ad hoc* international tribunals achieved landmark decisions in a short space of time, but it would be wrong to assess success only in terms of convictions. These will probably always be a matter of circumstance rather than pure judgement. Ken Roth, the director of Human Rights Watch, makes the point that indictments themselves have a significant effect:

> The experiences of former Yugoslav President Slobodan Milosevic and former Liberian President Charles Taylor suggest that international indictment profoundly discredits even a ruthless, dictatorial leader. That enormous stigma tends to undermine support for a leader, both at home and abroad, often in unexpected ways.[25]

The effect of the courts also went beyond a simple extension of national standards to an international level. They set new standards for the accountability of powerful people, which many nations had not achieved, particularly in relation to the abuse of women. In February 2001, three Bosnian Serbs were convicted of systematic rape and sexual slavery. This was the first conviction for sexual offences as crimes against humanity. And at Arusha, the trial of Akayesu, in relation to the rape of thousands of Tutsi women, set another precedent for the prosecution of sexual violence as an aspect of genocide in Africa. Sierra Leone became the first court to hold that forced marriage of so-called 'bush wives' to enemy combatants was a crime against humanity.

The Yugoslavia Tribunal had come about as the result of a footnote in the report of an otherwise abortive international conference about Yugoslavia in 1992.[26] The note had been added by the Germans, who were probably more aware of the dormant precedents of the Nuremberg trials. In May 1997, Dusko Tadiic became the first person to be convicted for crimes against humanity at The Hague, and by 2001 the tribunal had sentenced 14 Bosnian Serb, Croat and Muslim suspects. The domino effect was astonishing. In January 2001, former president Biljana Plavsic became the highest-ranking Bosnian Serb official, and the first woman, to face charges. The 'Iron Lady' made the first guilty plea from a well-known leader. Three months later Bosnian Serb commander Dragan Obrenovic was arrested and charged with the killing of 5,000 Muslims at Srebrenica, the worst massacre in Europe since the Second World War. Slobodan Milosevic became the first head of state to appear at the tribunal, and later the first to be tried for genocide. The same day, the former Serbian president Milan Milutinovic surrendered himself to the court. The next week, the Bosnian Serb government instigated legislation to permit the arrest of war crimes suspects including Radovan Karadzic and Ratko Mladic, and the Croatian government agreed to hand over two war crimes suspects from the army. The impetus became so evident that leaders such as Plavsic and former Bosnian Serb mayor Blagoje Simic surrendered themselves voluntarily to the court. The court's power was furthered when, in March 2001, the Serb police made their first arrest of a suspected war criminal, former mayor Milomir Stakic, on behalf of the tribunal. The Bosnian police made their first arrests in August, a few hours after Serb general Radislav Krstic became the first person to be convicted of genocide since the Nuremberg trials. His 46-year prison sentence was the longest handed out by the tribunal.

These events showed how the courts could be reinforced by alternative international strategies and coordinated incremental 'smart sanctions'.[27] Before the presidential elections, in September 2000, the EU promised to lift sanctions if Milosevic was voted out of power, and that happened. He was questioned about an infringement of planning law, arrested for abuse of power and corruption, and then also accused of shooting at the police who were arresting him. In 2001, the Hague Tribunal's chief prosecutor Carla Del Ponte put pressure on the new

Yugoslav government to hand over Milosevic by the end of March. This coincided with the US Congress decision about continuing a $100 million aid package to Yugoslavia. Human Rights Watch called for the EU to tie its aid to a promise that the Yugoslav government would cooperate with the UN War Crimes Tribunal,[28] and then wrote to US secretary of state Colin Powell, making a similar argument in relation to a forthcoming donors' conference.[29] Milosevic was sent to the Hague court early in the morning of 29 June, the day of a multilateral meeting in Brussels to discuss aid for Yugoslavia, which the US had threatened to boycott if Milosevic was not handed over. The subsequent change in Yugoslav law in April 2002, to permit hand-overs to the Hague Tribunal, was consequent upon the US freezing $40 million of the promised aid.

Symbiotic with bringing senior leaders to trial is that other senior leaders will be called as witnesses. In April 2002, Kosovo president Ibrahim Rugova became the most senior politician to give evidence at The Hague. He accused Milosevic of oppressing Kosovo Albanians, and of triggering the 1998–99 war. In the same month, the Yugoslav government had passed a law permitting extraditions to The Hague. General Dragoljub Ojdanc, the head of the military under Milosevic, surrendered to the tribunal, along with five others, including the former deputy prime minister Nikola Sainovic for his 'command responsibility'. Kosovo's prime minister, Ramush Haradinaj, was then forced to resign in March 2005 when the court called him to account for war crimes.

In Arusha, in September 1998, Jean Kambanda, the former Rwandan prime minister, entered the first guilty plea to an international court, and became the first head of state to be convicted by a tribunal. In 2003, the court made its first conviction of a church leader, Elizaphan Ntakirutimana, for genocide. The tribunal also became the first court to try journalists for war crimes, since the trial of Nazi publisher Julias Streicher, publisher of the anti-Semitic paper *Der Stuermer*. Three media executives were accused of genocide and inciting genocide through radio broadcasts and newspapers. This set a precedent about using false information to cause harm to a population, which is discussed further in Chapter 5. By August 2003, the court had convicted 100 people, following a two-year mass trial for crimes against humanity. The impetus continued when four former Rwandan ministers went on trial for inciting the slaughter of 800,000 people, in November 2003. In 2004, Pasteur Bizimungu, Rwanda's first post-genocide president, was sentenced to 15 years in prison for creating a militia and inciting ethnic violence.

The first to appear at the East Timor court was the former governor of the territory, Abbilio Soares, who was called to account for the conduct of his subordinates, and later given a three-year prison sentence for failing to prevent mass murder. In 2003, Brigadier Noer Moeis became the highest-ranking military leader to be convicted at an Indonesian court, and Sriyanto Muntrasan, head of Kopassus, the notorious special forces, was charged with the massacre of civilians twenty years earlier. In May 2004 it indicted General Srianto Wiranto, an Indonesian militarist commander wanted for war crimes. He was running for presidency at the time. Human rights organizations were concerned that most convictions were overturned on appeal, including those of General Sriyanto and Abbilio Soares. But a healthy appeals process symbolizes that a court errs properly on the side of caution – it is not victors' justice – and this is likely eventually to strengthen public trust in the system.

Sierra Leone was the first tribunal to be constituted through direct agreement between a local government and the UN, with Sierra Leonean and UN judges sitting together. And it was the first to be based where the atrocities happened. By May 2005, it had started hearing cases against the Revolutionary United Front (RUF) leaders, including the military chief, Issa Sesay. These men had overseen 50,000 killings and extreme violence including widespread mutilations, rape and sexual slavery of children and women. For his role in funding the RUF, Liberian president Charles Taylor faced 17 charges, and went into hiding in Nigeria.

The world's media were so absorbed by Milosevic that the arrest of Sylvestre Gacumbitsi in the same week was hardly noticed. Gacumbitsi, a former Rwandan mayor, was alleged to have supervised the murder of thousands of people. Charges against him included allegations that he had personally stabbed a pregnant Tutsi woman and dragged the foetus from her body. The global reach of the Arusha Tribunal was made apparent two weeks later when three suspects were arrested in Switzerland, Belgium and Holland, and transferred to Tanzania. Whatever the apparent difficulties, international justice had evolved from simply resolving disputes between nations to holding individuals accountable for harm – irrespective of their nationality or status, or where they hide.

By October 2004 Cambodia's parliament had finally ratified the legislation to set up the tribunal with three Cambodian and two UN judges. The ongoing power of Khmer Rouge leaders may subvert the intent of the court, but the symbolism of the endeavour was important, not least because it showed that such initiatives could not be timed out by obfuscation. At the start of 2004, Khmer Rouge leader Khieu Samphan accepted that there had been genocide, but pleaded ignorance. He claimed, 'I have found it difficult to believe what people told me of what happened under the Khmer Rouge regime ... I never conspired with any senior Khmer Rouge leaders to kill the people of Cambodia ... Within the regime I was only a leader in name.'[30] His defence bears uncanny resemblance to that of Albert Speer, Hitler's minister of armaments, at the Nuremberg Trial.

Perhaps the most interesting tribunal was in North Korea, and it received little attention from the West. In July 2003, the Pyongyang International Tribunal on US Crimes in Korea charged all US presidents from Harry Truman to George W. Bush with war crimes, particularly during the 1950–53 conflict. The endeavour was not entirely theatrical. The judges were from outside Korea, chaired by Jitendra Sharma, the president of the International Association of Democratic Lawyers. Prosecutors included Beth S. Lyons of the International Association of Democratic Lawyers at the UN.[31] The judgment was seemingly based on mainstream international law, the resultant 'verdict' was more moderated than the familiar North Korean rhetoric, and its use of 'Koreans' rather than 'North Koreans' throughout seems an interesting attempt to unify Korea against the US (Figure 1.1). The significance of the event is that it symbolizes that North Korean leaders accept the common ethics of global accountability for war crimes. They may be setting yet more dormant precedents but, whether or not their own standards are eventually used against them, the initiative is part of a broader reassessment of the history of international abuse of power in the North East Asia region.

These judicial initiatives were paralleled by firmer forms of accountability under the concept of 'humanitarian intervention'. French and subsequent UN intervention in the Democratic Republic of Congo aimed to prevent factional leaders killing thousands more innocent people. French and West African armies enforced a peace plan in Liberia and Côte d'Ivoire. Such interventions were approved, although not initially sanctioned, by the UN, and legitimate local governments eventually supported them. Intervention in Kosovo and Afghanistan seemed to reflect this trend, but then the invasion and occupation of Iraq broke the pattern because it did not gain formal international support. The distinction was not missed by the international community and civil society, which then rounded on the leaders of the countries responsible for the invasion, US president George Bush and British prime minister Blair, and others in Australia and Spain. This seemed to demonstrate that the new ethos of accountability for political violence was being built on objective global principles, not the ethics of victors' justice, and this change is discussed further in the next chapter.

> Something very profound has happened in the past decade, a movement so significant that it will register among the greatest achievements in the history of humanity. The horrors of Yugoslavia and Rwanda have forced the world to accept that leaders should be made accountable for the orders they give; the myth that genocide and war crimes are merely the consequence of atavistic hatred has been exploded. Ever since Nuremberg the law has said war crimes are the responsibility of political and military leaders. But with [the arrests of Milosevic and Gacumbitsi] the law at last showed that it had teeth.
>
> Fergal Keane, 2001[32]

The international panel of judges of the Pyongyang International Tribunal on U.S. Crimes in Korea announced its verdict on July 25. According to the verdict, the international panel of judges considered that all the criminal acts committed by the United States in Korea from 1945 to 2003 are grave violations of the UN Charter, the Universal Declaration of Human Rights, the charter and the principles of the international military tribunal of Nuremberg, the codes on crimes against human peace and security, the 1949 Geneva and other international conventions, regulations and principles, and held that the U.S. government should bear full responsibility for them. The verdict reads:

1. The U.S. government and the other accused mentioned in the indictment are guilty of the charges leveled by the prosecution and detailed in the indictment submitted to the tribunal.
2. The U.S. government must make an official apology for all its criminal acts committed in Korea, and make due compensation for the physical, mental and material losses inflicted upon the Korean people.
3. The U.S. must find out all those involved in planning, preparation, organization, instruction, execution and backing of the crimes against the Korean people, and punish them as criminal offenders.
4. The U.S. must enact a relevant law for it to assume full responsibility for its crimes on the Korean Peninsula, and establish a special institution in Congress and the Administration with a mandate to investigate and address this issue.
5. The U.S. government must immediately abandon its hostile policy towards the DPRK, put an end to its military threat against it, sign a non-aggression treaty with it, and settle the issue of peace on the Korean peninsula in a peaceful way through DPRK–U.S. talks.
6. The U.S. must immediately pull out its troops and all nuclear weapons from the south of Korea, and end its political pressure on, economic sanctions and blockade, and psychological warfare against the DPRK.
7. The U.S. government must refrain from interfering in the internal affairs of Korea, contrary to the will of the Korean people to reunify the country by the Korean nation itself in a peaceful way, true to the June 15 North–South Joint Declaration.

This verdict has been reached on the basis of objective and fair principles concerning the setting up of their tribunal and its procedures and the U.S. government has a legal and moral obligation to take practical measures in this regard.

Figure 1.1 Verdict of Pyongyang International Tribunal on US crimes

Source: International Action Centre. www.iacentre.org/Koreafiles/pyongyang-verdict.htm

National accountability

Reflecting the innovations within the international tribunals, domestic judiciaries conspicuously started to extend their remit beyond national borders and normal time limitations to address political violence. However effective the ICC and related tribunals become, their scale of operations will always be limited. It is therefore important that national courts become the primary means to redress international and national crime by power elites. National courts can operate on a much bigger scale than international forums, and that will probably continue to be the case. The international Arusha Tribunal is only trying around fifty of the key perpetrators of genocide, whereas the Rwandan courts have arrested more than 130,000 suspects and are hearing 600 cases a year. In Rwanda, a compromise system has evolved to deal with the insurmountable number of cases awaiting trial at local courts for more than seven years. At the traditional *Gechacha* ('grass') courts, defendants are brought before a mass meeting in their local community, and court officials hear evidence and make decisions, often with the aid of a megaphone. Traditionally this has been restricted to domestic disputes, but in June 2002 President Paul Kagame formally extended the remit of the courts, which brought into action 250,000 new judges who could impose life sentences, working across 11,000 jurisdictions and dealing with 115,000 defendants. The courts demonstrated their international remit when they arrested and tried a Belgian priest, Father Guy Theunis, for alleged incitement to genocide, in 2005. Initiatives like these will leave the international courts free to tackle cases that cannot be brought in national courts, or to deal with novel circumstances where precedents need to be established.

Since the mid-twentieth century, there have been many milestones marking the trajectory of leadership accountability. Vietnam was, of course, central. The public challenge to the US invasion and atrocities included the belief that President Lyndon Johnson had lied about the Tomkin Incident, which was essentially a fiction but justified the war. Questionable government 'dossiers' had been produced, which argued that 'counter-terrorism' initiatives were needed against the Vietnamese. Eventually even US secretary of defense Robert McNamara changed his mind and became doubtful about the motives and value of the war. The uncovering of the so-called Watergate scandal, from 1972 to 1974, provided a significant message to world leaders about changing pubic attitudes. The disclosure of the Pentagon Papers by Defense Department analyst Daniel Ellsberg, which evidenced American political deceit concerning four US presidents in relation to the Vietnam war, were followed up through investigations by two *Washington Post* reporters, and finally by a Senate committee. Attempts were made to deter Ellsberg and others through a case for treason against him, which collapsed but would have carried a prison sentence of 115 years. The eventual outcomes included convictions of several White House aides and the impeachment of President Nixon.

The trials of military leaders in Greece and Argentina were less opaque than events in the US, and were seen as part of an ongoing trend. Sir Nigel Rodley, of the UN Human Rights Committee, concluded:

> These years have seen a growing awareness that individuals and rulers can be held to account for their actions … it is significant that before they were toppled, Argentina's military dictators in the late 1970s and early 1980s talked of their fears of ending up in a Nuremberg-style trial.[33]

There were other landmark events. For example, Ferdinand Marcos, 'Baby Doc' Duvalier and Nicolae Ceausescu were all eventually overthrown by popular democratic movements in their own countries, and they had all at some point been supported by US leaders. By March 2004, Serbia had held its first war crimes trial, of six Serbs charged with killing 200 civilians. There were reservations that the court would try to apportion blame to those who carried out orders and ignore those who gave the orders. But the broader message that obeying orders is no defence was reinforced.

Although less acknowledged internationally, South Korea provided another significant example. During the first decades of the new country's history, the political and military rulers were usually brutal and corrupt. Then in 1996 former president Roh Tae Woo was sentenced to 22 years in prison for corruption, mutiny and treason by a Seoul court, and former president Chun Doo Hwan was sentenced to death for his additional involvement in the massacre of Kwangiu students and other demonstrators in 1980.[34] Like Nixon, both were eventually pardoned, but the trial marked a new era of greater leadership accountability in the country. This was part of a growing challenge to the claim that democracy and human rights were incompatible with successful development, which had been promoted by many post-war leaders in East Asia for the purpose of maintaining their power. These events in South Korea are not widely known because the Korean dictators had been supported by the US. In 2005 there were indications of a new public uprising in North Korea. Videos were found containing slogans such as 'Down with Kim Jong IL! People let's rise up and drive out the dictatorship.' This type of action is completely new in the post-war North.[35]

Within less punitive frameworks, the truth and reconciliation commissions and tribunals in around twenty countries, notably within South America and South Africa, have also demonstrated a continued will to address serious crime by political and military despots.[36,37] Other restorative initiatives included the Indonesian Human Rights Commission (KOMNAS), which has been working with the UN since 1997, and the Nigerian Human Rights Commission which has particular relevance for the Ogoni people and to the judicial killing of their leader Ken Saro-Wiwa. The Nigerian president, Olusegun Obasanjo, set an example by giving evidence to the Commission and he urged other leaders to follow. Ghana's National Reconciliation Commission, which was set up to investigate military abuses from 1979 to 1981, had the powers of a high court, and was closely modelled on the South African initiatives. In 2004, it summoned former president Jerry Rawlings to give evidence. Under Vojislav Kostunica's influence, a similar forum was set up in Yugoslavia in April 2001, and the idea was also proposed in relation to Northern Ireland but not pursued. Indonesia then set up a truth and reconciliation panel to investigate thousands of killings and abductions under the Suharto regime, which have never been mentioned in the country's official history books.

The principle of restorative justice – 'truth for amnesty' – has provided a pragmatic approach for new governments that have taken over from despotic regimes. The idea that citizens should 'know but not punish' their despotic leaders was also evident in Central and Eastern European countries such as Hungary. Public records have been made freely available, and families and communities have been able to identify and document officials who abused their power. Later Mexico adopted a similar approach when, in June 2002, millions of secret files, relating to human rights abuses, were made public.

From a Western viewpoint, truth and reconciliation is commonly criticized as the triumph of expediency over justice.[38] But this does not perhaps acknowledge the traditional roots of a restorative approach.[39] Back in 1968 Michael Barkun started to question the unassailable image of Western-style justice in the book *Law without sanctions.*[40] John Braithwaite describes characteristics of indigenous restorative justice:[41]

- disapproval while sustaining a relationship of respect
- ceremonies to certify deviance terminated by ceremonies to decertify deviance
- disapproval of an evil deed without labelling the person as evil
- deviance is not allowed to become a master status trait.

These seem remarkably applicable to the conundrums of leadership accountability in both the traditional and modern worlds.

Desmond Tutu, the principle actor in restorative justice in post-apartheid South Africa, provides a compelling yet balanced argument:

> In forgiving, people are not being asked to forget. On the contrary, it is important to remember, so that we should not let such atrocities happen again. Forgiveness does not mean condoning what has been done. It means ... drawing out the sting in the memory that threatens to poison our existence ... It involves trying to understand the perpetrators and so to have empathy, to try to stand in their shoes, and to appreciate the sort of pressures and influences that might have brought them to what they did.[42]

But the South African experience is not quite as optimistic as many advocates would claim. It seems that while those within religious circles accepted the ethos, there was less impact on the standard view within mainstream thought that justice intrinsically entails retribution.[43] South Africa's demonstration of truth and reconciliation often overshadows another interesting attempt, in Mozambique. At the end of the civil war in 1992, leaders from both sides agreed not to copy the Rwandan tribunal model, nor to adopt the South African approach in its original form. The aim of social peace and reintegration into village life was facilitated by reconciliation ceremonies by traditional healers.

In 2000, Haiti's courts made a number of convictions concerning the 'Raboteau massacre' during the country's 1991–94 dictatorship, including 37 senior officials who were convicted *in absentia*. The next year, Mayan communities filed the first lawsuit in Central America to accuse a sitting politician of genocide. It was claimed that the head of congress, Efrain Rios Montt, carried out racial extermination policies in the civil war in the 1980s. Earlier in June, the former Guatemalan head of military intelligence, Colonel Disrael Lima, his son, Captain Byron Lima, Sergeant José Obdulio Villanueva and a priest were convicted of the murder of a Roman Catholic bishop in 1998 and imprisoned for 30 years. Bishop Juan José Gerardi was killed after presenting a report, *Never again*. It concluded that government forces committed 90 per cent of the 200,000 deaths and other atrocities during the civil war.[44] The next month, the former president of Argentina, Carlos Menem, and three senior members of his 1989–99 administration were indicted concerning illegal arms sales to Croatia and Ecuador,[45] and Serbia announced the setting up of its own war crimes court. By April 2004, an arrest warrant had been issued for Menem, then aged 73, concerning corruption charges. The idea that leaders are responsible for the crimes of their subordinates was then reinforced through the civil courts in El Salvador, in July 2002. It was agreed that two generals living in the US, Casanova and Garcia, had ignored acts of brutality carried out by their troops twenty years earlier, and should pay damages to the victims of torture. Then 2004 saw the trial of one of those responsible for the assassination of El Salvador's Archbishop Romero. No proceedings had been instigated during the previous 24 years following his death. This was a civil case against Alvarvo Saravia who was implicated with the leaders of the death squads. The case was brought through a court in California, and demonstrated that time and place were no longer barriers to accountability. Later the former Nicaraguan president, Arnoldo Aleman, was tried in Florida for money-laundering.

In July 2004, Italy then delved back into its history and trials were started in relation to the fascist massacres in the village of Sant'Anna di Stazzema, in 1944. The end of Cold War politics, the demise of the old political elites and ground-breaking corruption trials against senior politicians in the country left the way clear for a reassessment of what had happened during the Second World War. The accused had been senior military leaders and were all in their eighties, and extradition from their hiding place in Germany seemed unlikely. But the symbolic importance of the trial was important, and at last 'Italy's Nuremberg' which, in the minds of local people, had been delayed for half a century, could take place.[46] Ten former Nazi SS members were eventually convicted for killings that had happened 61 years ago.

Throughout East Asia, there were numerous small but significant signs of change. In 2004 a Japanese court made the first compensation payment to other Asians for wartime abuses. The victims were Chinese and had been used as forced labourers in northern Japan in 1944, by

Nishimatsu Construction. This was then overturned on the grounds that too much time had expired, but then reversed again by the Hiroshima High Court. The judge ruled that the statute of limitations 'seriously goes against justice'.[47] People in Hiroshima understand that victimization in the modern world can take a long time to redress. This judgment also challenged a long-standing argument that the post-war peace agreements annulled responsibility for compensation, and followed a previous formal apology to Korea for the wartime abuse of Korean 'comfort women' by Japanese military leaders. A week later, another Japanese court ruled for the first time that Prime Minister Junichiro Koizumi's visits to the Yasukuni shrine, which honours Japanese war criminals, was unconstitutional. This resulted from a case brought by 211 private citizens who were relatives of war victims. It is unprecedented for the Japanese public to hold a prime minister to account in this way. On the 60th anniversary of the end of the Second World War Koizumi did not make a customary visit to the shrine, but expressed 'deep remorse' for the 'tremendous suffering' that Japan's colonial leaders had inflicted on Asia.

One further aspect of North East Asia is important to consider. Like Europe, since the Second World War, the political leaders in the region have 'de-linked war from violence'.[48] There are major ongoing disputes in the region – the Korean peninsula, Japan and Russia, China and Taiwan, and Japan's difficult relationships with both Koreas and China – but in the past half-century there have been very few related deaths. America would claim this as an outcome of its regional foreign policy, and this has an element of truth. But North Korea demonstrates that the US has little real power in the region in the face of a determined challenge. Perhaps the de-linking ethos stems from deeper regional beliefs about war and leadership, such as that expressed in *The art of war* by Sun Tzu 2,500 years ago:[49] 'The supreme act of war is to subdue the enemy without fighting.'

Extending jurisdiction

National courts have slowly extended their reach beyond their traditional national jurisdiction. Since the Second World War, at least a dozen nations have implemented the principle of universal jurisdiction through national courts.[50] Initially this mainly concerned Nazi war crimes. The Israeli courts set the precedent in 1961 when they tried and convicted Adolf Eichmann for crimes against humanity in Europe. Paul Touvier became the first Frenchman to be convicted of war crimes.

His SS patron, Klaus Barbie, was returned from Bolivia to France in 1983 and jailed for crimes against humanity. They died in prison. Maurice Papon, jailed in 1998 for complicity in war crimes, was released in 2002 on health grounds following apparent intervention by Jacques Chirac. But by this time the French public had been made aware of his relationship with the French elites since the war. His record included overseeing the repression of an Algerian demonstration in 1961, in which 200 protestors were killed. In 1999, a Zagreb court sentenced Dinko Sakic, the last known living commander of a concentration camp. In the same month, Austria brought Nazi doctor Heinrich Gross to trial for the alleged killing of over 700 disabled children. Then in June, Anthony Sawoniuk became the first man to be convicted through the UK courts for Nazi war crimes committed in Europe. In April 2001 an 83-year-old SS commander, Julius Viel, was jailed in Germany for murdering Jewish prisoners.

The European Court of Human Rights affirmed the principle of leadership accountability for political violence when, in March 2001, it disallowed an appeal by former East German leader Egon Krenz. He had been convicted by the German courts in relation to his 'decision-making role' and the deaths of people who tried to cross the Berlin Wall. The final trial of former Communist Party officials was a retrial of 74-year-old Has-Joachim Bohme and Seigfried Lorenze, who was 73. They had been cleared by a court in 2000, but in August 2004 this was overruled and they were convicted. Since reunification, the German courts had convicted 126 East Germans including senior politburo members. Erich Honecker, who had built the Berlin Wall in 1961, spent the last years of his life on the run from German prosecutors. An 86-year-old Slovak and Nazi collaborator, Ladislav Niznansky, was charged with murdering 164 civilians, at a Munich court in September 2004. He will probably be the last person to be tried concerning Second World War crimes in Europe. In 2005, the Simon Wiesenthal Center launched 'Operation Last Chance', aimed particularly at bringing to account Nazi leaders based in Eastern Europe. There have been 100,000 indictments and 7,000 convictions for Second World War crimes.

Initiatives extended beyond Nazi crimes. Following the Chilean National Truth and Reconciliation Commission, set up by the government of Patricio Aylwin in 1990, the subsequent case against General Pinochet, initiated by Spain, pursued by Chile and supported technically if not practically by the UK in 1999, provided a sobering warning to all despots that world opinion was changing. He was, in the words of Geoffrey Robertson, 'the first to be held potentially liable to prosecution for a crime against humanity committed in peace time, notwithstanding the cloak of sovereign immunity which the state he headed was determined not to waive'.[51] In Senegal, in February 2000, the former dictator of Chad, Hissein Habré, was indicted for acts contravening the UN Torture Convention. This was the first time an African former head of state had been indicted by the court of another country. In 2005, a Belgian court indicted Habré and applied to extradite him from Senegal.

The US Alien Tort Claims Act of 1789 created what we would now call global jurisdiction and represents one of the most significant 'dormant precedents'. It permits cases to be brought in the US by US nationals and non-nationals on the basis of international law, and its remit appears prescient of a globalized world. It came to world attention in the 1970s during a case concerning torture by a Paraguayan policeman.[52] There is strong resistance to its contemporary use by multinational companies, but one important aspect of this law has not attracted much attention. The right to global jurisdiction has not been *given* to the US by an international court or agency such as the UN. Through an archaic law, the US courts have, in effect, *taken* the right. Any other country could introduce similar legislation at any time – China or Iraq for instance. By 2004, claims were in progress against Unocal, ExxonMobil, Chevron Texaco and Daimler-Chrysler, but none had come to court. A case against a group of garment manufacturers on the Pacific island of Saipan had been settled out of court.

In June 2001, Belgium utilized a new law, passed in 1993 and extended to include genocide in 1999, which permitted the trial of any person for war crimes, committed anywhere. Two Rwandan nuns, a university professor, Vincent Ntezimana, and a former minister, Alphonse Higaniro, were convicted for homicide.[53] All four were arrested while evading the Rwandan authorities by living in Belgium. The success inspired other developments, notably a case against Israeli president Ariel Sharon in relation to alleged crimes against humanity in the villages of Sabra and Shatilla in Lebanon in 1982.[54] Already in March 2000, the court had initiated an investigation into alleged crimes against humanity by former Iranian president Ali Akbar Hashemi-Rafsanjani. The case did not go further, but Rafsanjani stepped down from politics following the 2001 elections.

In February 2003, the Belgian Supreme Court ruled that the war crimes lawsuit against Ariel Sharon could proceed after he lost immunity as prime minister of Israel. Next, in March, seven Iraqi victims of the 1991 Gulf War lodged claims against George Bush senior, Norman

Schwarzkopf, Dick Cheney and Colin Powell, relating to the bombing of Baghdad's Al Amiriya shelter, during which 403 civilians were killed, including 52 children. But by June, the power of the court had frightened the US government sufficiently for Donald Rumsfeld, US defense secretary, to threaten to boycott NATO and to withhold funding for a new office in Brussels, unless the powers of the law were reduced. As he made no distinctions, it might be concluded that Rumsfeld thought the convictions concerning Rwanda were also improper. By July, the Belgian government had decided to replace the 1993 law, but the impetus of the initiative continued. In June 2004, a leader of the Hutu extremist militia group Interahamwe, which had killed 800,000 Tutsis, was detained in Brussels.

Elsewhere in Europe, Spain also took a more global perspective. The judge Baltazar Garzon was a central figure in bringing Pinochet to justice, but in 2003 he also achieved the extradition of the former Argentinian military officer and 'nun killer' Ricardo Miguel Cavallo from Mexico. In January 2005, the trial of an Argentine former navy captain started. Adolfo Scilingo was charged with throwing up to 2,000 political activists to their deaths from airplanes. He was convicted and sentenced to 640 years in prison, which was the first international law ruling of its kind – an individual had been convicted in person for human rights crimes committed in another country. Garzon was also central to the indictment of al-Qaida operatives. By 2003, 24 faced trial, and Osama bin Laden was on the wanted list. In 2005, a Tibetan human rights group started a case in Spain, for genocide and crimes against humanity, against ex-president Jiang Zemin and other Chinese leaders. Britain also extended its jurisdiction through incorporating the torture convention into national law. Faryadi Sarwar Zardad, an Afghan living in south London, became the first to be tried and convicted, for torture and kidnapping perpetrated in Afghanistan. Victims gave evidence from the British Embassy in Kabul, via a video link.

In 1940, Margaret Mead wrote a paper called 'Warfare is only an invention'.[55] During the same decade the UN developed this understanding and affirmed that 'War is made in the minds of men', and it is in the minds of particular 'men' – leaders. War would not happen if powerful people did not make it happen.[56] Over the next sixty years, a pattern of redress for political violence by leaders has emerged across the world. For the first time in history, power and status no longer provide immunity for wrongdoings in the context of conflict; instead it has become a justification for more severe sanctions. International war crimes courts were a novel idea, and paradoxically this victors' justice created strong 'dormant precedents' that came to realize their full potential after the Cold War had ended. International communications and cooperation permitted national courts to implement their latent abilities to extend jurisdiction across borders, another form of 'dormant precedent'. Increasingly, cases cannot be timed out, and age does not deter attempts at redress.

Of equal importance, war crimes against women were for the first time in history being treated seriously. This is not just an equal opportunities nicety. It is a major shift in global ethics. Throughout history, there has been a tacit acceptance of the use and abuse of women as tools of war. Steven Pinker points out that it was even mentioned as an acceptable practice in the Bible.[57] Victors were permitted to take women as prizes of war, and soldiers were permitted to rape as a reward for fighting and as a weapon of terror. That has now changed, and this may have a more significant effect on the way that leaders construct armies and conflict because it removes one of the primary rewards for men to engage in an otherwise unrewarding and potentially suicidal endeavour.

Although there are technical distinctions between international and national courts, in practice their remits are becoming very similar. Both can address serious crimes of national or international nature, borrow precedents from one another, and enforce similar sanctions to redress wrongdoing increasingly anywhere in the world. Most significantly, working in tandem they are increasingly closing the loopholes through which powerful people have evaded justice in the past. The significance of this synergy has not yet been fully noticed.

Political and economic corruption

> Leaders must become more accountable to their peoples. Transactions must become more transparent, and funds must be seen to be properly administered.
>
> World Bank[58]

The initiatives to achieve accountability for political violence have been paralleled in the sphere of political and economic corruption, although observers make no direct link. The end of the Cold War seemed to mark a turning point. From the 1990s, international aid was less obviously a major tool of international security and the aim was more clearly to achieve stated development goals. There was a demand for 'structural adjustment', 'good governance' and other measures by the international donor agencies to increase public service accountability in recipient countries. In 1996, the World Bank's director, James Wolfensohn, had talked of the need to deal with the 'cancer of corruption'. For the previous forty years, few donor countries had even reported to their own parliament about how World Bank money was used.[59] But from the 1990s, the World Bank expressed the view that it 'cannot afford to look the other way when a country is plagued by deeply dysfunctional public institutions that limit accountability, set perverse rules of the game, and are incapable of sustaining development'.[60]

Good governance – the South

The 'good governance' ethos became evident at the national level in diverse ways. India's Central Vigilance Commission developed an innovative home page which permitted direct complaints from the public about corrupt officials.[61] Kenya set up a similar initiative, the Electronic Graft Management project, under the Kenya Anti-Corruption Authority. It planned to use youth volunteers to inform the public about the use of the e-accountability system.[62] Thailand's new Constitution created the National Counter Corruption Commission, and in the wake of this, in March 2000, the country's powerful interior minister and secretary-general of the ruling party was required to resign from the cabinet and was banned from political activities for five years.[63] By 2003, International Monetary Fund (IMF) pressure culminated in the setting up of a formal anti-corruption commission in Indonesia, which at the time was ranked among the ten most corrupt countries in the world by Transparency International.

A decade on from the end of the Cold War, the turn of the millennium seemed pivotal. In September 2000, the seemingly invincible President Fujimori of Peru had promised to stand down because of a corruption scandal which heralded his subsequent exile in Japan and the issue of an international arrest warrant by Peru. One year later he was charged with murder. By interesting coincidence, both Japan and Peru had passed new anti-corruption laws by the end of 2000, in Japan even prohibiting dinners between public officials and business friends. In August, Nigeria's Senate president was impeached for corruption and other Senate members resigned.[64] In October, one week after the fall of Slobodan Milosevic, Joseph Estrada became the first Philippine president to be impeached through Senate. He was charged with corruption, bribery, betrayal of public trust and culpable violation of the constitution. At the same moment, a parliamentary committee in Indonesia was hearing evidence about financial corruption implicating President Wahid. The evidence was formally accepted five months later, leading to his subsequent impeachment. Within two years Wahid had become the first democratically elected leader of Indonesia, and the first to be impeached. In November, forty corrupt government officials were sacked for bribery in Burma,[65] and an Azerbaijani court jailed 16 senior government officials for embezzlement, including two former ministers.[66] Events just in the final month of 2000 showed the increasing diversity and global spread of the challenge to errant leadership. Brown Mpinganjira, Malawi's former transport minister, was charged with corruption. A Chinese police chief, Yu Ding, was sentenced to death for taking bribes to ignore local crime. A former head of the antiquities department in Lebanon was jailed for embezzlement.[67] A top Russian general, in charge of finance at the defence ministry, was charged in connection with the loss of four hundred million dollars.[68]

Within South East Asia, Imelda Marcos is not now just remembered for her hundreds of pairs of shoes. Her name lives on because of the hundred or so charges made against her, concerning misuse of public office, her conviction in 1998, even though it was later reversed on a technicality,[69] and her subsequent rearrest in October 2001 in connection with money-laundering. The corruption conviction of Malaysia's deputy prime minister, Anwar Ibrahim, in 1999, which was upheld by the appeal court in 2002, demonstrated the ongoing determination of the courts in Malaysia. In August 2000, the Indonesian Attorney General's Office finally charged Suharto and others with corruption.[70] Although he evaded trial on mental health grounds, the symbolism was significant. Suhato's son, Tommy, was later jailed in connection with the assassination of the Supreme Court judge, Syafiuddin Kartasasmita, who had upheld sentences given to him for corruption. Indonesia later reflected the global trend to call senior politicians as witnesses, when former president BJ Habibie was summoned to give evidence against speaker Akbar Tandjung. In 2004, the former head of Perwaja Steel, Eric Chia, became the first focus for new initiatives instigated by the new prime minister, Adullah Badawi, who had promised to reduce corruption. Chia was involved in what was considered to be the most spectacular corporate collapse in the country's history. As the trial began, Chia was 71. The investigation had started in 1995. Badwadi also set up a commission to investigate the police which found evidence of corruption and brutality. This reflected the findings of an earlier survey by the Dutch Embassy, that the police were the least trusted body in Malaysia. Perhaps the most interesting aspect is that a foreign diplomatic mission had formally taken an interest in public malpractice in a host country. This initiative seems unprecedented.

Happenings of this nature were so common in Asia that the jailing of former Pakistani prime minister, Nawaz Sharif, in July 2000 attracted little press interest. Similarly, the imprisonment of former Indian prime minister PV Narasimha Rao, in October, for bribing opposition MPs, only received brief attention in the world's media. Although an appeal court permitted his liberty after the hearing, the decision remains significant. This was the first instance in Indian history of a prime minister receiving a prison sentence.[71] The prison sentence for Nepal's former prime minister, Sher Bahadur Deuba, in 2005 for embezzlement, was another landmark in Asian accountability. But the resignation of six senior Indian politicians, including the defence minister George Fernandes, six months later, was not ignored. Videos of them seemingly arranging bribes had been put on the tehelka.com website. Not only was the news picked up instantly, but it provided ongoing internet entertainment across the whole world. Four weeks later B.P. Verma, the chairman of India's Central Board of Customs and Excise, was remanded to the custody of the Central Bureau of Investigation to be questioned about impropriety in his department.[72] India's *Outlook* magazine carried out an 18-month search to reward an honest government employee in northern Punjab. It found 300 corrupt ones, but the 100,000 rupee prize for honesty was never awarded.[73]

The impetus in Asia included Bangladesh where, by the start of 2003, almost all senior politicians were facing corruption charges, including a former prime minister, Sheikh Hasina. Similarly in Pakistan, the National Accountability Bureau was set up (see Figure 1.2) following a presidential ordinance for 'free, transparent and across the board accountability' in 1999.[74] The aim was to prevent 'misconduct among politicians and administrators', as had surrounded the presidency of Benazir Bhutto. It was so effective that being caught was presented by some elites as a symbol of success rather than shame. But whatever its ultimate impact, it certainly had the best acronym – NAB.

The ethos was also very evident in North East Asia. In 2002, Kim Eun Sung, the deputy chief of the Korean national intelligence service, was arrested for receiving a $38,000 bribe. In the wake of this, President Kim Dae-Jung's two sons were then charged with corruption, and the president publicly apologised for their conduct. Then in 2003, presidential candidate and former high court judge Lee Hoi-chang admitted that his campaign had received illegal funding of £25 million, and admitted that he should go to prison. Other Korean leaders distanced themselves from their corrupt peers. Lee Man-Sub, who was twice a former speaker of the

WHY
For better future of our generations.
Corruption cannot be eliminated without full public participation.
For speedy accountability drive.

HOW
Provide evidence against **CORRUPT PUBLIC OFFICE HOLDER**
Guide us through constructive critique & suggestions.
Provide information regarding money being siphoned abroad/foreign assets of fugitives and their activities at Contact Us.

What Do You Get In Return
Informers are rewarded, if evidence leads to conviction.
More details available on personal contact.
While Passing Information Fill In Following:

1. Identity.
Name of the individual or group involved in corruption. For example Mr. XYZ or ABC Company or ABC Group of Companies etc.

2. Occupation.
Occupation/status or position of the individual. For example Chairman XYZ, Political figure, Civil Bureaucrat Name, Ministry of XYZ, Director of ABC Group etc.

3. Address.
Official / Business / Residential or Hideout.

4. Type of Corruption.
Type of corruption indulged in. For example Corruption and corrupt practices, Misuse of Authority, Bank default and Loan write off.

5. Assets.
The known or suspected assets of the culprit.

6. Evidence.
a. Evidence Held.
b. Where evidence is held or can be obtained.
c. Name(s) and addresses of witnesses.

7. Miscellaneous information.
Any thing which is not covered above.
Please provide us your comments and suggestions on the following links:
Feed Back Form, Survey Questionnaire (click for further Information)

Figure 1.2   NAB Pakistan

Source: http://www.nab.gov.pk/

South Korean Congress, stated:

> If our leaders want to lift Korea to be a fully developed country, where people are happy to live, the president and his family and staff have to be very clean. There must be no corruption or bribery so that the people will be encouraged to sacrifice for the nation, and plant the seeds of hope and dreams. In the future, this will be the most crucial thing.[75]

In the context of the past fifty years, this marks a remarkable change in Korean political ethics. This mood was reflected in a finding from a unique survey by Lee Yun-Joo in 2002. When asked what the main development challenges were, the Korean public put 'corruption' first and 'leadership skills' second, above the goal that has been paramount for 50 years, 'economic development'.[76]

In the context of this came the announcement in 2004, by President Roh Mo-hyun, that former collaborators with the Japanese occupying forces were to be investigated, together, in the words of Roh, with 'the encroachment on human rights and the illegal acts perpetrated by past administrations'.[77] This issue had remained dormant for fifty years, in part because the US did not want to complicate its relationships in the region. A few months later, Kim Woo-Choong, former CEO of Daewoo, voluntarily returned to Korea and surrendered to the courts. Seven of his colleagues had already been found guilty of fraud surrounding the collapse of the Daewoo group six years earlier. Kim was 69 when he returned, and had apparently been hiding in Vietnam. Elites like elite lifestyles, and hiding in a remote land denies them the rewards of power.

South Korea has become one of the most advanced ICT nations in the world, and this has been used in the accountability movement. The hi-tech OPEN anti-corruption project now permits the state licensing systems and other bureaucratic processes to be transparent through online tracking.[78] The ethos even extended to bribery concerning university exam results. More significantly, 'netizens' – citizens who use the net politically – are a new strong dynamic which can make or break politicians. Roh Mo-hyun came to power in the wake of this movement, and one of his first acts was to send four million emails to netizens addressing their concerns.

But China was probably the most active country. In March 2000, the deputy provincial governor of Jiangxi, Hu Changqing, was found guilty of corruption and of stealing 5.4 billion yuan. He became the most senior official to be executed in fifty years of Communist China's history.[79] The Guangxi party leader, Cheng Kejie, suffered a similar fate for stealing 41 million yuan, as did the security chief of Chende's Relics Protection Department, Li Haitao, for stealing antiquities. Even those with close party connections were not immune. By the end of 2000, the Discipline Inspection Commission's anti-corruption campaign had led to the disciplining of over 136,000 communist officials and nearly 43,000 cases had been brought to court.[80] The need was urgent. It is estimated that between 4 and 8 per cent of China's GNP stemmed from corruption.[81] A banker and friend of Premier Zhu Rongji was jailed for taking bribes in 2003. A year earlier, the head of the China Construction Bank, Wang Xuebing, lost his membership of the Communist Party, and was described as 'debauched' and 'corrupted' in the state media because he was implicated in the same case. Former Beijing mayor Chen Xitong was similarly shamed, and a trial of senior officials in charge of a large road building project followed. During the same period, the Chinese courts started trials of 200 'impure' officials resulting in the death sentence for fourteen. A year later the former deputy minister of police became the highest-ranking official to be given a death sentence (suspended) for taking bribes. The initiatives were not only about financial malpractice. As a result of the initial cover-up of the SARS epidemic, the health minister and the mayor of Beijing both lost their jobs. A new slogan, 'take the blame and resign', arose and a government anti-corruption film became compulsory viewing for all Communist Party officials – its title, *Choice between Life and Death*.[82]

Good governance – the North

The resignation of Edith Cresson and 19 members of the European Commission in 1999 generated a fresh approach to integrity within Europe. France was particularly active, where there were constant efforts to bring President Chirac to account for alleged corruption when he was mayor of Paris. These were deflected by old French immunity laws, but although Chirac may have avoided accountability through the courts, journalists sensed an era of change. One commentator concluded:

> What is being investigated is the ways of an older France, which not long ago would have flourished with impunity. Today, however, a new breed of younger, hard-nosed magistrates is cleansing the system. The real question is whether the politicians of the old order accept that the rules of the game have changed.[83]

In August 2001, *Le Monde diplomatique* published an article called 'Presidents under pressure', which linked events in France to the broader global picture.[84] Other French leaders under investigation included former prime minister Alain Juppé, a former finance minister, the mayor of Paris, and Christophe Mitter and, son of the late president. A number of other former mayors had previously been convicted of impropriety.[85] By 2004, Juppé had been convicted of corruption. The judge who had convicted him, Catherine Pierce, then claimed that she and her colleagues had endured a campaign of harassment during the trial, including computer hacking, break-ins and anonymous threats.[86] Events in Paris seemed very similar to those that the wealthy nations had been condemning in the so-called less developed countries a decade previously.

In January 2001, Roland Dumas, the former French foreign minister and president of France's highest court, went on trial together with executives from the oil company Elf-Aquitaine for misappropriating company funds and was given a prison sentence. In true French style, he implicated his former mistress who had already published her version of events in a book *The whore of the Republic*.[87] This was the same Roland Dumas who had been president of the Constitutional Council when it affirmed Chirac's presidential immunity.[88] Dumas later won an appeal against his conviction, but other senior Elf officials did not, including a former president of the company, Loïk Le Floch-Prigent, second in command Alfred Sirven, André Tarallo and 34 other officials. Le Floch-Prigent's former wife was also fined – her $5 million divorce settlement had been paid by Elf. The globalizing nature of corruption, the political and commercial aegis of the world leadership club, and accountability were very evident. Allegations included illicit payments to Kohl's German Christian Democratic Party. Alfred Sirven was then arrested in Manila, having evaded French authorities since 1997.[89] On his way back to France he was intercepted for questioning by the German authorities. A former Elf boss claimed that de Gaulle, Pompidou, Giscard d'Estaing and Mitterand had all been aware of what was happening.[90] The French law of 'defence secrecy' prevented further investigation. Henri Perrier and other heads of the Concorde programme did not evade accountability so easily when they were put under investigation in 2005 concerning the death of 113 people in the Concorde crash five years earlier.

In Italy, during the start of the 1990s, senator Antonio Di Pietro was responsible for an initiative that became known as 'Operation Clean Hands'. He generated 2,565 accusations of corruption, extortion and tax fraud against politicians and business administrators. He claims that this caused 'a major revolution that resulted in the near total replacement of our ruling political class'.[91] His endeavours were soon subverted, but as leader of the Italia de Valori (Italy of Values) party, he had established a new ethos of accountability. In November 2002, Giulio Andreotti, who had been prime minister seven times and was known as the 'little Caesar', was sent to prison for 24 years for the murder of a journalist.

Prime minister Silvio Berlusconi was then charged with bribery, and initially evaded justice through gaining special immunity, largely because he was about to become president of the EC Council and MPs wanted to avoid embarrassment. This was then overturned by Italy's Constitutional Court – after Berlusconi had completed his EC post, in January 2004. Di Pietro, who had collected millions of signatures to force a referendum on the self-immunity law, made the obvious statement: 'This ruling affirms that no one is above the law, not even the Prime Minister.'[92] The comment may seem banal, but this was a novel idea in Italy. If nothing else, Berlusconi will certainly be remembered in history as the first serving Italian prime minister to be forced to appear at his own criminal trial. An earlier successful related case, which involved many of Berlusconi's associates, was described by the court as the largest corruption case in post-war Italy.[93] The courts eventually found Berlusconi 'responsible' for paying a $430,000 bribe to a judge, but he could not be convicted because of time limitations. A day later his close colleague, Marcello dell'Utri, was given a seven-year jail sentence for colluding with the Mafia. Berlusconi's former defence minister, Cesare Previti, was also convicted of bribing judges in Rome and given an 11-year prison sentence.

In January 2001, the world's most powerful leader, Bill Clinton, was finally forced to admit that he 'knowingly' misled a court about his relationship with Monica Lewsinski. He accepted a $90,000 fine. A month later Helmut Kohl agreed to pay a fine of DM300,000, following his receipt of illegal party donations in excess of DM2 million. This spared Kohl becoming the highest-ranking German politician to be tried for corruption since the Second World War. At a lower level, but still demonstrating the ongoing impetus of the clean-up in Europe, a former Irish justice and foreign minister, Ray Burke, was imprisoned for tax evasion at the start of 2005.

The US came to public attention again when, in July 2002, Congress expelled James Traficant who was convicted of bribery and racketeering. He is only the second politician to be expelled since the Civil War. Three years later, the House majority leader, Tom DeLay, was indicted and forced to resign because of criminal conspiracy charges. He was seen as the most powerful man in Congress. This was in the wake of major revelations of corporate corruption in the US, involving companies such as Enron, WorldCom and Anderson. The Enron bankruptcy was the biggest ever experienced in the US. At first, investigations were hampered by corporate obfuscation, and it was predicted that senior managers would evade accountability, as usually happened in cases of this nature. But in September 2003 Enron's treasurer, Ben Gilson, was jailed for criminal conspiracy and the following month the chief financial adviser, Andrew Fastow, pleaded guilty to fraud and helped prosecutors with other cases to lessen his sentence. Both he and his wife received prison sentences. By February 2004 the highest-ranking former executive, Jeff Skilling, was charged with 36 counts of fraud, and by August chairman Ken Lay was indicted. These events led to new regulations requiring the chief executive and finance officers of 14,000 companies personally to sign sworn statements that their company accounts were accurate and not misleading. Then the world saw the 'Australian Enron'. Ray Williams, the CEO of insurance company HIH, was jailed for four-and-a-half years after misleading shareholders and the largest corporate collapse in Australian commercial history. By 2005, Bernie Ebbers, the former head of WorldCom, was convicted of a $11 billion fraud that resulted in the biggest bankruptcy in US history, and he was given a twenty-five year prison sentence. Soon after, Dennis Kozlowski, the CEO of Tyco, and his chief financial officer faced a 25-year sentence having been found guilty on 22 counts including grand larceny and securities fraud. They had apparently arranged 'special bonuses' and other payments for themselves. John Rigas, of Adelphia Communications, and his son both received long prison sentences in June 2005. Rigas was by then eighty years old.

The press were talking of an 'Enron effect' when the Lithuanian parliament started impeachment proceedings against President Rolandas Paksas because of his links with Russian gangsters and other apparent wrongdoings. By July 2004 the former Ukrainian prime minister, Pavlo Lazarenko, had been convicted in the US for money-laundering and extortion. The Russian courts then tried and convicted the country's wealthiest man, head of the oil company Yukos, Mikhail Khodorkovsky, for fraud tax evasion and embezzlement. The trial was seen by some as a crude attack on Yukos by the government. But it also shows the strength of peer accountability among elites even if it amounts to rough justice, and the broader message to commercial leaders in Russia was clear. Even in Afghanistan the trend was evident. Investigative journalists at the new Tolo TV station brought about the trial and imprisonment of two junior ministers who had exploited pilgrims making the Haj.

A few months later, a bastion of the British economic establishment, Shell, was held to account for the biggest corporate scandal of the past two decades in Britain. Senior managers had deliberately overstated the company's oil and gas reserves. As with Enron, emails provided the trail of deceit. In one, the head of exploration and production, Walter van de Vuver, told the chairman, Sir Philip Watts, that 'I am sick and tired about lying about the extent of our reserves'. Watts, van de Vuver and Judy Boynton, the finance director, left the company. Along with other senior directors, they then faced lawsuits from shareholders.[94]

January 2004 saw another striking example of economic accountability, of some of the most powerful establishment elites in the world. The Bank of England was put on trial for misleading the British government about the collapse of the Bank of Credit and Commerce International (BCCI). The trial for misfeasance in public office was the first of its kind in British legal history. The accusations, of dishonesty and reckless conduct, were against 22 specific supervisory staff. But the most significant case was in Thailand in 2005, when the former governor of the Central Bank, Rerngchai Marakanong, was blamed for the Thai financial crash in 1997, and fined £2.5 billion for gross negligence. This set a groundbreaking precedent for public servants to be held personally liable for their mistakes or misdeeds.

'Good governance' initiatives that had originally been conceived in terms of improving accountability in the South were also soon applied in the North. In May 2002, a chief executive from the Lesotho Development Authority was found guilty of taking bribes from multinational companies including Balfour Beatty.[95] A year later, a Canadian company, Acres International, was found guilty of paying a $260,000 bribe. The significance was expressed by Guido Penzhorn who led the investigations: 'This turns on its head the perception in first world countries that consultants are obliged to pay bribes in Africa … it is very important that the briber was convicted. People here are very aggrieved when the rich world writes this off as just an African problem.'[96]

The anti-corruption strategies developed by the OECD, notably the 1999 Bribery Convention, had started to create a consensus between world leaders in rich and poor countries alike about not paying or taking bribes. By 2003, the UN Convention against Corruption, which dealt with prevention, criminalization, international cooperation, asset recovery and implementation mechanisms, was in place. Public officials who live in a style in which 'he or she cannot reasonably explain in relation to his or her lawful income' will be subject to criminal investigation. National legislation started to adopt the principles, 'corporate social responsibility' became more central to the business practice of many national and transnational companies, and Transparency International reframed its view of corruption to include conduct such as leaders from the rich nations using development aid for their nationalistic political ends.

An ethos that originally aimed to bring errant leadership to account in less developed countries had turned to apply the same standards in the wealthy nations. This form of dormant precedent is very similar to those following the Second World War war crimes trials. Standards set by countries such as the US and Britain to hold others to account eventually came to be applied to those nations themselves. Hugh O'Shaughnessy explained the paradox that this created. Concerning the UN Corruption Convention, he pointed out in 2004 that 'developing countries [were] showing more enthusiasm for its ratification than EU countries and the US, none of which have so far ratified it'.[97] And in comparison with the response to violence, corruption has a significant gap. The powerful nations have not yet argued for an equivalent of the ICC – an international forum to prosecute individuals for international economic crime.

Environmental security

Although the international community was clearly starting to redress the up-system aspects of political violence and corruption, this was much less evident in relation to harm instigated by commercial, industrial and political leaders which affected environmental security, including food and public health. Even successful legal cases against the tobacco and asbestos industries, or successful resistance to the imposition of genetically modified (GM) crops, was focused on corporations, not individuals. International organizations such as the UNEP, WHO, FAO and EC promote good practice and enforce regulations, but do not concern themselves with personal accountability.

Agreements such as the Genome Declaration (DHG), the UNEP Code of Ethics on the International Trade in Chemicals (ITC) and the Persistent Organic Pollutants Treaty[98] signed in December 2000 create an ethic of caution but do not create positive obligations on leaders to ensure that ethic. But there is one interesting and relevant exception within the 1993 Chemical Weapons Convention (Part VII, 6(a), 7(a), 10(a)). Hidden away in the technical detail is a requirement that declarations of a plant site must include 'The name of the plant site and the name of the owner, company, or enterprise operating it'. This seems to be a unique example of building in the principle and means of personal accountability within an international law.

Perceptions about the importance of environmental threats are changing among power elites. In March 2004, the former UN weapons inspector in Iraq, Hans Blix, surprised an American TV audience by stating that

> the question of the environment is more ominous than that of peace and war ... the environment, that is a creeping danger. I'm more worried about global warming than I am of any major military conflict.[99]

This was a direct criticism of the policies of George Bush, and was paralleled by the views of the British government's chief scientific adviser,

Sir David King. He claimed specifically that climate change was a far greater threat to the world than international terrorism. King criticized American leaders for 'failing to take up the challenge of global warming'.[100] Prime Minister Tony Blair agreed, but avoided direct criticism. Then the head of the oil company Shell, Ron Oxburgh, echoed the concern, and said that he was 'very worried for the planet' and that 'no one can be comfortable at the prospect of continuing to pump out the amounts of carbon dioxide that we are at present'.[101] This was an astonishing U-turn for the chief of an oil company. Similarly, Ray Anderson, CEO of the US carpet company Interface, became known for his complete change of mind about the environmental impact of industry. In 2005, the president of the Royal Society, Lord May of Oxford, directly accused George Bush of irresponsibility for not supporting the Kyoto agreement on climate change. This challenge, by a former chief scientific adviser to the government, was seen as 'virtually unprecedented' for a scientist in his position.[102] Are evolving ethics such as these starting to set the scene for direct personal accountability, as in the other two sectors?

A justice framework

The 'environmental justice' movement has provided a conceptual framework for civil society action, particularly in relation to the victimization of minority groups.[103] NGOs such as Greenpeace, Friends of the Earth and Genewatch challenge entities whose actions threaten the global environment, but bringing power elites personally to account has not been a major strategy. Global Witness, which works to 'expose the link between environmental exploitation and human rights abuses' concerning forests, oil and diamonds, is similar.[104] In a more developmental mode, the California Global Corporate Accountability Project addresses 'environmental governance dilemmas faced by US corporations in their global operations' in three spheres – law on corporate responsibility, ethical investment and training journalists.[105] LEAD International aims to train and create a global network of leaders who promote sustainable development, and the work of the UK's Forum for the Future is similar, but these initiatives aim to influence the minds of potential leaders rather than challenge the conduct of current elites.

People's tribunals are one of the more interesting initiatives, of which the Permanent People's Tribunal (PPT) is probably the best known. Based in Rome, this was set up in 1979 following the Bertrand Russell tribunals on Vietnam and South America. The Russell tribunal had addressed the absence of accountability for political violence through national and international courts at that time, and provided a model for subsequent national and international developments. Since then, the PPT has visited different countries and heard evidence, and provided judgments concerning environmental victimization such as the Union Carbide/Bhopal disaster and the conduct of oil companies, particularly Shell in Nigeria. This includes naming and judging accountable commercial leaders, such as Union Carbide chairman Warren Anderson, and the creation of a Charter of Rights Against Industrial Hazards.[106] Although often dismissed as tokenistic, these initiatives are becoming good indicators of future global ethics, because they instigate embryonic precedents that eventually fuel an accountability movement. In 2004, Shell was formally asked by the Nigerian government to pay $1.5 billion as compensation for oil pollution in the country. This had been unthinkable a few decades earlier, when the PPT was passing its judgments about Shell's activities in the context of the former regime and the judicial murder of the environmental activist Ken Saro-Wiwa.

The PPT seems to have perpetuated Russell's prescience about leadership accountability and political violence, through its more recent response about environmental security. It seems probable that formal national and international forums will again follow the lead of the people's tribunals, and also extend their view of the accountability of leaders in this third area of concern. The idea of an international Environmental Court is being mooted. But perhaps before this, we will see environmental cases at the ICC, in relation to environmental damage and resultant harm to populations caused by weapons such as depleted uranium-tipped shells. In 2004, the European Commission set a new precedent when it started court proceedings against the British government over radioactive waste at the infamous Sellafield reprocessing plant.

Personal responsibility

Although most legal redress for environmental victimization has not brought specific individuals to account,[107] there have been instances of a changing mood, particularly in North East Asia. One of the first examples was in relation to the Chisso mercury poisoning of Minamata Bay in Japan, which resulted in death and injury to thousands of people in the 1950s–60s. The effectiveness of survivor activism had been demonstrated by the Hiroshima and Nagasaki A-bomb victims, and the Minamata survivors learned from this. They became one of the first campaigning groups in the world to use direct action at a shareholders' meeting, and company directors were taken completely by surprise.

The director of Chisso, Kenichi Shimada, was eventually forced to perform a public *dogeza* – bowing until his head touched the floor – the ultimate shame for a Japanese leader. Compensation was paid, although this happened many years later. Government officials and the courts impeded redress and the international community remained silent.[108] At the time, Western environmentalists showed little direct interest, presumably because of a reluctance to show any form of support towards Japanese people during the immediate post-Second World War period. Had the event happened more recently, the dynamics would probably have been very different, and the outcome would have been perceived as having more significance in marking personal responsibility for environmental victimization. But, as is so often the case in the history of accountability, the case created dormant precedents that were utilized decades later in Japan and elsewhere.

In the interim period, notorious cases of environmental poisoning have seen responsible leaders seemingly avoid accountability.[109] Most of those responsible for the nuclear power disaster at Chernobyl evaded trial. The Soviet Union ceased to exist three years later, and a few token individuals were blamed by the new Ukrainian state, without any trial, and real culprits became high-ranking officials in the new government.[110] Those responsible for the Union Carbide disaster in Bhopal, which resulted in more than 22,000 deaths (7,000 immediate; 15,000 later) and 100,000 people injured, also seemed to evade accountability.[111] And this failure was presented in comparison with the forces of 'accountability' that were unleashed following the terrorist attack on the World Trade Center on 11 September 2002, in which fewer than 3,000 people were killed. In July 2004, a US court again dismissed a case for damages against The Dow Chemical Company (which had taken over Union Carbide and masked responsibility for the poisoning) and the responsible director, Warren Anderson, on the pretext of time limitations even though the delays had been caused by the company. At the same point a Bombay court issued a summons against the representative of Dow to explain why the company should not be held responsible. New fax evidence showed the link between Union Carbide's US and Indian operations.[112] Then one month later, Dow was summonsed by a court in Bhopal, and this was the first time an Indian criminal court had issued a direct summons about the poisoning.[113] The frustrations of the victims masked the significance of these actions. First, the challenge is active and getting stronger twenty years after the event. Second, in many instances individuals were being called to account, not just amorphous companies, and that was almost unheard of in former years.

Even if the Indian courts do not have many powers of enforcement, it becomes uncomfortable for anyone summonsed to remain and operate effectively in the country.

In contrast to the nuclear power disaster at Chernobyl, following a nuclear accident at the Tokaimura reprocessing plant in Japan in 1999, six managers, including the head of the facility, Kenzo Koshijima, were charged and sentenced for professional negligence and contravening nuclear safety laws in 2003. The accident caused two deaths and 600 people were exposed to radiation. The sentences were tokenistic – suspended prison sentences and fines of a few thousand dollars – but the fact that a case against senior managers reached the courts was notable. It perhaps demonstrates how national history can influence accountability for environmental victimization. The Minamata survivors showed that the Japanese public can act effectively, and there is great sympathy for anyone affected by nuclear radiation. The conviction, in 2004, of the leader of the Aum Shinrikyo cult, responsible for the sarin gas attacks in the Tokyo subway in 1995, which killed twelve people and injured thousands, also seemed to reflect Japanese history. Shoko Asahara was found guilty of involvement in murder on the basis of his 'grave responsibility' for his followers, not for any direct involvement. His defence was that they were out of his control at that time. Paradoxically, this echoes the precedents about command responsibility that were established at the Tokyo (and Nuremberg) war crimes trials.

China too seems to be setting stronger standards. In December 2003, the release of toxic fumes from a well in Chongqing, operated by the state-owned gas producer China National Petroleum, killed 233 people and injured many more within a ten-kilometre radius. This was China's worst industrial accident in recent years. Investigations found safety violations, and within days responsible company executives were held to account.[114] It is not unusual that Chinese local officials are held directly responsible for industrial accidents.

There were also signs of change in the UK, albeit on a small scale. Health and safety laws were extended to create personal responsibility for corporate crime, and the first instance of individual accountability for environmental crime in Britain came in February 2000. The director of a company that handled radioactive waste was given a suspended prison sentence and fined for illegally disposing of waste, within the UK Radioactive Substances Act.[115] A year later the prosecution service was considering charges against Ministry of Defence scientists for poisoning volunteers during experiments concerning nerve gas, during the 1950s and 60s at Porton Down. At first the cases did not proceed, but this was the first time that government scientists had faced prosecution for carrying out official research. Cases were instigated again after an inquest into the death of a British soldier at Porton Down which found unlawful killing by the state, and the Canadian government paid compensation to 2,000 Canadian soldiers who were dosed with mustard gas as part of the same series of tests.[116] Soon afterwards, the managing director of IMPCO Plastics faced manslaughter charges for the death of three people who caught legionnaires' disease from bacteria discharged from the factory cooling tower. Charges were stayed as he was unfit for trial, but the evolving message about personal accountability was clear. In 2004, the Environmental Agency fined the directors of six waste management companies, and the agency director stated, 'Company Directors ... who try to increase profits at the expense of the environment should know that a fine or a criminal record could be on the cards.'[117] The scale of these initiatives seemed small, but they marked a new trend in personal responsibility in Britain.

Eventually America seemed to be following the trend. In 2005, Federal officials announced criminal charges against seven of the senior executives of the mining company Grace, concerning lethal contamination of the locality with asbestos, which presented them with the possibility of prison sentences of between 50 and 70 years. The head of the US Environmental Protection Agency, Lori Hanson, called the case 'one of the most significant criminal indictments for environmental crime in our history'.[118] Government officials were also themselves being caught in the new accountability net. A few months later Brazilian police arrested 89 suspects implicated in illegal logging in the rain forest. Among them were 40 officials from the state branch of the government environment agency Ibama, who were accused of supplying false transport permits to illegal loggers. They included Ibama's executive director and one of the agency's senior directors in Brasilia. Then in August 2005, the director of Newmont Minahasa Raya, Richard Ness, found himself facing a possible ten-year prison sentence for arsenic and mercury pollution in Buyat Bay, Indonesia. The story of Minamata Bay seemed to be repeating itself, but this time the responsible leader was being held to account for his supervisory role.

Leadership accountability in the area of environmental security seems slow compared with initiatives in the other sectors, except perhaps in North East Asia and, outside of this book, developments in this sphere are not being related to those concerning political violence and corruption. But this may change as the science of establishing causation improves, and paradoxically the delay may have created the Achilles heel of errant industrial leaders. As a result of their perception of immunity they have not thought it necessary to cover their tracks, and so audit trails are well-established. In 2004, a study from the NGO Friends of the Earth calculated that ExxonMobil (and its predecessors) caused 4.7 to 5.3 per cent of the world's man-made carbon dioxide emissions between 1882 and 2002.[119] The claim that this could lead to future victims of climate change suing the company might appear fanciful, but then probably so did any prognosis a few decades ago that tobacco companies could be sued for harming the health of smokers. Then in 2005 a California court agreed that Greenpeace and Friends of the Earth, together with three US city authorities, could sue the US government for permitting US companies to increase the risk of global warming through its overseas operations. This was the first case based on the threat of climate change.

Industrialists seem unaware that legal precedent can be extended very creatively, as public ethics evolve. The cases concerning tobacco were based on arguments such as those from the US Attorney General Janet Reno that the companies 'conducted themselves without regard to the truth, without regard to the law, and without regard to the health and life of the American people'. A similar charge could well be made against polluting industries. The tobacco cases in 2004 were based on 'fraud and deceit' laws which were originally created to counter the mafia.[120] In a common law system, precedent and practice can evolve to address harm that was not even considered by those who framed the original legislation.[121]

One further emergent characteristic of accountability in the environment sector may turn out to be the most significant – its ability to unite people with otherwise disparate views. In 2005, the British press announced 'The end for GM crops', following field trials of genetically modified crops that had shown environmental damage.[122] This was in the run-up to a general election, and immediately the Conservative Party announced that, if elected, it would prevent any planting of GM crops until they were properly tested for environmental and health impacts. Labour leader Tony Blair had supported the introduction of GM crops. This may seem insignificant until we remember that the action against GM crops stemmed from leftist activist organizations such as Greenpeace. Their direct action included destroying fields of GM crops. Activists had been arrested for criminal damage, but were acquitted in a virtually unique way by a jury which accepted the defence that their action was to prevent a greater harm. At the time, this outcome was condemned by Conservatives, but by 2005 Greenpeace activists and the Conservative Party had seemingly started fighting on the same side. This fits an ongoing theme of this book, that global accountability unites adversaries and creates new allegiances around specific circumstances. The belief that leaders can depend on traditional groups of followers and 'sides' is eroding, and environmental issues may become the main catalyst for that social evolution.

Immunity and extradition

One of the biggest barriers to the accountability of heads of state and senior politicians has been the immunity principle and refusal to extradite. But the so-called 'Pinochet precedent', established by Spain and the British courts in 1999 and later affirmed by the Chilean judiciary, started to challenge this.[123] The momentum continued when Spain then requested the extradition from Mexico of the former Argentinian military officer and 'nun killer' Ricardo Miguel Cavallo, for genocide, terrorism and torture. He was then extradited in June 2003. The ongoing ethic resurfaced in 2004, when two senior junta officials were convicted of stealing babies born to imprisoned Uruguayan parents. This was the first case of its type. By the end of 2001, Pinochet's own commanders had turned against him. Ten retired army officers filed a criminal complaint against him that they were tortured and dismissed for opposing human rights abuses during his rule. By May 2004, the Chilean Supreme Court had totally removed his long-standing immunity, and judges ordered Pinochet to testify in writing if he was too ill to attend court. By December he was found fit for trial by Judge Guzman and was indicted. Not least of the outcomes was that he was made to pay $2.5 million in unpaid taxes, and his wife and son were charged with tax fraud.

One week after Pinochet was charged with kidnapping and murder, a judge in Paraguay issued an order for the arrest and extradition of former dictator General Stroessner, who had claimed immunity in Brazil, and of his interior minister Sabino Augusto Montanaro, from Honduras. José Miguel Vivanco, Human Rights Watch America's regional director, concluded: 'Like the Pinochet prosecution, it is proof of the growing international consensus that those responsible for gross human rights abuses should not escape punishment.'[124] By the end of the year, France had demanded the arrest of 15 Chilean officials in relation to the disappearance of French citizens during the Pinochet regime, including Manuel Contreas, former head of the secret police. The Nicaraguan parliament also challenged immunity when it removed former president

Arnoldo Aleman from the leadership of Congress in 2002. This permitted Congress to take away his immunity and charge him with the theft of $100 million from state funds.

In February 2001, Mexico agreed to extradite Cavallo, and Vivanco called this 'an extraordinary step toward accountability for human rights abuses … Mexico is making history'.[125] A few days later, the Lithuanian authorities issued an arrest warrant for 85-year-old Anton Gecas. They wanted him to be extradited from Scotland to face charges for the mass murder of Jews and other civilians during Nazi occupation.[126] He evaded extradition on health grounds and died shortly afterwards, but the decision was one of the first major international relations cases for the newly devolved Scottish executive, and it affirmed the message that global leadership accountability is not just a game played among the powerful nations. Two weeks later the Philippines Supreme Court voted to deny Estrada immunity, and the next week an Argentinian judge declared two immunity laws unconstitutional, meaning that hundreds of military officers could be prosecuted for human rights violations during the 1976–83 dictatorship.[127] In the same wave of change, the Indian National Commission to review the constitution proposed to amend Indian laws so that MPs cannot claim immunity, as had Prime Minister Rao.[128] The seemingly strong former president of Zambia, Frederick Chiluba, was then charged with 59 counts of 'theft by a public servant' – of stealing two million dollars of public money while in office. In 2002, the government had made the charges possible by removing Chiluba's presidential immunity. Mexico made further history in 2004 when an 82-year-old former president, Luis Echeverria, was indicted for the killing of student protestors in 1971. The courts had circumvented the 30-year statute of limitations for murder by charging him with genocide. Echeverria became the first modern Mexican president to face a criminal trial, and others, including a general, interior minister and attorney general, were being investigated.[129]

Less conspicuous but no less interesting is the case of George Speight, who became known to the world in May 2000 when he violently ousted the elected prime minister of Fiji, Mahendra Chaudhry. Originally he was given amnesty in return for releasing his hostages. After much deliberation, particularly among the Great Council of Chiefs, Speight was eventually put on trial for treason and an election was called.

The challenge to immunity was also evident in Europe.[130] In October 2000, the French courts had ruled that Libyan leader Colonel Gaddafi did not have immunity in relation to the shooting down of a French airliner over West Africa in 1989. Although this was later overruled on a technicality, the message still contributes to the broader picture. The judges concluded, as did the UK House of Lords, that the immunity of a head of state did not extend to acts of terrorism.[131] Ironically, two weeks earlier, President Chirac had evaded being placed under investigation by the French courts for allegations of misconduct while he was mayor of Paris, because of disputed immunity provided by the French Constitution.[132] Under the direction of its then president, Roland Dumas, the Constitutional Council had made a judgment affirming Chirac's immunity. This still leaves the possibility of an investigation when his term of office ends. It was also argued that although a 1999 ruling by the Constitutional Council holds that a head of state cannot be placed under investigation, this does not relate to a witness summons. This precipitated another historical landmark. Although he ignored it, in March 2001 Chirac became the first head of state of the French Fifth Republic to receive a formal witness summons by an investigating judge. A petition for his impeachment was then started. Its proponent, socialist deputy leader Arnaud Montebourg, argued:

> How can we explain to our compatriots that crimes committed by presidents Joseph Estrada, Alberto Fujimori and Richard Nixon can be tried, but that no judge can be found in France to try President Jacques Chirac?[133]

A month later, the investigators realized another possibility. A president may have immunity, but that does not apply to his family. Chirac's daughter and 'image adviser', Claude, was questioned about cash payments to family and friends. His wife, Bernadette Chirac, achieved another 'first' – the first French first lady to be required to give evidence in this way. The investigators then reported that they had 'evidence which points to the likely involvement' of the president in financial impropriety, and referred the question of whether a president has immunity for acts committed before the presidency to an appeal court.[134] The court did not uphold the summons, and the judge who issued it was sacked. The judge who investigated Chirac, Eric Haphen, eventually resigned in disgust at the perverse application of the immunity law, saying 'Nixon quit for less'.[135]

Estrada's fierce resistance to losing his status as president was not just because of a desire to lead the Philippine people, but because his immunity went with his presidency. Even after the Supreme Court affirmed the ruling, Estrada claimed that he was merely 'on leave' from his job. The fact that immunity is usually not for life hit the former

Serbian president Milan Milutinovic, at the end of 2002, when extradition proceedings were started by the Hague Tribunal a day after his term of office expired. In Argentina, a law passed in 1987 gave the junta leaders immunity, and a request by Spain for their extradition was blocked by presidential decree in 2001. But Argentina's new president Nestor Kirchner overturned this in 2003, and a judge immediately issued an arrest warrant for 46 former military leaders. In 2005 the Supreme Court then removed the amnesty for atrocities during the 'Dirty War' between 1976 and 1983, which opened the door for charges against 3,000 military leaders. Under Argentinian law, the precedent can be applied to similar cases. Also in 2003, former president of Zambia Frederik Chiluba found himself in court on corruption charges, because parliament had removed his immunity and the High Court ruled that there was no 'impropriety' in this decision. Perhaps the most significant example was the ruling by the Italian Constitutional Court in January 2004, which overturned the immunity that Prime Minister Silvio Berlusconi had created for himself through persuading his parliament that it would be embarrassing for him to be on trial as EU president. But the presidency is short, and soon after he lost his protection.[136]

These events provide very straightforward messages to leaders about immunity. It goes with the job, it is only a law, and laws can be changed or subverted. The Chilean government quickly overturned Pinochet's auto-immunity, following the UK House of Lords ruling. And although the Yugoslav Constitution formally prevented the extradition of Milosevic, it did not hinder a simple decree passed by the cabinet, which permitted a 'handover', not 'extradition', to The Hague. Although the French Cour de Cassation upheld Chirac's presidential immunity in 2001, it also suspended the normal time limit on legal proceedings, and this will permit his prosecution when he leaves office. The French courts demonstrated other innovative strategies to circumvent immunity. Although General Paul Aussaresses was protected by two amnesties passed by the French parliament, for his alleged misdeeds concerning Algeria, prosecutors were quick to spot that he could be charged for condoning such crimes in his book *Special Services, Algeria 1955–1957*. In Britain, the case against the Bank of England in 2004 could be brought because the prosecutors circumvented the bank's long-standing immunity against claims based on incompetence, by bringing a case of 'misfeasance in public office'.

The centuries-long mythology about the immunity and impunity of political leaders has been dispelled in a few years. Why? Perhaps one answer arises from remembering that, historically, leadership immunity did not come about only because those with power could get their own way. In past eras, it was also socially useful for leaders to be above the law because this created stability and strength against enemies during the era in which the civilizations and nation states were being constructed. Perhaps the reason for the current change is deceptively simple – we just do not need our political leaders to have total immunity any more.

But Mike Moore (then of the WTO) provides a reminder that the argument against immunity is not totally clear-cut. His sense of real politik leads him to point out:[137]

> The Russians have even suggested that war crimes tribunals such as the one in the Balkans can actually delay peace, because the fearful generals and politicians can actually delay peace. Peace would see them on trial, so why negotiate a settlement? Unfortunately there is some truth in this.

This may tell us more about Russian leaders than those in the Balkans, but campaigning organizations need to acknowledge if not accept this broader frame of reference. Moore continues,

> sometimes peace accords only come about if generals are guaranteed immunity for crimes. That's been the South American formula as nations such as Chile and Argentina moved from fascism to a more democratic system.

Perhaps the more significant question is not 'should despots be granted exile or brought to justice?', but 'when?' Charles Taylor's exile in Calabar, Nigeria, may demonstrate that courts can bide their time before they finally act. There is one further important distinction, made by Megawati Sukarnoputri when she lifted charges against her former adversary who was dying of pneumonia, on 'humanitarian grounds'. If done for the right reasons, pardon is different from impunity.

Creative immunity

A few leaders seemed to notice the fast-changing attitudes towards their protection and acted accordingly. Former Rwandan prime minister Pierre-Celestin Rwigema asked the US to grant him asylum in June 2000, after accusations that he misappropriated World Bank loans. Then in April 2001, the Rwandan government put him on a list of those suspected of genocide. A few days before Pinochet was charged with kidnapping and murder in December 2000, President Fujimori of Peru had decided to resign and remain in Japan, from where he cannot be extradited, and was simultaneously sacked by Congress as 'morally unfit' for office.[138] He was wise. Three months later, charges of 'illicit enrichment' and inappropriate use of public funds were filed against him, and then in March 2001 legal proceedings were started in relation to the murder of 14 Marxist rebels in 1997. By August, the Peruvian Congress had removed Fujimori's immunity to permit his arrest for murder. His aide and former spy chief, Vladimiro Montesinos, who was wanted for alleged corruption and human rights abuses, disappeared towards Costa Rica on his yacht.[139] By July 2002, he was in jail for corruption and awaiting trial for murder. But Milosevic had been less cautious. The same week saw him summonsed to give evidence in a Serbian court about election fraud, corruption and killings – the first step of his journey to The Hague.

The demise of traditional forms of immunity will probably cause power elites to construct other ways to achieve protection for themselves and their friends. By curious coincidence, in 2002 Russia's President Putin was arranging lifelong immunity for himself through the Russian parliament.[140] The US withdrawal of aid to 35 countries that would not give US personnel immunity from prosecution at the ICC was another strategy. Another US action, which received remarkably little attention, was in 2001 when President Bush gave President Mugabe something he called 'personal immunity' against the use of an old US statute of 1789, the Alien Tort Claims Act, to bring him to court for widespread killings and human rights abuses in Zimbabwe.

The pattern of accountability

Figure 1.3 provides an impression of what has happened since the mid-twentieth century. The reason for these different levels of progress reflects the relative visibility of the harm and problems of establishing causation. Political violence is highly visible, and there is usually little problem to establish cause and effect. The main defence left for responsible leaders is to lie or run away. Wrongdoings and causal trails are harder to identify in terms of corruption, and evasion strategies are therefore easier to implement, but accountability is still practicable especially as e-trails improve. Clarifying causation for environmental impacts, many of which are invisible because of dispersal of causal agents spatially and temporally, is fraught with difficulty, and tracking responsible leaders is like following footprints in a snowstorm.[141] But it

Violence	Corruption	Environmental security
International initiatives	***International initiatives***	***International initiatives***
War crimes trails	1990 World Bank 'good governance'	EU Regulations
1945–6, Nuremberg and Tokyo	1996 OECD Code, Public Officials	1993 Chemical Weapons Convention, 'name of
UN tribunals and courts	1999 EC anti-corruption measures	owner of chemical plants must be recorded.
1993 Hague Tribunal (Yugoslavia)	2002 OECD Bribery Convention	?International Environmental Court?
1994 Arusha Tribunal (Rwanda)	2003 UN Corruption Convention	
1997 Indonesia	1996–2002 Regional codes: inter-American, Asia &	
2001 Sierra Leone special court.	Pacific, Council of Europe	
2001 Cambodia Tribunal		
2002 International Criminal Court		
National initiatives	***National initiatives***	***National initiatives***
Extended jurisdiction	1997 Italy, Operation Clean Hands;	1960 Chisso mercury poisoning, Minamata Bay, Japan,
1789 US: Alien Tort Claims Act	India, Central, Vigilance Commission;	*dogeza* by company directors; 1998 damages paid to
1988 UK: Torture	Korea, OPEN Public Service monitoring	victims
1993/9 Belgium: Torture, Genocide	1999 Pakistan, NAB	1990s Health and safety laws used against
Truth and reconciliation	2000 Thailand, Counter Corruption Commission;	senior industrial managers, UK, China, Japan
1982 Bolivia, 1983 Argentina,	China, Discipline Inspection Commission;	2005 US EPA, asbestos cases against company
1985 Uruguay, 1990 Chile,	Japan and Peru, anti-corruption laws	executives of *Grace*
1991 El Salvador, 1995 South Africa, 2001	2004 Bank of England managers held personally	2005 Brazil, EA *Ibama* directors charged
Yogoslavia, 2002 Nigeria, 2003 Ghana	responsible for 'misfeasance'	
War crimes tribunals	2005 Thailand, Central Bank governor personally	
2003 Iraq War Crimes Tribunal	responsible for 'negligence', fined £2.5bn	
Immunity challenged	***Immunity challenged***	***Immunity challenged***
2000 Pinochet, 2000 Habré,	2000 Fujimori, 2001 Chirac, Estrada, 2004	Attempts to extradite senior managers of Union
2000 Gaddafi, 2003 Argentine Junta	Berlusconi, 2003 Chiluba	Carbide/Dow Chemicals by Indian courts
Civil society organizations	***Civil society organizations***	***Civil society organizations***
e.g. Human Rights Watch,	e.g. Transparency International, Corporatewatch,	e.g. Earthaction, Genewatch, Greenpeace
Amnesty, Asiawatch, Permanent	St Petersburg Centre for Business Ethics, Turkish	Permanent People's Tribunal
People's Tribunal	Ethics Foundation	

Figure 1.3　　The pattern of leadership accountability

is very likely that this imbalance will be redressed in the future. New technologies such as biomarkers will make environmental causation easier to prove, and information technology is now copiously documenting networks of leadership responsibility. Judging by the cases concerning tobacco, asbestos, lead and mercury, a false sense of security has made industrial leaders very careless about leaving audit trails of their wrongdoing.

National jurisdiction is extending beyond national borders. Figure 1.4 provides examples, and it is interesting how eclectic and unpredictable these are. How many people know that piracy laws have readily been extended to cover hijacking, and that there has been international jurisdiction in the UK concerning the abuse of women with mental disabilities since the 1950s? Such laws provide the basis for arguing for extensions of jurisdiction in other areas. The British government was surprised to be told by the European court in 2004 that the UK Human Rights Act can extend to the protection of people in other countries, which included abuses by British soldiers in Iraq.[142] The 'dormant precedent' for this had been set by a challenge against Margaret Thatcher concerning her decision to sink an Argentinian battleship, the *Belgrano*, during the Falklands War in 1982. Relatives of the 323 Argentinians killed took a case to the European Court of Human Rights. It did not proceed, only because of time limitations.

In absentia judgments and sanctions are another characteristic of national initiatives against despots, and arguably another aspect of extending jurisdiction, which are gaining legitimacy because of the extreme difficulty of enforcing court attendance of powerful people.[143] Early examples include the trial of Pol Pot and Ieng Sary by the People's Republic of Kampuchea, in 1979. The trial of those involved in the Raboteau massacre in Haiti ended with 37 convictions *in absentia*, including that of former lieutenant general Raoul Cedras. Similarly, in August 2003, a Croatian court in Osijek convicted and sentenced eight Serbs found guilty of abducting and beating Croats between 1991 and 1995. The Elf corruption case in France went ahead despite the four-year absence of its senior manager, Alfred Sirven, who was finally arrested in Manila in February 2001 and brought to court. There is often great value in the ritual of court hearings or investigations, even if defendants are absent and sanctions seem improbable. In April 2000, the Greek Supreme Court found that Germany should make reparation for war crimes in the village of Distomo in 1944. Potential sanctions were to include the seizing of German state property in Greece.[144] If nothing else this reminded the international community that the Nuremberg trials

Who can be held legally accountable?	For harm done where?	Examples
Nationals and non-nationals	In the nation of the court	National criminal law. Internet law – irrespective of the location of the perpetrators at the time
Nationals	In another nation	In countries with Roman law systems – treason, murder, bigamy. 'Sex tourism'. Prostitution of women with mental disabilities.[1] Specific war crimes.[2] Offences in the Antarctic.[3] EC human rights law[4]
Any public official	Anywhere	Torture (UK).[5] Corruption (UK).[6] Human rights abuses (Spain)[7]
Anyone	Global commons, any nation, or ship	Piracy, High Seas Convention (1958). Hijacking
Anyone	Anywhere	Hostage Convention (1979). UN Torture Convention (1986), related Belgian (1993/1999) and German (2002) Law. Crimes against humanity – International Criminal Court. USA Constitution (1787).[8] Alien Tort Claims Act (1789)[9]

Figure 1.4   The extension of national jurisdiction beyond national borders

[1] UK Sexual Offences Act (1956), s29 (1), 'anywhere in the world'.

[2] UK War Crimes Act (1991). If a person is a British national at any time, irrespective of nationality at the time of the act. War crimes committed between 1939 and June 1945 in Germany or in an occupied territory. The Act therefore avoids claiming global applicability by being place and time specific.

[3] UK Antarctic Act (1994), sec. 21.

[4] European soldiers operating in another country that is controlled by an EU country are bound by EC human rights law. ECHR ruling, November 2004, RE Iraq.

[5] UK Criminal Justice Act (1988), sec. 134(1), 'A public official or person acting in an official capacity, whatever his nationality … if in the UK or elsewhere'. See also Offences Against the Person Bill (1999) 12(3) – 'in the UK or elsewhere [irrespective of] the nationality of the persons concerned'.

[6] UK Corruption Act (1998) 9(4) – an 'agent … even if the person has no connection with the UK, and "public" is not confined to the public of the UK'.

[7] Conviction of Argentinian military officer and 'nun killer' Ricardo Miguel Cavallo, 2005.

[8] Congress is empowered 'to define and punish … offences against the law of nations' (Art. 1, sec. 8, cl.10).

[9] Anyone can sue for acts committed by anyone 'in violation of the law of nations or a treaty of the United States'.

had failed to provide redress on behalf of Greek victims. The *in absentia* strategy is, of course, available to all sides of the global accountability debate. In September 2000, President Milosevic set up a symbolic trial of Bill Clinton, Tony Blair and others concerned with the NATO bombing of Yugoslavia. Charges included crimes against humanity, initiating an aggressive war, using illegal weapons such as cluster bombs and violating sovereignty. The trial took place a few days before the presidential elections. A defence was presented, but by lawyers appointed by the court.[145]

Pinochet, Suharto and others such as Nazi doctor Heinrich Gross[146] evaded the courts through claims of mental incapacity. But the possibility of a 'hearing of the facts' in this circumstance, with or without the defendant, is already established in some legal systems. The rationale of these hearings is to avoid unjust sanctions for defendants with mental disabilities. There seems no reason why a hearing of the facts could not have been held despite *and because of* Pinochet's plea of mental incapacity. In December 2000, having put the original charges on hold, the Chilean Supreme Court ordered Judge Guzman to interview the general, 'regardless of whether medical tests had been carried out to establish ability to stand trial'.[147] This affirmed that the basis of accountability – answering reasonable questions to establish a record of fact – need not be inextricably linked with court procedures and mental competence.

One partial precedent for *in absentia* hearings is arguably rooted in England's first attempt at regime change, the trial of the monarch Charles I who was charged with harming his own subjects in 1649. He was taken to the trial, but would not acknowledge the authority of the court and refused to participate. That did not prevent the trial from proceeding, and he was then executed. The 'dormant precedents' for the trial were from Magna Carta. It is unlikely that King John foresaw the impact of his expedient deal with his barons in 1215 on his royal successors, or that he would be famed as the first British ruler to agree that the king was not above the law. The British monarchy restored after the trial and execution of Charles I considered Oliver Cromwell to blame for the execution, and also used the *in absentia* principle. They tried Cromwell, hung him from gallows and beheaded him – two years after he had died.

Throughout history, peer accountability has been a central aspect of bringing miscreant leaders to account, and its significance continues. The open questioning of the US-led invasion of Iraq – by senior figures such as Pope John Paul II, Nelson Mandela, Desmond Tutu and the Archbishop of Canterbury – provides an example. Other courageous endeavours were evident in diverse countries. At the end of 2000, in Iran, President Khatemi persuaded the Intelligence Ministry to take responsibility for the murder of dissident intellectuals. Forty officials, including judges and court officers, were put on trial to redress what the new head of the justice system, Ayatollah Mahmud Hashemi-Shahrudi, called a 'ruined judiciary'.[148] Three defendants were later sentenced to death and two to life imprisonment. The year-long anti-corruption campaign in Libya received personal backing from Colonel Gaddafi when he publicly questioned why some of his officials owned numerous taxi cabs and shops, while public money was going missing. The result was prison sentences for 47 government and bank officials, including finance minister Ujayli Abdelsalam. Perhaps the most significant example was the new ethos introduced in Kenya by Moi's successor, Mwai Kibaki, in 2003. The new permanent secretary for Governance and Ethics soon provided evidence that former president Moi had transferred sums abroad equivalent to a third of Kenya's GDP – half its foreign debt. The head of Kenya's anti-corruption initiative, John Githongo, had previously run the local branch of Transparency International.

Global leadership organizations occasionally produce interesting ideas. The InterAction Council was established in 1983 to 'mobilize the experience, energy and international contacts of a group of statesmen who have held the highest office in their own countries'.[149] It produces prescient reports on matters of peace and security, economy and development, and in May 2000 it produced a report on 'Enlightened leadership and human responsibility', which proposed that state leaders should agree to be bound by the UN Human Rights Declaration. This is an almost unique example of a group of leaders proposing that leaders should be bound by the same rules as everyone else, although it remains to be seen if current heads of state concur with this *post hoc* proposal by their predecessors, who would be little affected. The Commonwealth Ministerial Action Group has greater legitimacy and therefore its actions – for example, its role in addressing errant leadership in Nigeria, Fiji and Zimbabwe – are less contentious and all part of the broader pattern.

Personal surveillance of potential corruption is another aspect. In Jordan, King Abdullah made a visit to observe procedures in a tax office in Amman, disguised as an old man in traditional Arab dress. Similarly, over the winter holiday period, Mexican president Vicente Fox and his cabinet ministers personally stood at the US border to deter customs agents who extract bribes ('shake down') from migrant workers. Later, all but four customs supervisors and all 50 customs police chiefs were sacked and state revenue increased fivefold. But the endeavour was not wholly successful. During the same period, a £31,000 bribe was sufficient to permit an elephant to be smuggled across the border at Matamoros.[150]

> It is Africans who are now holding their leaders to account. Anybody with memories of the 1970s and 80s must be inspired by this new scenario. It is an awakening, every bit as powerful as the pan-Africanist movement of the 1960s but sure to have a much more profound impact on every day lives.
>
> Fergal Keane[151]

Most of the events that came to the attention of the world community during this period concerned high-profile political violence by notorious national leaders. But the 'domino effect' also includes a significant 'second track' challenge to powerful people who abuse their positions at lower levels of society – senior doctors, local government officials, workplace managers, police chiefs, head teachers, university staff, husbands – and this is clearly an aspect of the new 'up-system' accountability ethos. For centuries, child abuse by Catholic priests has been hidden because church leaders thought themselves answerable only to canon law. They considered that there was no moral requirement to involve civil authorities, even for serious cases. In April 2002, the Pope put an end to that belief, and made it clear that religious leaders were not above the law.[152] A report two years later concluded: 'These leadership failings have been shameful to the church.'[153] In 2004, the Pakistani government started to expose sex abuse by clerics in the country's Madrassas. In parallel, senior leaders of the Greek Orthodox Church were investigated and arrest warrants issued concerning the bribery of judges and other corruption.[154] The Polish Dominican Order was also reexamining whether or not some of its leaders had collaborated with the former communist regime, and alleged bribes.

At all levels of society, the impunity of elites is being dismantled. One little-known example of second-track accountability concerns the abuse of people with disabilities, particularly mental disabilities. Throughout the world, these people have traditionally been seen as invisible victims of violence by those with more power, which it was thought impossible to redress.[155] Now this is changing: in many countries new legislation is coming into place to protect them, and justice is at last extending to all citizens irrespective of their personal power.

By 2005, not only had the war crimes courts firmly established that rape and abuse of women are unlawful, but the prosecutors from

> In the last two decades, the quest for greater accountability has penetrated all our lives, like great draughts of Heineken's, reaching parts that supposedly less developed forms of accountability did not reach.
>
> Onora O'Neill, *A question of trust,*
> BBC Reith Lectures 2002[156]

the courts had met to discuss international criminal accountability and the rights of children. This included the protection of child witnesses before, during and after giving evidence. David Crane, Sierra Leone prosecutor, said the message was now: 'If you go after women and children, you will pay the price.'[157] Perhaps the eventual indicator of leadership accountability may not be how many international despots have been brought to justice, but how many unknown and formerly powerless people have achieved justice against local despots.

The new accountability ethos is likely to create new relationships between leader and followers. Leaders will increasingly be challenged by those they perceive as their supporters. A seemingly small example came in the wake of the US-led occupation of Iraq. Defense secretary Donald Rumsfeld had seen the conservative right faction of the US population as clearly on his side. But when it was discovered that his signature on the letters to the families of soldiers killed in action was printed, not personally signed, he was vociferously challenged by pro-war Americans. The example may seem insignificant, but it encapsulates two arguments that run throughout this book. The first is that leadership accountability is less now a matter of 'sides' – the challenges are becoming circumstance-based rather than political. The second is that the most significant single factor fuelling these challenges is deceit, even about a signature. Rumsfeld would probably have not been attacked had his name been typed instead of being printed as a forged signature, in the manner of a piece of junk mail from a disreputable fly-by-night mail trader. The centrality of deceit as the catalyst for accountability is explained further in the next two chapters.

The 'public order of the international community'

If global leadership accountability is to become an established check on abuse of power at personal and institutional levels within a globalizing world, what central concept might provide the ethical basis and rationale for accountability initiatives? If 'intervention' and 'regime change' are to become acceptable in extreme circumstances, what is the guiding principle that could prevent this regressing into spirals of retributive accountability as described in the next chapter?

Within the UK House of Lords judgments on the Pinochet extradition case in 1999, Lord Hope of Craighead spoke of acts that 'offend against the public order of the international community'.[158] This simple statement is very valuable as it proposes a workable concept that can link ethics, law and accountability on a global scale. It represents an extension of the notion of domestic public order law, which has clear and relevant parameters. It extends 'order' to an international level, but also, logically, 'public'. This is already reflected in recent legislation, for example the UK Corruption of Foreign Public Officials Act 1998, which states that ' "public" is not confined to the public of the UK' (section 9(3)).

The main elements of public order offences are force, violence, fear and provocation. These can readily be applied more broadly. The UN Charter declares that members 'shall refrain in their international relations from the threat or use of force' (Article 2(4)), and it is increasingly argued that this can concern economic force such as sanctions or blockades.[159] It seems reasonable to extend the notion to embrace the other elements, for example to the violent force of adverse environmental impacts.[160] Fear arising from food or water insecurity or an ageing nuclear power station across a border is relevant, as is provocation such as testing weapons close to another country.

If powerful individuals become above the law in a village community, disorder and local retribution will follow. If powerful individuals become above the law in the global community, disorder and global retribution will follow. If there are no agreed global rules to regulate world rulers, the world's peoples will make up their own rules and invent their own means of deterrence, punishment and retribution. Ongoing global feuding is not an attractive prognosis, as the next chapter shows.

Implications

- **Up-system personalized leadership accountability** is increasing globally. Power and status no longer ensure impunity; leaders become more culpable than others.
  - There is a **domino effect** around the world.
  - Responsible leaders cannot **time out justice** – people in their eighties and nineties are made to account for their misconduct.
  - Coordinated **alternative international strategies** complement and strengthen the courts.

- There is **second-track** accountability of minor power elites – local religious leaders, doctors, teachers, managers – on behalf of powerless groups – children, people with disabilities, women.
- Leaders are challenged **irrespective of traditional loyalties**, by their own supporters and by their peers.

- Redressing **political violence** is central.
  - The Second World War tribunals established **strong standards** – it was not foreseen that these could eventually be utilized against leaders in the same countries that set the standards.
  - **New standards** emerge, for example the **abuse of women and children** becomes a war crime.
  - There is a **top-down-bottom–up synergy** as national courts and international forums work in tandem.
  - Leaders **de-link war and violence**, notably in Europe and North East Asia.

- **Corrupt** leadership is challenged.
  - Post-Cold War initiatives (for example the World Bank) to ensure **good governance** in less developed countries extend to include corrupt leaders in the rich nations.
  - Particularly strong action is taken in **North East Asia**.

- **Environmental harm** is more difficult to redress because causation is less visible.
  - Industrial leaders are therefore less guarded and leave **audit trails** which fuel future challenges.
  - **Small-scale cases** set significant precedents.

- 'Dormant precedents' are activated and extended.
  - The **WWII tribunals** provide the basis for addressing political violence fifty years later.
  - Measures against **corrupt leaders** in less developed countries are applied in the rich nations.
  - **Environmental** cases draw on seemingly unrelated case law, for example corruption.
  - Precedents **extend across sectors**, for example environmental war crimes.

- **Jurisdiction extends.**
  - **National courts** claim or are given international jurisdiction.
  - **International law** is incorporated into national legislation.
  - The EC extends its reach within and outside the EU.
  - **Trials *in absentia*** and **hearings of the facts** become increasingly legitimate.

- **Immunity** is overturned and subverted; extradition increases.
  - Leaders create **innovative forms of self-protection** – mutual sanctuary, authoritarian laws, creating fear, media control, distraction through blaming and challenging others.

- A **precautionary approach** emerges within power elites, because dormant precedents and the extension of precedents and jurisdiction create an uncertain and unpredictable context for the misuse of global power.

- The 'public order of the international community' provides a central concept to frame legitimate global accountability.
  - Internationally agreed **codes of leadership conduct** emerge to form the basis for future international action.

2
Global Feuding: Regime Change and Retribution

> A democratic society in its thirst for liberty may fall under the influence of bad leaders.
>
> Plato, Tyranny, *The Republic* (*c*.400 BC, 8:563)

> You can fight on the side of the angels and nevertheless commit crimes against humanity.
>
> Desmond da Silva, Deputy Prosecutor at Sierra Leone Special Court, 2004[1]

In 2001, global leadership accountability seemed to go wrong. The plane attacks on the World Trade Center and the Pentagon and over Pennsylvania on 11 September (9/11) which killed around 3,000 civilians, subsequent further crimes termed 'terrorism' and the US-led military responses all represented retributive accountability. The 9/11 attacks rationalized US-led military retaliation, first in Afghanistan because it hosted al-Qaida, and then in Iraq, which was falsely linked with al-Qaida. The US-led action was presented in relation to a so-called 'axis of evil' – which included Iraq, Iran and North Korea – within the slogan a 'war against terrorism'. The Iraq invasion appeared to mimic terrorist tactics – it was named 'shock and awe'.

The purpose here is not to provide a complete account of events surrounding the 9/11 attacks, nor to assess whether the actions of the US or other parties were morally or legally justified. The aim is to describe and explain these happenings in the context of an era of accountability, in the light of information that was in the public domain and would therefore influence the calls for accountability. Why did action to oust a nasty despot, which should have attracted global praise, instead attract global criticism? What was the nature of the challenges to US, British and other leaders in relation to the broader accountability movement? And why did these leaders pursue policies that were founded on so little evidence and seemed so unaccountable by contemporary norms?

Noam Chomsky points out that the public challenge to the military action against Iraq was categorically different to that in Vietnam, because it started before the invasion, and this 'reflects a steady increase over these years in unwillingness to tolerate aggression and atrocities [by states]'. He talked of the ' "second superpower", public opinion'. And continued: 'Not only was "revisionism" of the [US] political leadership without precedent; so to was the opposition to it.'[2] The argument in this chapter is that the events surrounding 9/11 fitted a bigger pattern of change about global leadership accountability, on all sides.

The context

The 9/11 attacks appeared as last-resort deeds by frustrated and ideologically extreme groups who could see no other means to question the way in which the US government used its power throughout the world. There were no threats or demands associated with this new form of international crime. It was not blackmail. The targets and the timing were the message – a dislike of the economic, military and political use of power by US institutions, their leaders, and those who supported them. The weapons were also new. They were, as the Cambridge Security Seminar in 2004 argued, 'instruments of mass effect',[3] not weapons of mass destruction as popularist politicians claimed. They deployed a combination of spectacular, small-scale (in terms of war) violence and large-scale media reporting to achieve their impact. The Islamist network al-Qaida and its apparent leader Osama bin Laden were presented as culpable for most of the attacks.

In Iraq the work of UN weapons inspectors, led by Hans Blix, had been suddenly curtailed to permit the invasion in March 2003. A copious written response from the Iraqi government to the UN, to questions about its weapons programmes, was only made public by US authorities after thousands of pages had been removed. Bush justified the invasion by claiming that Iraq had posed a 'grave and gathering threat to America and the world'.[4] A CIA report, *Iraq's mass destruction weapons programs*, claimed in 2002:

> Iraq has continued its weapons of mass destruction (WMDs) programs in defiance of UN resolutions and restrictions. Baghdad has chemical and biological weapons as well as missiles with ranges in

excess of UN restrictions; if left unchecked, it probably will have a nuclear weapon during this decade ... Baghdad hides large portions of Iraq's WMD efforts.[5]

A letter from the US government to the UN Security Council in March 2003 stated that the operations 'are necessary steps to defend the United States and the international community from the threat posed by Iraq'.[6] British prime minister Tony Blair had asked the House of Commons to 'support the decision of the government that the UK should use all means necessary to ensure disarmament of Iraq's weapons of mass destruction'.[7] He presented selected intelligence information that appeared to provide evidence of a significant threat, in a 'dossier' published in September 2002. He said that he believed it was 'established beyond doubt that Saddam has continued to produce chemical and biological weapons', and that 'his military planning allows for some of the WMD to be ready within 45 minutes of an order to use them'.[8] In 2003 Bush had claimed, 'We won't be proven wrong ... Saddam Hussein produced and possessed chemical and biological weapons and was trying to reconstitute his nuclear weapons program.'[9]

By the end of the year, Bush had to accept that there were no weapons of mass destruction in Iraq, but his response was, 'So what's the difference?'[10] The head of Iraq's nuclear weapons programme, Jafar Dhia Jafar, told the world that Iraq's WMD programmes had stopped in 1991, on the orders of Saddam Hussein.[11] Blair had claimed, 'There are literally thousands of sites ... As I have said throughout, I have no doubt [the Iraq Survey Group] will find the clearest possible evidence of Saddam's weapons of mass destruction.'[12] In October 2004, the Iraq Survey Group confirmed that there were no WMDs and no WMD programmes when the invasion took place. In July 2003, Blair had said, 'I don't concede at all that the intelligence at the time was wrong.'[13] At the 2004 Labour Party Conference he made a stilted apology for the faulty intelligence, but not for the invasion. Two weeks later the claim that WMDs could be ready for use in 45 minutes was formally withdrawn by the British government, and the intelligence services said that half their sources were unreliable. The Mexican ambassador to the UN, Adolfo Aguilar Zinser, revealed that an MI6 officer had admitted to him that there was no 'clear' evidence of WMDs.[14] By 2005 the British government was introducing new rules for intelligence-gathering and report-writing, the biggest revision for sixty years. Among others, Lord King stated that it was unlikely that there would ever be another dossier of this nature. In the US, a commission set up by Bush concluded that 'The intelligence community was dead wrong in almost all of its pre-war judgments about Iraq's weapons of mass destruction.'[15] In April 2005, Blair finally admitted that his ill-famed dossier was a mistake: 'In retrospect, it would have been better to have simply published the Joint Intelligence Committee reports.'[16] By 2005 even Blair's home secretary David Blunkett had admitted during a TV interview, 'We were wrong.'[17]

By the start of 2004, one year after the invasion, Iraq seemed to be imploding, with effective resistance movements killing many US soldiers, hostage-taking, ongoing killing of civilians by the US-led forces, and an American administration that wanted to exit because of growing domestic pressures. It was initially estimated that 11,407 Iraqi civilians had been killed by the US-led forces during the invasion and occupation[18] and by September 2004 over 1,000 US troops had died. In November, *The Lancet* published a paper calculating that up to 100,000 civilians had died from various causes. Most were women and children, and the risk of death from violence after the invasion was 58 times higher than in the period before.[19] In addition, 50,000 Iraqi soldiers were killed; most were unwilling conscripts. The occupying forces claimed that they did not keep statistics, even though this is necessary to fulfil the Geneva Conventions.[20,21] But an American aid worker, Marla Ruzicka, reported that she has been told by a US brigadier general that recording enemy deaths was 'standard operating procedure',[22] yet the figures were not publicly available. By June 2005, a *Washington Post/ ABC News* opinion poll indicated for the first time that most American people thought the invasion was a mistake.[23] And the press announced that 'American officials lied to British ministers over the use of "internationally reviled" napalm-type firebombs in Iraq'.[24]

The public questioning

The US

In the US, strategies deployed in Iraq were quickly questioned by significant political figures. Carl Levin, the senior Democrat in the Senate Armed Services Committee, claimed that the CIA had deliberately misled Blix and other UN arms inspectors. A NATO supreme commander, General Wesley Clark, argued that it was the wrong war at the wrong time in the wrong place.[25] Reports, repeated by Bush and Blair, stating that Niger had been providing nuclear material to Iraq, were shown to be based on false documentation. Through a book called *The price of loyalty* by Ron Suskind, the former US treasury secretary Paul O'Neill stated that invading Iraq was 'topic A' at the first meeting of Bush and the

National Security Council, ten days after he came to office. O'Neill claimed that the president was constantly asking, 'Go find me a way to do this', and September 11 provided the justification. When confronted with this claim, Bush did not deny it, and he argued that regime change in Iraq had been an ongoing policy from the Clinton era. Countless similar challenges were from within the US political establishment, not from aggrieved victims, and were paralleled by ongoing anti-war demonstrations throughout the US.[26]

Al-Qaida and the 9/11 attacks were incorrectly linked to Iraq by US leaders, particularly by US vice-president Dick Cheney, who had said that there is 'overwhelming evidence ... of a connection between al-Qaeda and Iraq'. In November 2002, US secretary of state Donald Rumsfeld stated that 'Saddam could give his WMD to al-Qaeda', and in June 2004 Bush had claimed: 'The reason I keep insisting that there was a relationship between Iraq and Saddam and al-Qaeda is because there was a relationship between Iraq and al-Qaeda.'[27] But a report from the Carnegie Endowment for International Peace, in January 2004, found that 'there was no evidence to support the claim that Iraq would have transferred WMDs to al-Qa'ida and much to counter it'.[28] Secretary of state Colin Powell then concurred with this, seemingly contradicting his own assertions before the invasion.[29] By October, Rumsfeld had changed his mind, claiming at a Council of Foreign Relations meeting in New York: 'I have not seen any strong, hard evidence that links the two [Saddam Hussein and Osama bin Laden].'[30] Subsequent government inquiries in the US and UK found no evidence of links, but by that time around 80 per cent of Americans had been led to believe that al-Qaida and the Iraqi regime were jointly implicated in the 9/11 attacks.

The head of the US Iraq Survey Group and former UN weapons inspector, David Kay, resigned, claiming that stockpiles of WMDs had never existed. He stated simply, 'we were all wrong and that is most disturbing'.[31] Kay had been a strong supporter of the invasion, but a few weeks later said even more bluntly that the US leaders should 'come clean with the American people'.[32] He later said that if anyone, specifically Blair, still believed that there were WMDs, they were 'delusional'.[33] Following Kay's resignation, US secretary of state Colin Powell then said that Iraq's possession of WMDs was 'an open question'.[34] The press noted that Bush had moved from a concern with WMDs to a concern about 'weapons of mass destruction programmes', to a concern about 'weapons of mass-destruction-related programme activities'.[35] Bush then changed his rationale for war from eliminating WMDs to eliminating Saddam Hussein – 'a dangerous man in a dangerous part of the world'. His security adviser

Condoleezza Rice talked on *CBS News* of 'differences between what we knew going in and what we found on the ground'.[36]

This left one line of defence, to blame the intelligence services for statements that had, it was claimed, misled the politicians and public alike. And the defence specialists moved quickly to defend themselves. CIA director George Tenet claimed that the Agency had 'never said there was an imminent threat'. Yet Bush had stated, 'The Iraqi regime is a threat of unique urgency.'[37] In February 2003, Powell had said, 'Every statement I make today is backed up by sources, solid sources. These are not assertions. What we are giving you are the facts and conclusion based on solid intelligence.'[38] By April he admitted that the intelligence 'appears not to be ... solid'.[39] Bush announced an inquiry into the apparent problems with the intelligence that had led to his belief that Iraq had WMDs, and within a day Blair had set up a similar inquiry in Britain. Two weeks later, Australia followed. These were immediately criticized for being too narrow. (See 'Forums', later.)

In parallel with these events, for over two years around 680 so-called 'enemy combatants' from Afghanistan and Pakistan were imprisoned indefinitely without being charged at the US Guantanamo Bay base in Cuba. Cells had no windows, exercise was restricted, and abusive questioning techniques were permitted. British law lords, EU leaders and many others pointed out that this was illegal by the standards of international and US law going back at least a century. In February 2004, five British detainees were released without charge, then French and Australian, and many more followed. In June, the US Supreme Court ruled that detainees must be told why they are being held, and have a right to appeal against detention, a fundamental national and international human right which the Bush administration had claimed did not apply. A further ruling held that the detainees should be treated as prisoners of war and given protection under the Geneva Conventions. The Australian Prime Minister, John Howard, in relation to Australians held in the camp, concluded, 'My understanding is that the American Supreme Court has ruled that the detention has been unlawful.'[40] A subsequent report form the International Committee of the Red Cross (ICRC) stated that practices at the prison amounted to 'an intentional system of cruel, unusual and degrading treatment and a form of torture'.[41]

Britain and elsewhere

Similar challenges in Britain were more sustained. Two senior government ministers resigned in protest against Blair's presentation of the case for invading Iraq. Cabinet minister and former foreign secretary

Robin Cook accused Blair and other ministers of 'not presenting the whole picture' and of a 'missionary zeal', and secretary of state for international development Clare Short said that the prime minister was guilty of 'honourable deception'.[42] She also claimed that she had been misled by Blair because he promised that Britain would be able to contribute fully to the reconstruction and future development of Iraq. Instead, the US took total control. A junior health minister, Lord Hunt, also resigned, and his 14-year-old son took part in anti-war protests as did many other schoolchildren. The press ran stories under headlines such as 'The lies that led us into war',[43] and anti-war protestors carried posters reading 'B.liar' at the biggest such protest ever to take place in London.

The questioning intensified, especially from senior politicians. Robin Cook said, 'I just don't see how Blair can hold to the line that he was right when everyone else is admitting that they were wrong.' US and British leaders then tried another line of defence, arguing that an announcement by Libya that it was not continuing its WMD programme was a broader outcome of his strategy against the 'axis of evil'. But this was then contradicted by Libyan foreign minister Abdul Rahman Shalgam, who pointed out that the Libyan decision to do this had been taken ten years earlier.[44] David Albright, head of the Washington-based Institute for International Security, later stated that the US government claims about Libya's ability to produce WMDs had been 'exaggerated'.[45]

Meanwhile, in Australia, a parliamentary inquiry had been told by a former senior intelligence analyst that the Australian government 'skewed, misrepresented, used selectively and fabricated' the intelligence it used to justify Australian involvement in the war.[46] Prime minister John Howard dismissed the claim in August 2003, but by February 2004 he was saying, 'In the fullness of time, it might be demonstrated that the [intelligence] advice was inaccurate.' In Spain, the opposition party was directly accusing the retiring prime minister, José Maria Aznar, about 'the lies' that had led to Spanish support for and involvement in the invasion.[47] It is estimated that on the same day as the protest in Britain, throughout the world, a record ten million people had taken part in simultaneous protests against the war.[48]

The day after the UK inquiry was announced, Brian Jones, a former head within the Defence Intelligence Staff (DIS) went on record as saying, 'In my view, the expert intelligence analysis of the DIS were overruled in the preparation of the dossier back in September 2002, resulting in a presentation that was misleading about Iraq's capabilities'.[49]

A former deputy chief of intelligence at the Ministry of Defence, John Morrison, said on a BBC TV interview that when he heard Blair talk of Iraq as a 'serious and current threat' to Britain, 'I could almost hear the collective raspberry going up around Whitehall'.[50] The invisible leaders of the CIA, MI6, MI5 and the Joint Intelligence Committee (JIC) were being pulled into the accountability frame in a way never seen before.

Then a British Security Council official, Katherine Gun, was charged with breaking the Official Secrets Act. She had disclosed to a newspaper that the US had asked the British intelligence services to monitor the phones of Security Council members who might vote against a resolution for war, which she believed was illegal. The action against her acted as a catalyst for protest. She was supported by Hollywood actor Sean Penn, black civil rights activist Jesse Jackson, the British accountability NGO Liberty, five US congressmen and Daniel Ellsberg, whose whistle-blowing had led to Watergate and the downfall of Nixon. The trial was set for the end of February, but in court the government prosecutor dropped the case on the basis that there was no realistic prospect of conviction. This appeared strange as Gun had openly admitted what she had done. The outcome spared the government further embarrassing revelations, one of which might have been the disclosure of the Attorney General's full advice about the legality of invading Iraq which had been kept secret. It was pointed out that the Attorney General also has the ultimate power to discontinue prosecutions.

In the wake of this, Clare Short, the former development secretary for Blair, was asked on a radio interview if it were true that 'British spies have been instructed to carry out operations within the United Nations on people like Kofi Annan?' Her reply was, 'Yes absolutely'.[51] Her disclosure seemed itself to be a breach of the Official Secrets Act and customary cabinet confidentiality, and the UN made clear that such spying would be illegal. Blair was publicly challenged to say that Short had lied. He did not. She had set up an accountability catch-22 for Blair. If she were found guilty of breaking the law, then her claim would be right, and therefore the government had acted illegally too. Two days later, a former deputy legal adviser at the Foreign Office, Elizabeth Wilmshurst, stated that 'I left my job because I did not agree that the use of force against Iraq was lawful.'[52] She, and others, it seemed, had disagreed with the Attorney General. Former prime minister John Major then added his name to those, including Greenpeace, who were calling for Blair to disclose the Attorney General's full legal advice. Blair's office claimed this was an official secret; other MPs pointed out that the rules of parliament permitted such a disclosure.

Further criticism came from a spectrum of eminent sources. One of the most surprising was the International Institute for Strategic Studies (IISS), which by February 2004 was stating that the US could no longer 'assume a high moral position' in the world. Its report elaborated:[53]

> The credibility of America's externally directed human rights message has been damaged by US curtailment of the rights of its own citizens and non-citizens.

The phraseology at the end of the sentence echoes the criticisms levelled at Saddam Hussein by Bush and Blair as a rationale for invasion. A previous report, in 2002, by the IISS claimed that Iraq had used, and would use, chemical and biological weapons. Much of this had been used by Blair in his own 'dossier', which came out two weeks later.

Individuals also continued to fuel the challenge. In August 2004 a member of the Iraq Survey Group (ISG) claimed that British JIC chief John Scarlett had urged members to include so-called 'golden nuggets' of intelligence that had already been discredited. The ISG members were reluctant to include claims that Iraq had a smallpox programme, mobile chemical weapons laboratories and a nuclear rail gun. A member of the ISG was reported as saying, 'Inclusion of Scarlett's nuggets would have been grossly manipulative of the truth. Let's face it, he wanted to include lies.'[54] The Prime Minister's Office refused to deny the claims.[55] Before the Iraq war, this sort of disclosure was virtually unheard of within the British establishment.

The public mood was summed up simply in an open letter to Blair from Maxine Gentle, the 14-year-old sister of a British soldier who had been killed in Iraq. She wrote:

> My feelings are that I think you are rubbish at your job. You don't care about the British public, armed forces or anyone in fact. My big brother died at the age of 19, and what for? A war over oil and money, that's what I think the war is all about. There was no such thing as weapons of 'mass destruction', if there were Saddam Hussein would have used them at the start of the war.

Ms Gentle was invited to a meeting with the deputy prime minister, John Prescott, but she walked out after a few minutes, accusing him of 'talking rubbish'.[56] A few years ago it would have been unthinkable that senior leaders would pay so much attention to a 14-year-old girl, and even less thinkable that she would accuse a prime minister of causing death by starting an improper war, firmly challenge a deputy prime minister, and walk out because she was not impressed by his answers. The new accountability movement transcends age. It also transcends traditional views of loyalty. In 2005, another British subject was reported as saying, 'Two years ago, I marched against the war ... I still reckon the invasion was wrong – there were surely more discriminating means of removing one man from his job.'[57] The view was from a British army major, Giles Harris, serving in Iraq. But perhaps the greatest indicator of accountability came from a simple statistic from the British Prime Minister's Office. The number of letters sent to the prime minister has steadily increased over ten years. But in 2004 'surge' had caused the office to hire extra staff. There had been over a million letters to the prime minister.[58]

By the time of the election in 2005, 17 MPs from Blair's own Labour Party were campaigning on the basis of a declaration stating, 'I remain totally opposed to the war on Iraq', and most local Labour parties were opting to use a version of the Labour Party leaflet that did not include a photo and message from Blair, because of his unpopularity.[59] Independent candidates and political parties emerged, asking for support to hold Blair to account for the war. George Galloway, a former Labour MP who had formed is own party, Respect, ousted an established Labour candidate. In Blair's own constituency, the father of a soldier killed in Iraq stood against him, questioning his integrity and honesty about the war. The day before the election he defended his decisions on the basis that he felt Iraq was 'the place to start' on weapons of mass destruction after the 9/11 attacks.[60] Yet American rumouring about a link between 9/11 and Iraq had been shown to be false, and the 9/11 attacks were not carried out with 'weapons of mass destruction' in the form that Iraq was wrongly accused of possessing. The Labour Party was reelected, essentially because there was no viable opposition, but its majority was cut by more than half and the Blair factor was seen as the reason.

By 2005, cases against Blair and his supporters had been put before the International Criminal Court, Scotland Yard, the Parliamentary Standards Commissioner and Information Commissioner, British courts and the Bar Council, by British, Irish, Belgian and Greek lawyers. He had faced four separate public inquiries. His own civil servants, diplomats, party members and ministers had openly attacked him, and efforts had been made to impeach him in parliament. Families of soldiers killed in Iraq demanded an inquiry threatening judicial review and other legal action if he refused, including a case to the ICC. It is hard to think of another such significant accountability challenge against a British prime minister, from the type of people who in previous eras would have supported their leader through tradition or loyalty or at worst would have stayed silent.

Human rights abuses

Public calls for accountability escalated when photos and videos by US personnel of the abuse of Iraqi prisoners in Abu Ghraib jail outside Baghdad appeared in the press in May 2004. These included hooded and chained inmates, beatings, naked women and men being threatened with dogs, naked prisoners forced to lie on top of one another in sexually demeaning positions, apparent rape and threat of rape, inmates hooded and wearing women's knickers, and guards exerting unbridled power over prisoners including a female US soldier leading a man on a lead like a dog. One of the victims later said, 'The Americans told us about democracy and freedom. Then they did this to us ... It was humiliating. We didn't think we would survive.'[61] At first Pentagon officials tried to prevent CBS from broadcasting the images, but soon Bush said he was 'sorry for the humiliation suffered by the Iraqi prisoners'.[62] It was noted that this is not the same as apologizing for the conduct of US personnel under his command. The astonishing aspect was that the pictures were not taken by investigative journalists, but by the perpetrators on their own digital cameras.

Similar allegations appeared in relation to British troops, and the defence secretary Geoff Hoon was forced to admit that hooding prisoners was illegal because of British laws dating back to 1971 and the ill-treatment of prisoners in Northern Ireland.[63] Blair then apologized for abuses by British troops. At this point defence minister Adam Ingram had stated to the House of Commons that 33 cases of civilian deaths, injury and ill-treatment were being investigated, but was then forced to admit that the figure was 61.[64] An Amnesty report talked of 'serious human rights violations' by British troops, and that 'torture and ill-treatment by coalition forces were widespread'.[65] It was found that another report expressing concern about the treatment of prisoners, by the Red Cross (ICRC), had been received by the government. Pierre Krahenbuhl, the ICRC Director of Operations, stated, 'We had identified a series of elements and patterns in terms of treatment and conditions that appeared to us contrary to some of the provisions contained in the Geneva Conventions.'[66] A British commander whose loyal service in Iraq had earned him considerable praise, Colonel Tim Collins, then stated publicly that the abuse arose partly because 'leaders of a country, leaders of an alliance' constantly referred to Iraqi civilians as 'enemy ... rather than treating them as people'. And this attitude spread to ordinary soldiers. He continued:

> Either it was a war to liberate the people of Iraq, in which case there was gross incompetence, or it was a cynical war that was going to happen anyway to vent some form of anger on Saddam Hussein's regime with no regard to the consequences on the Iraqi people. In that case it is a form of common assault – and the evidence would point towards the latter.[67]

Previously a speech made by Collins, to increase troop morale, had been hung in the Oval Office by Bush.

US and British troops faced courts martial over the allegations, and there were many claims that they were acting on the instructions of, or with the tacit permission of, more senior military and political leaders.[68] The apparent goal was to make the prisoners compliant for questioning by intelligence agents. The senior officer at Abu Ghraib prison said that she had been told by a senior intelligence officer to treat prisoners like 'dogs'.[69] In the formal inquiry into these events, Major General Antonio Taguba concluded that 'there was a failure of leadership ... from the brigade commander on down. Lack of discipline, no training whatsoever, and no supervision. Supervisory omission was rampant.'[70] There were eleven separate inquiries into the abuses, and subsequent reports blamed top civilian military officials, including Rumsfeld and his advisers.[71] Similarly, British soldiers claimed they had been following orders from officers to 'work them [the prisoners] hard'.[72]

John Gray provided a reminder of the significant point underlying these abuses:

> the Bush administration evaded international law ... [because] They outsourced security duties at Abu Ghraib and other detention facilities to private contractors not covered by military law and not regulated by the Geneva convention. In effect, the Bush administration deliberately created a lawless environment in which abuse could be practiced with impunity.[73]

But this evasion tactic opened up other unexpected and novel routes for accountability. Two US-based security firms – Titan Corporation and CACI International – were taken to court by prisoners for conspiring to 'direct and conduct a scheme to torture, rape, and in some instances, summarily execute plaintiffs', in breach of the Racketeer Influenced and Corrupt Organizations Act, which is intended to redress organized crime.[74] The 'next step agencies' and 'agents' are a significant aspect of contemporary leadership accountability, and of how despots try to evade accountability.[75] Leaders who are being made increasingly accountable are likely to attempt to distance themselves from problems by contracting out risky activities. But this distancing often opens other routes for accountability, and senior leaders are then implicated to an even greater degree because of the perceived deceit.

World leaders

Calls for accountability also came from highly respected world leaders, who were better-known for their discrete diplomacy than for damning political criticisms. Both Pope John Paul II and the Archbishop of Canterbury openly questioned the invasion. Former UN weapons inspector Hans Blix contributed his view about the presentation of the threat posed by Iraq's WMDs:

> the intention was to dramatise it, just as the vendors of some merchandise ... exaggerate the importance of what they have. But from politicians, of our leaders, in the Western world, I think we expect more than that – a bit more sincerity.[76]

He later talked of British and US governments 'distorting' the reports of the weapons inspectors.[77] A week later Archbishop Desmond Tutu was even more direct. In a speech in London he claimed that Bush and Blair had implemented a policy of 'might is right – and to hell with the rule of international law':[78]

> An immoral war was thus waged and the world is a great deal less safe place than before. There are many who resent the powerful who can throw their weight about so callously and with so much impunity ... President Bush and Prime Minister Blair would recover considerable credibility and respect if they were able to say, 'Yes, we made a mistake.'

As a Nobel Peace Laureate and former chair of the South African Truth and Reconciliation Commission, Tutu is an international accountability icon. A few months later he appeared in a play staged in New York, *Guantanamo: honour bound to defend freedom*. The play challenged the Bush view of the legality of the prison camp.

Another Nobel Laureate, former US president Jimmy Carter, then put the argument in stronger terms:

> Iraq ... was a war based on lies and misrepresentations from London and from Washington, claiming falsely that Saddam Hussein was responsible for [the] 9/11 attacks, claiming falsely that Iraq had weapons of mass destruction. And I think that President Bush and Prime Minister Blair probably knew that many of the allegations were based on uncertain knowledge ... a decision was made to go to war [then they said] 'Let's find a way to do so.'[79]

Carter had succinctly encapsulated the questions that were being asked daily in the US and Britain by the end of March 2004. Questioning by those seen as embodying the highest moral authority in the world continued when Nelson Mandela said in his farewell speech to the South African legislature:

> We watch as two of the leading democracies of the free world get involved in a war the United Nations did not sanction ... We look on with horror as reports surface of terrible abuses against the dignity of human beings held captive by invading forces in their own country.[80]

Following a bomb attack and election in Spain, the new prime minister José Luis Rodriguez Zapatero immediately declared, 'The war was a disaster, the occupation of Iraq is a disaster.'[81] The next day he continued, 'Military intervention in Iraq was a political mistake ... It divided more than it united, there were no reasons for it. Time has shown that the arguments for it lacked credibility. You cannot bomb by chance. You can't lead a war with lies.'[82] Two days after taking office, Zapatero had recalled Spanish troops from Iraq. Other countries, including the Philippines, followed.

Then in April, a group of 52 former British diplomats, including former ambassadors and senior officials with direct experience of the Arab Middle East, wrote an open letter to Blair, which was another unprecedented initiative. It claimed, 'we are portrayed throughout the Arab world as partners in an illegal and brutal occupation of Iraq', and continued:

> The conduct of the war in Iraq has made it clear that there was no effective plan for the post-Saddam settlement. All those with

experience of the area predicted that the occupation of Iraq by the coalition forces would meet serous and stubborn resistance, as has proved to be the case. To describe the resistance as led by terrorists, fanatics and foreigners is neither convincing nor helpful … However much Iraqis may yearn for a democratic society, the belief that one could be created by the coalition is naïve.[83]

One of the signatories, Sir Crispin Tickell, commented, 'I have never seen such a level of worry and despair among those who have been involved in the diplomatic field before.' A former ambassador to Libya, Oliver Miles, went further, 'The Iraq war was illegal … whatever policy George Bush and Tony Blair had appears to have been badly planned and badly executed.'[84] In June, a US group called 'Diplomats and Military Commanders for Change' made a similar statement, and stated that they had 'lost confidence [in] the Bush administration to advocate for American interests to provide the kind of leadership that we think is essential'.[85] Three months later, Australia followed. A letter to the prime minister from former heads of the defence force, senior intelligence offers and diplomats stated, 'We are concerned that Australia was committed to join the invasion on the basis of false assumptions and deception of the American government.'[86] In December around 40 British ambassadors, military commanders and senior politicians publicly petitioned Blair to set up a formal inquiry into the civilian deaths in Iraq. Ambassadors broke with all tradition in their criticisms. The British former ambassador to Uzbekistan, Craig Murray, talked of the 'web of illegality' spun by the Bush administration, and argued: 'We have abandoned the notion of a foreign policy based on the rule of international law, in favour of one that says that might is right.'[87]

The media

The contribution of the newly digitalized media was its prodigious ability to record and recall what had been said by senior politicians anywhere, and to highlight apparent contradictions through compressed continuous comparisons. Politicians appeared very naive in their grasp of this new dynamic. The new skill of the digitalized media was to edit relevant comments in such a way that a dialogue could be created between disparate actors across the world and across time. Many 'docudramas' presented views that were clearly contradictory and sometimes self-contradictory. The word 'deceit' became common.

> Our objectives are clear ... because the Taliban have chosen to side with al-Qa'ida, to remove them.
>
> Tony Blair, UK Prime Minister, 30 October 2001
>
> The objectives are clear, and the one about the removal of the Taliban is not something we have as a clear objective.
>
> John Prescott, UK Deputy Prime Minister, 31 October 2001[88]
>
> The assessed intelligence has established that Saddam has continued to produce chemical and biological weapons.
>
> Tony Blair, 24 September 2002
>
> I have to accept it seems increasingly clear that Saddam did not have stockpiles of chemical or biological weapons.
>
> Tony Blair, July 2004[89]

The public was reminded that in February 2001, Powell had said in Cairo:[90]

> Frankly [sanctions] have worked ... [Saddam] has not developed any significant capability with respect to weapons of mass destruction. He is unable to project conventional power against his neighbours.

But less than two years later he claimed at the UN Security Council:

> Leaving Saddam Hussein in possession of weapons of mass destruction for a few more months or years is not an option.

There was no explanation or evidence base for the evolved view. On the BBC Radio 4 *Today* programme, defence secretary Geoff Hoon maintained that he did not think that the public believed that the 45-minute warning referred to WMDs. Within half an hour of this statement, the programme played back Hoon's evidence to the Hutton Inquiry in which he appeared to say that he *did* recall newspapers suggesting that the 45-minute claim concerned WMDs. The British public was also reminded that, speaking in March 2003 just before the invasion, Blair has said:[91]

> If military action proves to be necessary, it will be to uphold the authority of the UN and to ensure Saddam is disarmed of his weapons

of mass destruction, not to overthrow him. It is why, detestable as I find his regime, he could stay in power if he disarms peacefully.

The public perception was that a few days later, Blair and Bush went to war without clear authority from the UN, no WMDs were found, Saddam had disarmed well before the invasion and, later, 'to overthrow him' was presented as an intended outcome that rationalized the invasion. In a TV interview in February 2005, Blair was asked, 'Knowing what you know now … knowing there were no WMD … would you have invaded Iraq?' His reply was: 'I would still have continued with it',[92] which appeared to be a direct contradiction of his promise before the invasion, and of the legal advice given by the Attorney General (see later, 'The legal context').

Blair had stated in the dossier, 'I believe the assessed intelligence has established beyond doubt that Saddam has continued to produce chemical and biological weapons, [and] that he continues in his efforts to develop nuclear weapons.'[93] But the BBC pointed out that a few months later, his reply when asked if he thought WMDs would be found was reported as, 'I don't know'.[94] By July, he was saying that 'we haven't found them and may never find them'.[95] If nothing else it had become clear that Blair knew that he did not know for sure about WMDs.

The daily reporting was complemented by numerous instant books by key figures such as weapons inspector Hans Blix and former US ambassador James Wilson, which were highly critical of US and UK leaders. A senior White House anti-terrorist expert, Richard Clarke, claimed, in a book called *Against all enemies*, that Bush had put immense pressure on him and others to find a link between Iraq and the September 11 attacks. He said that when no evidence of a link was found, Bush 'came back at me and said, "Iraq! Saddam! Find out if there's a connection." And in a very intimidating way … I mean that we should come back with that answer.'[96] An anonymous CIA Islamic specialist wrote *Imperial hubris*, in which he claimed that the Iraq war was 'a gift to Bin Laden and those like him'.[97]

Another less publicized but perhaps more remarkable perspective came from Stafan Halper, a traditional Republican, and Jonathan Clarke, who works for the conservative Cato Institute in Washington. In *America alone* they argue, in the words of Godfrey Hodgson, that a small but powerful sect of US 'scholars', journalists and political personnel, using funding from a biased US media:

used September 11 as an opportunity to put into effect a preconceived design for bringing democracy to the Middle East by force of arms. They conned the US public that Saddam Hussein possessed weapons of mass destruction and was in cahoots with al-Qu'ida ... They have thrown away the benefits of 50 years of American alliances and international institutions.[98]

From Britain, Milan Rai published *Regime unchanged*, which included chapters headed 'George Bush lied' and 'Colin Powell lied'. Under 'Tony Blair lied' he provided a transcript of a BBC interview with Blair before the invasion, and argued that the statement was then contradicted by Blair himself.[99] A former editor of *The Times* concluded, 'It is quite phenomenal that so many books are coming at us with such force and candour.'[100]

In parallel with the books was Mike Moore's film *Fahrenheit 9/11*, which showed links between Bush and the Saudi royal family and presented strong evidence against the invasion of Iraq. At first the Disney subsidiary Miramax tried to prevent its screening, but it had great success at the Cannes Film Festival, and then broke box office records for a documentary film in the US and Britain. When Bush nominated a Republican congressman, Porter Goss, to be the new head of the CIA, Bush claimed that he was the 'right man ... with strong experience'. Moore put an interview with Goss on his website, which had been edited out of his film. Goss said:

> I couldn't get a job with the CIA today. I am not qualified ... I don't have the language skills ... I don't have the cultural background probably ... I certainly don't have the technical skills.[101]

A more serious documentary film, Robert Greenwald's *Uncovered: the war on Iraq*, presented numerous senior US officials who were directly critical of Bush's actions. It also showed a series of clips in which senior leaders contradicted themselves, and the presentation by Colin Powell to the UN in which he showed satellite images of supposed weapons installations in Iraq which were fictitious and known to be suspect by CIA officers at the time. Another film, *Control room*, showed the work of the Qatar-based satellite TV network al-Jazeera. The station represented a brave attempt to create a free media across the Arab world, and showed graphic pictures of military atrocities perpetrated by both sides. It was condemned for 'constantly lying' and being anti-American by Rumsfeld, but in parallel its Baghdad office was closed down by the Iraqi regime because it was considered to be anti-Iraqi. The film shows the attack on al-Jazeera's Baghdad office, by an American plane, and the death of journalists. Across the US and Britain, audiences applauded the films and laughed in despair at the duplicitous conduct of their leaders.

The formal forums

By August 2003, three nations were holding parliamentary inquiries into the intervention in Iraq – the US Congress, Australian Senate and British House of Commons. The terms of reference differed slightly, but the central question was: what were the intelligence failures that led to the invasion of Iraq? Later, the US 9/11 Commission also assessed the failings leading to the attacks on 11 September. But what the public wanted to know was: had heads of state, senior MPs and civil servants lied or otherwise misled governments and the public? The inquiries in all three countries came to common conclusions, that the intelligence upon which the decision to invade and occupy Iraq had been made was highly inaccurate, based on little credible evidence, and presented by politicians with unwarranted certainty. But they were also ground-breaking in terms of hearing evidence from senior politicians and hitherto invisible civil servants including intelligence officers. The precedents for accountability were more significant than the findings. Never before had parliamentary inquiries in three countries asked the same questions of their senior leaders about the same overseas event at the same time. It seems unlikely that there was no communication and networking between those administering the inquiries, and certainly the public had access to the data and findings across the world, and so arguably they represented a quasi-global inquiry, something which had never happened before.

The US inquiries

The US Senate Intelligence Committee heard evidence from the director of the CIA, George Tenet, the first time that such a senior official had given evidence to Senate. It seemed clear that scientists had told the CIA that Iraq did not have WMDs, but this had been ignored, and relatives of Iraqi scientists had told the CIA that the WMD programmes had been abandoned, but the CIA did not tell Bush. The committee found that, 'Most of the key judgements in the ... *National Intelligence Estimate, Iraq's Continuing Programmes for Weapons of Mass Destruction* were either overstated or were not supported by underlying raw intelligence'.[102] The CIA was guilty of uncritical 'groupthink' and did not make any attempt to redress wrong information that had been presented to the public, for example the claim that Iraq had tried to buy uranium from Niger.

Greg Thielmann, a former intelligence analyst, claimed that intelligence provided by the State Department Intelligence Bureau was routinely ignored.[103] In June, Tenet resigned, his deputy James Pavitt retired, and the vice-chairman of the Senate Intelligence Committee concluded simply, 'Congress would not have authorized the war had we known what we know now.'[104]

A Congress commission examined the failures leading up to the September 11 attacks. At first Condoleezza Rice refused to appear before the commission on the grounds that security advisers never gave such testimony. Two days later she agreed to give evidence. On 23 March 2003, she had written in the *Washington Post*: 'we received no intelligence that the terrorists were preparing to attack the homeland using airplanes as missiles'.[105] Yet a Senate Select Committee on Intelligence had found that from 1994 to 2001, 'the intelligence community received information indicating that terrorists were contemplating, among other means of attack, the use of aircraft as weapons'. The contradictions were furthered by the release of a classified White House briefing, entitled 'Bin Laden determined to strike in United States'.[106] An FBI translator, Sibel Edmonds, termed Ms Rice's claim 'an outrageous lie', because she used the word 'we' instead of 'I', which implied the whole intelligence community.[107] Similarly, Bush's claim that there was no intelligence information about the 9/11 attacks was only true because he had specified the date 9/11 – there was a lot of evidence of a likely attack but, of course, no specific date.

The commission heard evidence from Bush and his deputy Cheney in secret, and concluded that 'Terrorism was not the overriding national security concern for the US government under either the [former president Bill] Clinton or pre-9/11 Bush administration.'[108] 'The most important failure was one of imagination. We do not believe [US] leaders understood the gravity of the threat.' One of its recommendations was that the US should 'stand as an example of moral leadership' in the world.[109] The public perception was that Bush's preoccupation with invading Iraq had caused him to downplay the real threats to national security, and that it is necessary to listen very carefully to how US leaders present their evidence.

The British inquiries

In response to the apparent suicide of a senior British intelligence expert on WMDs, David Kelly, Blair set up an inquiry led by Lord Hutton to establish the circumstances leading up to the death. Kelly, a highly respected weapons expert, had spoken to the press about his concerns, which was virtually unprecedented for someone in his position. The remit of the inquiry was not to assess the rationale for going to war, or whether politicians had lied about this. But evidence disclosed that the process employed by the British government in its presentation of the case for a war against Iraq, in what the press had by then dubbed its 'dodgy dossier', had been questionable. Important caveats had been taken out in later drafts, for example that Saddam Hussein would only use WMDs 'if he believes his regime is under threat'. A sentence pointing out that Iraq could not attack London had been removed. From this, even politically disinterested parties such as the editor of *New Scientist* concluded, 'it is what is missing that is most worrying. The changes made turned the dossier into a blatant advert for going to war – and never mind what it did for public trust in government.'[110] Later Middle East expert Robert Fisk found that the Arabic version of the dossier had been subtly changed to win support from Arabs.[111]

The statement 'Intelligence indicates that the Iraqi military are able to deploy chemical weapons within 45 minutes of an order to do so' appeared in various forms four times, and had been highlighted by the prime minister in his own copy of the dossier. It was taken to apply to long-range missiles because of its proximity to statements about WMDs, and because the title of the dossier was *Iraq's weapons of mass destruction*.[112] But, according to John Scarlett, chair of the Joint Intelligence Committee, the claim concerned 'battlefield mortar shells or small calibre weaponry'.[113] The important word 'munitions' had also been cut in the drafting process. The BBC later showed a film in which Kelly stated that 'Iraq's intrinsic capability has been reduced since 1990/91' and that weapons could be 'deployed within a matter of days and weeks', but not 45 minutes. From a conference paper he gave in 2002 Kelly believed that Iraq had biological weapons,[114] but the impression he gave in the BBC film was that he thought that such weapons would only be used defensively by Iraq because it would have been suicidal to use them aggressively.

The inquiry was very critical of BBC management, which was also not specifically within its remit, and this caused the hasty resignations of senior BBC managers. Hutton was especially condemnatory of a statement based on an interview by a BBC journalist with Kelly, which claimed that the 'dossier' had been 'sexed up'. The Hutton report concluded:

467. (vii) However I consider that the possibility cannot be completely ruled out that the desire of the Prime Minister to have a

dossier which, whilst consistent with the available intelligence, was as strong as possible in relation to the threat posed by Saddam Hussein's WMD, may have subconsciously influenced Mr Scarlett and the other members of the JIC to make the wording of the dossier somewhat stronger than it would have been if it had been contained in a normal JIC assessment.[115]

The idea reemerged in 2005 when a microbiologist who had worked for the Australian intelligence services for twenty years said that John Scarlett had asked (as then head of JIC) for 'new elements' to be included in a report he was producing. He told ABC TV, 'Both Washington and London wanted other things put in to make it – I can only use these words – to make it sexier.'[116] The report seemed to show the globalizing scale of both deceit and accountability.

The Hutton Inquiry had been set up by Blair on his terms. A British QC, Anthony Scrivener, pointed out that Blair had not been cross-examined like many other witnesses during the second stage of the inquiry. He was simply permitted to present his evidence during the first stage. Scrivener also questioned why minutes of certain government meetings were not available, and why parts of emails had been blacked out.[117] Press, public and politicians were not convinced by the Hutton Report. The day it was published a British newspaper, *The Independent*, had one word on an otherwise blank front page – 'Whitewash?'[118] This was picked up by numerous other commentators. Protestors from the Oxford Citizens for Truth group disrupted a House of Commons debate about the report, the first such disruption since 1987. Just like Bush and Blair, Lord Hutton was himself brought into the accountability frame by public opinion. This is perhaps more significant than it appeared. Centuries of mythology had constructed a view that heads of state were above accountability, and by inference so were judges. But the British public had suddenly made it clear that this was no longer the case. Judges are not immune from common-sense questioning. A judge can make a judgment, but now the public will judge the judge. A few weeks later it was reported that Hutton 'was shocked by public anger at his report', and by the BBC resignations.[119]

Blair denied that he had known that the 45-minute claim only applied to small tactical weapons. Of this Robin Cook, former foreign secretary, said, 'I find it difficult to reconcile what I knew and what I'm sure the Prime Minister knew at the time we had a vote [about going to war] in March.'[120] The defence secretary, Geoff Hoon, said that he had known that the claim referred to smaller weapons. The shadow foreign secretary said that it 'beggars belief' that both Cook and Hoon knew the truth of the claim, but the Prime Minister did not.[121] The aberration also appeared strange because on the day following the publication of the 'dossier' the press had run front-page headlines such as that in *The Sun* '45 minutes from doom', and in the *Evening Standard*, '45 minutes from attack'. Did the prime minister's staff not read the newspapers? Why did the government not correct this public misperception? Blair had also been criticized for releasing Kelly's name to the press. In April 2005 he stated in a TV interview, 'I don't believe we had any option but to disclose his name.' The press recalled that originally when asked why he had revealed the name, he had claimed that 'That is completely untrue'; he said he had 'emphatically not' disclosed Kelly's name.[122]

Blair's appearance at the Hutton Inquiry was only the second time a British prime minister had appeared in court to answer questions. His immediate predecessor John Major was the first. Another of the many unprecedented events during the inquiry was the appearance of Sir Richard Dearlove, who became the first head of the intelligence agency MI6 to give evidence at a public inquiry, albeit from behind a screen. The inquiry placed nearly 9,000 pages of material on its website. This included government memos and minutes of meetings, which journalists and academics quickly used. The whole accountability debate about the prime minister's conduct became instantly public, rather than confined to a courtroom.

No one should underestimate how extraordinary is the judicial inquiry going on into the death of David Kelly. The apparent suicide of one of the country's top experts on Iraq's weaponry, shortly after being revealed in July as the source for a BBC radio report alleging the government had knowingly misled the public over those weapons, has brought the greatest spate of official openness that Britain has ever seen. Documents and e-mails have been released that would normally have been held secret for 30 years or more; civil servants, senior ministers and even spies have been questioned in public; and to top it all the prime minister himself took the witness stand.

Editorial, *The Economist*[123]

At first it seemed that the next British inquiry, under Lord Butler, would not consider the actions of individuals, only 'structures, systems and processes'. It would be held in secret, and looked like an internal organizational review. The Liberal Democrat Party refused to take part, and even members of Blair's own party, who sensed the public mood, criticized the terms of reference. In a press letter, Labour MP Glenda Jackson wrote:

> The country was sent to war; thousands are dead; an entire region is destabilised; and the weapons of mass destruction that were supposedly the justification for this mayhem are nowhere to be found. People want to know why and, rest assured, if Lord Butler does not intend to find the reasons then, one way or another, the people will.[124]

Critics like Jackson had nothing to gain, and much to lose, from taking this stance against their own party. A week later, the Conservative Party withdrew its support for the inquiry. The Inquiry Committee then claimed that they had, all along, intended to 'start by looking at structures, processes and systems before considering which, if any, individuals should be held accountable'.[125]

The Butler Report was published a few days after the US Senate Report. Like the US inquiry, it was critical of intelligence agencies and the use that had been made of intelligence. It largely confirmed all the claims made by the press and other critics of the government, but it stopped short of holding specific individuals to account. As with the Hutton Report, Blair claimed that it cleared him of blame yet, as before, that was not the remit that Blair had set for the inquiry. In his response Blair argued that even if there were no WMDs, removing Saddam was still a good thing. It was noted that, when he addressed the House of Commons on the eve of war, Blair had said, 'I have never put the justification for action as regime change.' Yet after the Butler Report he stated that although neither in the case of Afghanistan nor Iraq 'was the nature of the regime the reason for the conflict, it was decisive for me in the judgement as to the balance of risk for inaction'.[126] The public were left to decide the degree to which 'justification for' and 'decisive for me in the judgement' had different meanings.

Butler considered the intelligence about the 45-minute claim to be 'vague and ambiguous', but it was used as an 'eye-catching' part of the dossier. Butler concluded, 'More weight was put on the intelligence than it could bear.' He was clear the important caveats in the original intelligence reports had been removed by the time the information was presented to the public and parliament: 'We conclude that it was a serious weakness that the JIC's warnings on the limitations of the intelligence underlying its judgements were not made sufficiently clear in the dossier.'[127] Among other experts, CIA weapons inspector David Kay then concluded that there was no basis for Blair to make the claim that Iraq had WMDs or presented an imminent threat.[128] A few months later Butler accused Blair of being responsible for 'bad government in this country' and 'too much emphasis on selling'.[129] This was remarkable from a man who had led a formal inquiry.

Then it was noticed that MI6 had withdrawn two key reports because they had been discredited before the Hutton Inquiry, and these reports had weakened the case for the invasion. Yet no one, including Blair, had told Hutton. Blair denied knowledge of this withdrawal, yet it was pointed out that a memo sent by foreign secretary Jack Straw stated, 'The Prime Minister and other Ministers who are members of the Committee on Security and Intelligence see all Joint Intelligence Committee (JIC) papers.'[130] It was then admitted that MI6 had made a deliberate decision not to advise the Hutton Inquiry, because the information was 'too sensitive' to be made public.[131] A few days later, the Flood Report in Australia concluded that the government had relied on 'thin, ambiguous and incomplete' intelligence when deciding to join the US-led invasion.[132]

As following the Hutton Report, the criticisms of Blair continued. Among the critics was Sir Geoffrey Chandler who wrote simply, 'In no other walk of life would it be possible to cause the death of thousands on a false prospectus and walk away scot-free.'[133] This and many similar claims amounted to direct accusations of unlawful killing. Yet those who made such claims were never challenged by Blair or his supporters, either through the press or through the courts. A few months later, in the light of further evidence and ongoing conflict in Iraq, Butler reemphasized particular conclusions:

> the government's dossier in September 2002 does not make clear that the intelligence underlying those conclusions was very thin even though the JIC assessments had been quite clear about that … How grave a fault that was in the context of the lead up to the war is a matter on which people will and should reach their own conclusions. But we regard it as a serious weakness, a weakness which subsequently came home to roost as the conclusion about deployable stocks of chemical and biological weapons have turned out to be wrong.

He added that the claim that Saddam was linked to international terrorism was 'not really supported by the intelligence'. Blair then edged a little further towards an apology: 'I have no doubt when you look back over this you can always see things that could have been done better or mistakes that were made.'[134]

Two other inquiries, by the Intelligence and Security and the Foreign Affairs Committees came to similar conclusions. But all hearings were seen as unprecedented examples of accountability. A former chair of the JIC, Lord Wright, concluded that, 'Both the Hutton report and ... the Butler Report have revealed evidence and argument about intelligence which would have been unthinkable in the 1980s.'[135] But the type of military action was also unprecedented. It was the first significant pre-emptive (or preventive) war in modern times, and the first invasion ever to be based on intelligence rather than a perceptible threat. That in part explains why the only defence left to British and US leaders was to claim that it was not their fault if the originally highly caveated intelligence information was presented and used in a misleading way.

The Iraq tribunal

In parallel with these inquiries, arguments about how Saddam Hussein and his colleagues should be brought to justice also reflected narrow political interests. The possibility of a US-led court had obvious difficulties, not least that President Bush was on record as saying that he wanted 'the ultimate penalty [for] the guy who tried to kill my dad'.[136] A South African-style peace and reconciliation process was presented as improbable on the grounds that Islamic justice tends to be punitive rather than restorative, yet recompense and reparation have always been traditional elements of Iraqi tribal courts.

A tribunal based on those concerning Yugoslavia and Rwanda was thought to be problematic because these use a Western-biased system and international judges. More importantly, the US did not like the idea of judges from countries that had opposed the war, including France and Germany, hearing cases. These tribunals were also considered expensive, and the predicted volume of cases in Iraq was large. At the start of 2004, 5,500 Iraqis were in prison awaiting a trial of some sort. A treaty-based tribunal, as in Sierra Leone and Cambodia, appeared the most logical way forward,[137] but the US was unlikely to want much UN involvement.

The proposed Washington model was that cases would be tried by Iraqi judges and presented by Iraqi lawyers, with international (that is, American) experts serving as advisers. There was no explanation about how to find Iraqi judges with no personal interest in what had happened in Iraq over previous decades, nor how judges who had only had expertise of dispensing cursory justice in politically led domestic trials never lasting more than a few days would have the technical experience to hear long complex cases based on international law. There was concern from the EU, but not from the US, that an Iraqi court would use the death penalty. British foreign minister Jack Straw stated that although Britain was against the death penalty, Iraq 'may make sovereign decisions with which we don't agree, and they may include the death penalty'.[138] Straw suddenly appeared to respect the sovereignty of Iraq at a point when it had no formal government, yet did not see the need to respect sovereignty at the time of the invasion when it did.

Unsurprisingly, the eventual Iraqi Special Tribunal for Crimes Against Humanity, set up by the US-appointed Governing Council, closely reflected the original US proposal. But this represented a policy change, which was not noticed. In 1996, Congress had passed the Iraq Liberation Act within which Section 6 urged the president to call upon the UN to set up an 'international criminal tribunal', not a national court controlled by the US. The Statute of the Tribunal,[139] published quietly just before Christmas on 10 December 2003, covers the standard war crimes, including:

4. Intentionally launching an attack in the knowledge that such attack will cause incidental loss of life or injury to civilians or damage to civilian objects which would be clearly excessive in relation to the concrete and direct overall military advantage anticipated;

5. Intentionally launching an attack in the knowledge that such attack will cause widespread, long-term and severe damage to the natural environment which would be clearly excessive in relation to the concrete and direct overall military advantage anticipated;

6. Attacking or bombarding, by whatever means, towns, villages, dwellings or buildings which are undefended and which are not military objectives;

It also covered the mistreatment of prisoners.

In modern international law, it is usually taken that such crimes can apply to any party in a conflict. The Statute of the Yugoslavia Tribunal,[140] for example, concerns any crime 'in the territory of the former Yugoslavia', and it has straightforward 'jurisdiction over natural persons', without qualification. The Sierra Leone Special Court is very specific about non-national offenders. Ultimately, anyone properly accused of war crimes must face trial in some way.[141] The court has

> the power to prosecute persons who bear the greatest responsibility for serious violations of international humanitarian law and Sierra Leonean law committed in the territory of Sierra Leone since 30 November 1996, including those leaders who, in committing such crimes, have threatened the establishment of and implementation of the peace process in Sierra Leone.

Any transgressions by peacekeepers and related personnel present in Sierra Leone 'shall be within the primary jurisdiction of the sending State'. However, 'In the event the sending State is unwilling or unable genuinely to carry out an investigation or prosecution, the Court may, if authorized by the Security Council on the proposal of any State, exercise jurisdiction over such persons.'

But the Iraq statute was different. It limited the jurisdiction of the tribunal to Iraqi nationals or residents, and only for crimes committed up to 1 May 2003:

> b) The Tribunal shall have jurisdiction over any Iraqi national or resident of Iraq accused of the crimes ... committed since July 17, 1968 and up until and including May 1, 2003, in the territory of the Republic of Iraq or elsewhere, including crimes committed in connection with Iraq's wars against the Islamic Republic of Iran and the State of Kuwait. This includes jurisdiction over crimes ... committed against the people of Iraq (including its Arabs, Kurds, Turcomans, Assyrians and other ethnic groups, and its Shi'ites and Sunnis) whether or not committed in armed conflict.

Throughout the world, even the lowest domestic courts can hear cases against non-nationals, if the standard criteria for jurisdiction are fulfilled. Whether or not the tribunal should have embraced cases against non-Iraqis, for example against US or British military and political leaders, was not discussed publicly. If the genuine intent were to ensure that the tribunal was not to be seen as a theatre for victors' justice, presenting trials acted out by a puppet judiciary, why was this not considered openly?

It was pointed out that the tribunal would not, for example, be able to hear a case against three US soldiers who were dismissed from the army for mistreating Iraqi prisoners. Its remit would not cover a complaint like that brought in March 2003 by seven Iraqi victims, through the

Belgian courts, about the US bombing of Baghdad's al-Amiriya shelter, which killed 403 civilians including 52 children.[142] The court is precluded from considering cases against non-Iraqis for previously supporting the regime of Saddam Hussein by providing the chemicals that had been used to torture women prisoners, for example.[143] It could not investigate the US bombing and killing of 40 civilians who were shown, on a video, simply to be at a wedding.[144] The British troops accused of killing an eight-year-old girl and 36 other Iraqi civilians could never be brought to justice in Iraq.[145]

The new Iraqi court's first case was against Saddam Hussein, who was charged in a secret location by judges who were not officially named but who were lawyers, not trained judges. Saddam had no defence lawyer, and censored CNN video excerpts of the hearing were in boxes labelled 'Cleared by the US Military'. He asked to call senior Western leaders as witnesses, and this was ignored. Future hearings were to exclude the media completely. The first chief executive of the court was Salem Chalabi, whose uncle, Ahmed, had been convicted of fraud in Jordan and given a 22-year prison sentence.[146] While he was in the UK, the Iraqi US-appointed judge of another court issued a warrant for Chalabi's arrest for alleged involvement in a murder.

The Iraqi Tribunal seemed to take us back sixty years to the victors' justice of the Nuremberg and Tokyo hearings. After the formal return of sovereignty to a nominally Iraqi government, Elizabeth Wilmshurst, a British Foreign Office lawyer, pointed out that the immunity granted to UK and US troops and civilians was without precedent. The occupying military could kill with impunity, their protections applied to criminal and civil claims, and operatives were exempted from taxes and did not even need driving licences. She concluded, 'A host state, certainly so far as I know, has never been given such wide immunities.'[147] But that could all change. In July 2005, as the power base of the new Iraqi government became Shia, the Iranian government contacted the tribunal to seek justice for victims of Iraq's chemical weapons attacks in Iran. At that time Saddam was supported and assisted by US and British leaders.

The International Criminal Court (ICC) and other forums

The International Criminal Court (ICC) was not formally considered in relation to the Iraqi trials, on the grounds that it could only hear cases based on events after its inception in July 2002. But more significantly, the US did not support the court. However, the ICC could still play a part irrespective of the wishes of US and British leaders, because it *can* hear cases about alleged crimes during or after the invasion and occupation. In July 2003, in a 47-page document presented to the ICC, British leaders were accused of 110 crimes concerning 'The repeated, blatant violations by the United States and Britain of the stipulations of the four 1949 Geneva Conventions, the 1954 convention of The Hague as well as the character of the international criminal court, which constitute war crimes and crimes against humanity.' The complainants were not aggrieved Iraqis or Muslim lawyers. They were from the Athens Bar Association, lawyers with no direct interest in the case, who were implementing the Association's remit to 'safeguard international law'.[148]

The Greek complaint, and a similar one from Belgian lawyers, was not taken forward by the ICC. But in January 2004, a group of British legal experts, including law professors from Oxford University, LSE and the Irish Centre of Human Rights, held an independent 'war crimes inquiry' in London, and heard evidence from eyewitnesses and experts. On the basis of this, they put forward a similar case against British leaders, which was formally considered by the ICC prosecutors. This was focused on harm to civilians and non-military targets, the use of cluster bombs, the targeting of power stations which affected water supplies, and the use of depleted uranium shells.[149,150,151] In parallel, lawyers from Legal Action Against War wrote formally to Scotland Yard asking for a police investigation of Blair. French lawyers prepared similar cases. Saddam Hussein's defence lawyer, Jaques Verges, was broadly in agreement, and he added a further dimension. He claimed that the US government was guilty of 'complicity' because it had previously supplied the Iraqi regime with the means to commit war crimes, in the form of poison gas and biological weapons. He also pointed out that the US chiefs of staff had termed Fallujah a 'rats' nest'.[152] The Rwandan Tribunal had previously held that referring to the Tutsis as 'cockroaches' had contributed to the guilt of those convicted of war crimes.

Then in August 2004 a group of British MPs, led by Adam Price, set in motion impeachment proceedings against Blair. The process dates back to the seventeenth century, but was prescient of the power of leaders to evade justice systems. It can be used for 'high crimes and misdemeanours beyond the reach of the law or which no authority of the state will prosecute'. It was last used in 1805. In a detailed report – *A case to answer*[153] – Blair was accused of 'gross misconduct ... deliberate repeated distortion, seriously misleading statements and culpable negligence'. It argued, 'If his actions go unchallenged then we will have established a new precedent that will say that a minister can mislead the people and still govern with his conduct unpunished.' The initiative had little hope of succeeding because it would require agreement from parliament, but the symbolism was strong.

Irrespective of the outcomes, these moves are very significant. They were not part of a mass uprising or direct party politics. They were painstaking efforts to use formal processes of accountability against leaders, often from other countries. Political forces may have deterred and prevented cases from proceeding, but the public was made aware that those who proposed such actions were very well qualified to understand whether or not a *prima facie* case could be made. The future could see other innovative initiatives, for example other war crimes courts hearing cases concerning Iraq.

In the long term, it may be national courts that fill the gap left by the Iraqi Tribunal and the failings of parliaments, and these may provide a deeper view of the truth of what happened in Iraq. American human rights lawyers instigated a case against Donald Rumsfeld, concerning the abuses in Abu Ghraib jail, in the German courts at the end of 2004. This was based on a German law of 2002 which gave the courts international jurisdiction for war crimes cases.[154] Shortly afterwards, a Dutch court prosecuted Frans van Anraat for supplying chemical weapons to Saddam between 1984 and 1988. A future Iraqi government could well change the remit of the tribunal, set up another special court, or extend the jurisdiction of its national courts. In March 2004, it was announced that Iraqi families were seeking compensation for the unlawful killing of family members by British troops. They planned to use the British High Court and the Human Rights Act. The cases included a 13-year-old boy who was killed by a cluster bomb, and a housewife who was shot while she was eating her supper.[155] By November, the European Court of Human Rights had ruled that European troops in another country that is under the control of that European country can be prosecuted under European (and therefore British) human rights law. In the same week, Britain was criticized by the UN for trying to claim that the UN Torture Convention (and therefore British law based on the Convention) did not apply to Afghanistan and Iraq.[156] The High Court then ruled that the Human Rights Act extended to 'outposts of the state's authority', and the judges were critical of the case put forward by the British government. They described their ruling as 'An unhappy submission to have to make about a country which was one of the cradles of civilisation.'[157] In parallel, the High Court had also ruled for the first time that British peacekeepers in a war zone could be liable for the deaths of civilians. Soldiers in Kosovo had shot and injured demonstrators.[158] A few months later the International Criminal Court Act 2001 was used for the first time to try British Military leaders for war crimes in Southern Iraq. Like the Tokyo and Nuremberg tribunals, EC human rights law had set the dormant precedents that were subsequently applied to a globalizing world.

The outcomes

The specific rights and wrongs of the events surrounding 9/11 will be argued over for decades. But the broad outcome was that none of these manifestations of extreme accountability, from any party, were accepted without question as having achieved genuine accountability. The explanation, which will be supported by the evidence throughout this book, is that contemporary leadership accountability does not equate with mass killings of the powerful or of those who symbolize their power, or with the elimination of 'regimes' or even of supposed 'terrorists' or despots through death or imprisonment, or with inquiries and tribunals with restricted terms of reference set by those whom they should legitimately investigate. Echoing the words of Justice Richard Goldstone (Chapter 1),[159] accountability entails the identification of the misdeeds of 'Specific individuals [who] bear the major share of the responsibility ... who need to be held to account, through the fair and meticulously detailed presentation and evaluation of evidence', by impartial judges and in relation to common reciprocal standards, and then preventing them from doing further harm, without collateral damage to institutions of state, organizations, or innocent bystanders.

The perception of deceit

Rightly or wrongly, a significant outcome of these events was the common belief that American, British, Spanish and other pro-war leaders had been deceitful. In April 2004, a CBS poll found that 72 per cent of Americans believed that the Bush administration were either hiding something or directly lying about what they knew before the September 11 attacks.[160] A *New York Times/CBS News* aggregation showed that in October 2003 65 per cent of the population thought that the invasion of Iraq was the 'right thing'; 28 per cent thought it was wrong. But by July 2004 45 per cent thought that it was right; 52 per cent thought the war wrong. The public perception had reversed following the inquiries, yet US and British leaders claimed that they were vindicated. But the inquiries had made a lot of information available to the public about the conduct of their leaders. At the start of 2005, a BBC global poll showed that in all the countries surveyed (Russia, Turkey, France, Germany, Mexico, Lebanon, India, China, UK and the Philippines), 70 per cent of respondents believed that Bush's reelection was 'negative' for world peace and security.[161]

In 2005, a Yahoo internet search for 'Iraq deceit' found half a million (504,000) sources; 'Iraq deceit Bush' found 386,000; 'Iraq deceit Blair' found 123,000 (Advanced search, English: 'all of these words'; exact phrase, 10 June 2005). Searching for the exact phrase: 'Bush lied' found 394,000 sources, 'Blair lied' 26,200, 'Saddam Hussein lied' 170, and 'bin Laden lied' 89. These numbers are, of course, only a crude indicator of the expression of public perceptions. But public perceptions make or break the integrity of leaders and in a globalizing world ICT is increasingly important, as discussed further in Chapter 3.

Similarly in Britain, Blair's 'approval rating' had fallen from +41, at the time of the September 11 in 2001 attack, to −30 at the start of 2004.[162] Although the Hutton Report made almost no mention of political wrongdoing, Blair's ratings in subsequent opinion polls (six in three days) remained poor. One poll found that 54 per cent of voters believed that Blair's reputation had been damaged by the Hutton Inquiry, even though it had made no direct criticism of him.[163] A further poll found that 51 per cent of those asked agreed that Blair should resign, 35 per cent did not; 54 per cent thought he had lied, 31 per cent did not.[164] A further longer-term survey found that the percentage of the public who thought that the government was 'honest and trustworthy' had moved from 56 to 25 per cent since 2001, and those seeing it as 'not honest' rose from 30 to 67 per cent.[165] A more formal survey by the Committee on Standards in Public Life found a 'widespread lack of trust in politicians' and that the war on Iraq was the most important event influencing public opinion. In the list of trusted professions, government ministers were third from the bottom, above estate agents and journalists on the tabloid newspapers.[166] By March 2005, an ICM poll found that just 28 per cent of British women thought that Blair was honest.[167] After the election, a survey showed that if Blair's name was related to questions about support for the EU Constitution, support for it fell by 35 per cent.[168]

In the past, periods of war have improved political ratings. But now the questions asked by the polls were about accountability issues and integrity, not just a simple assessment of likely party political votes. Although it was not shown that Bush and Blair had directly lied, it had been shown that the public had been deceived. The polls appeared counter-intuitive – inquiries that appear to find no fault with political leaders should increase their standing. The decline seems to show the influence of the broader forces of accountability and the significance of the perception of deceit.

In the US, a senior official, Greg Thielmann, former director of strategic proliferation and military affairs, said that the Bush administration had 'twisted, distorted and simplified' intelligence which led Americans to 'seriously misunderstand' the threat posed by Iraq. He added, 'I'm not sure I can think of a worse act against the people in a democracy than a President distorting crucial information.'[169] He then went further:

> The way the political leadership in Britain and America explained the intelligence to their populations was not an accurate rendition of what intelligence services were saying … Iraq did not pose an imminent threat to either its neighbours or the US or Britain.[170]

Bush's own envoy to the Middle East, General Tony Zinni, concurred, stating in relation to events before and during the occupation: 'I saw at a minimum true dereliction, negligence and irresponsibility; at worst lying, incompetence and corruption.' He concluded that the 'senior [civilian] leadership in the Pentagon' had 'twisted [intelligence] in a way that didn't make sense'.[171]

Daniel Ellsberg, the former State Department analyst who had instigated the events leading up to Watergate through publishing the Pentagon Papers detailing the political deception surrounding the Vietnam War, was interviewed on BBC Radio. He talked of 'The new Vietnam – Iraq', and claimed that 'We were lied into a war, as we were in Vietnam.' He believed that if classified papers about Iraq were released, the public would find that 'Bush and Blair had systematically and outrageously lied to their publics'.[172] Later, others developed the comparisons between Iraq and Vietnam. These included Senator Edward Kennedy, who talked of a 'breach of trust with the American people', and added that Bush had created 'the largest credibility gap since Richard Nixon'. He continued that the Bush administration:

> misled Congress and the American people because the administration knew that it could not obtain the consent of Congress for the war if all the facts were known.[173]

Jimmy Carter put the argument in stronger terms: 'Iraq … was a war based on lies and misrepresentations from London and from Washington.'[174]

In the UK, the recognition of the centrality of deceit also came from diverse sources. It was even noted by the British foreign secretary Jack Straw, who concluded:

> There has been a huge challenge to the integrity of the Prime Minister particularly – suggestions that he could not be trusted in some very personal moral way.[175]

Journalist Robert Fisk was among the most cogent of critics:

> A war founded on illusion, lies and right-wing ideology was bound to founder in blood and fire. Saddam had weapons of mass destruction. He was in contact with al-Qa-ida. He was involved with the crimes against humanity of 11 September. The people of Iraq would greet us with flowers and music. There would be democracy. Even the pulling down of Saddam's statue was a fraud. An American military vehicle tugged the wretched thing down while a crowd of only a few hundred Iraqis watched ...[176]

John Kampfner identified 'The five deceptions of Blair', that:[177]

1. Saddam could peacefully be disarmed
2. foreign governments agreed about the intelligence
3. the war was to protect the authority of the UN
4. the French prevented the 2nd UN Resolution
5. the WMDs threat was growing

The cover of an issue of *The Economist* had photos of Bush and Blair and was headed, 'Sincere deceivers'.

More conservative commentators presented a similar view. Writing in *The Times*, Simon Jenkins stated:

> Three public deceptions precede Britain's invasion of Iraq ... One was that Saddam Hussein presented an urgent and substantive threat to Britain. That was untrue. The second was that an attack on him accorded with international law. That was untrue. The third deception still lurks in the dark, shrouded in spin and fog. Yet it is massive in its presumption. It holds that the west can, by force of arms, bring stability, democracy and freedom wherever it chooses to set foot, even in Saddam's Iraq.[178]

At the demonstrations in London, on the anniversary of the invasion, two Greenpeace activists captured the prevailing sentiment when they climbed up to the clock face on Big Ben and displayed banners reading 'Time for Truth'. In 2005, the discourse then changed from 'deceit' to 'lies'. Among others, journalist Bruce Anderson claimed of Blair: 'This is a Prime Minister who lied to the House of Commons. He lied to the British people. He lied to Lord Butler. There is no truth in him.'[179]

Another interesting use of the discourse of deceit came, purportedly, from Osama bin Laden, in his statement offering a truce to European countries:

> your politicians ... exaggerate lies and falsification regarding our right in defence and resistance ... their falsification increases the shedding of your blood instead of sparing it ... It is the war-lords ... who are steering the world policy from behind a curtain. As for President Bush, the leaders who are revolving in his orbit, the leading media companies and the United Nations, which makes laws for relations between the masters of veto and the slaves of the General Assembly, these are only some of the tools used to deceive and exploit peoples ... [Bush] also would not have lied to people and said that we hate freedom and kill for the sake of killing. Reality proves our truthfulness and his lie.[180]

Bin Laden certainly seemed aware of the political weakness of his adversaries, and that in a world of global ICT deceit is the Achilles heel of all leaders who cause harm. Not least, deceit hands an informational 'instrument of mass effect' to the opposition.

Shortly afterwards the Archbishop of Canterbury Dr Rowan Williams provided a similar view. *The Times* gave front-page coverage to a sermon at Cambridge, where Williams talked of the 'weakening of trust in the political system of our nation'. Although he wanted to avoid 'the melo-dramatic language of public deception', he argued:

> Now we do not usually look in our rulers for signs of advanced con-templative practice ... But we do say that credible claims on our polit-ical loyalty have something to do with a demonstrable attention to the truth, even unwelcome truth.
>
> A government that habitually ignored expert advice, that habitu-ally pressed its interests abroad in ways that ignored manifest needs and priorities in the wider human and non-human environment, habitually repressed criticism or manipulated public media – such a regime would, to say the least, jeopardise its claim to obedience ...
>
> There were things government believed it knew and claimed to know on a privileged basis which, it emerged, were anything but cer-tain; there were things which regional experts knew which seemed not to have received attention ...
>
> Government of whatever kind restores lost trust above all by its willingness to attend to what lies beyond the urgency of asserting

control ... by patient accountability ... even to admit error or miscalculation.[181]

These views seemed especially pertinent in the light of the Christian-based morality that had been used by Blair and Bush to legitimize the invasion.

At first sight, the outcome of the Spanish election after the bombing in Madrid was not so surprising. Spain had seen the biggest anti-war demonstration in the world, and around 90 per cent of Spanish people opposed the war. But this dynamic had not changed since the prediction that the ruling Popular Party would win, and there had been a massive anti-terrorism demonstration in Madrid after the bombing. Observers then argued that a further factor had precipitated the change of view, and was probably more significant than the attack. When the bombing happened, the Spanish government immediately tried to blame the Basque group Eta, and play down any retributive motivation in relation to Iraq, even apparently circulating embassies to disseminate this message. In an article called 'Spanish lies', Ignacio Ramonet explained in *Le Monde diplomatique* that

Anazar's Popular Party, which all commentators backed as the likely winners before the bombings, attempted to turn this wave of emotion to its advantage by manipulating information, concealing evidence suggesting that Islamists were to blame and insisting on blaming its preferred enemy, the Basque organisation ETA.[182]

This was seen as a significant deception by the Spanish public, and it seems that the deception as much as the bombing may have precipitated the change of pubic opinion. Whatever the significance of the deceit, it appeared that retributive non-state violence had assisted a 'regime change' in Spain. History provides many examples of 'terrorists' or 'freedom fighters' overthrowing regimes, but this seemed the first time it had happened through directly influencing democratic processes. Whether or not this was planned, the attack showed that regime change can be a realistic objective for state and non-state actors alike.

In March 2004, Blair had asked the public to question his judgement but not his integrity. Like any astute politician, he seemed aware that he might be forgiven for a mistake or being inept, but not for cheating. The discourse of deceit focused on Blair's phrase 'no doubt' about the existence of WMDs and the genuineness of the intelligence. It is worth examining the exact words. In his dossier of September 2002, Blair claimed:

> What I believe the assessed intelligence has established beyond doubt is that Saddam has continued to produce chemical and biological weapons.[183]

It was hard to claim that the statement amounted to a lie, because it was carefully prefixed, 'What I believe ...'. It would be equally unassailable for anyone to state, 'I believe that Blair lied', or 'I believe in Father Christmas'. But the question this caution raises is: why did Blair not simply state, 'The assessed intelligence has established beyond doubt'? Similarly in testimony to the Commons Liaison Committee in July 2003, and in a press interview at the start of 2004, Blair had carefully used the phrase, 'I have absolutely no doubt' about finding WMDs and the intelligence.[184] Also in May 2003, his phrase was, 'I have no doubt' about WMDs. Why did he not just say in direct and objective terms, 'There is no doubt'? Does the care of the phraseology suggest that Blair did have doubts? When Blair's beliefs were subsequently shown to be wrong, he claimed that he may have made a mistake, but he did not lie. Had he not prefixed his claims with 'I believe', it is possible that he would have been seen to have lied.

Other important phrases arguably did amount to deception – the titles used on the reports making the case for war – but this point was missed by the press. In the US, the name of the CIA report in 2002, *Iraq's mass destruction weapons programs,*[185] represents an unambiguous claim that the programmes exist. The title of the October 2002 report, *National intelligence estimate, Iraq's continuing programmes for weapons of mass destruction,* is similar. In Britain, the title of Blair's dossier – *Iraq's weapons of mass destruction*[186] – implied that such weapons existed as a report entitled 'Tony Blair's lies' would imply that he had certainly lied. A slight rephrasing, for example 'Weapons of mass destruction in Iraq', would still have been disingenuous, but it would have left room for the possibility of a conclusion that there were no weapons. Who approved these titles, and what was their influence on busy officials who often read little more than a title? How do the dossiers fit with the UK Civil Service Code (Paragraph 3) which clarifies that public officials have

> a duty to give Parliament ... and the public as full information as possible about their policies, decisions and actions, and not to deceive or knowingly mislead them.

Unsurprisingly, elections provided the chance for opposition parties to develop the discourse of deceit. In his nomination speech as the US Democrat presidential candidate in July 2004, John Kerry claimed:

> I will be a commander in chief who will never mislead us into war. I will have a Vice President who will not conduct secret meetings with polluters to rewrite our environmental laws ...
>
> Saying there are weapons of mass destruction in Iraq doesn't make it so. Saying we can fight a war on the cheap doesn't make it so. And proclaiming mission accomplished certainly doesn't make it so ... .
>
> I will immediately reform the intelligence system so policy is guided by facts, and facts are never distorted by politics.[187]

From the Convention, former British foreign secretary Robin Cook concluded that the 'principle motivation of the delegates to defeat Bush [was] their conviction that he cheated America over the reasons for war. As Bill Clinton put it, "You cannot lead the world if you mislead America." '[188]

In Britain the opposition also made play of deceit. In September 2004, the leader of the opposition Michael Howard said, during an interview in *New Statesman*, 'I think people hold the view pretty firmly now that they were lied to over Iraq.'[189] A week later he told his party conference, 'In the run up to the war the PM did not tell the truth.' He announced that the central ideology of his campaign was 'accountability', and a campaign poster read: 'If he's prepared to lie to take us to war, he's prepared to lie to win an election'. The word 'lie' had never before been used so blatantly in an election.

In the context of the countless direct accusations that senior US and British leaders had lied or deceived the public, something seemed to be missing. There were no court cases for defamation against any of these writers or commentators who had publicly impugned the reputation of the most powerful people in the world, and few evidence-based repudiations of what they had claimed in their challenges.

All war is based on deception.

> Sun Tzu, *The art of war*, 500 BC[190]

'More inquiring times'

The bigger questions that these events raised in relation to accountability were obvious, but they were often overlooked in the turmoil of events. The capture of the Iraqi president, Saddam Hussein, was welcomed across the world. He was seen as among the worst despots of the past century. He was presented by the British government as a 'cruel and sadistic dictator' accountable for one million deaths in the Iran–Iraq war, the murder of 100,000 Kurds and 200,000 Shia Muslims, the invasion of Kuwait and thousands of Iraqi deaths.[191] Human rights organizations had been campaigning for the international community to hold him to account for decades. In 2001, the NGO Indict persuaded the British Attorney General to refer for police investigation a *prima facie* war crimes case against Saddam Hussein and his deputy, Tariq Aziz. So why did a seemingly successful outcome not deflect or mitigate an ongoing questioning of the means used to achieve this end, even after Saddam had appeared in court and sovereignty had officially been returned to Iraq? It was unclear who held the moral high ground in the new era of global leadership accountability, and history is likely to find this puzzling.

British defence secretary Geoff Hoon was one government official who also seemed to display awareness that these events formed part of a broader trend. He pointed out that the 'dossier' itself was an innovatory accountability initiative in 'more inquiring times'. He elaborated:[192]

> We live in less deferential times, we are more democratic, but it also means that the word of a prime minister is not taken for granted. We have the media in our face all the time. Inevitably [now] we have to substantiate what we are saying.

The introduction to the dossier claimed that 'It is unprecedented for the Government to publish this kind of report.'[193] And the debate in parliament, about invading Iraq, was presented similarly. Yet the public saw these ground-breaking accountability initiatives as ill-judged pieces of political spin. Even the resignation of Blair's director of communications, Alistair Campbell, who had been responsible for the dossier, did not remove the perception of deceit.

One distinctive aspect of the events surrounding the Iraq invasion was, as suggested in the previous chapter, that the old bipolar stereotypical social groupings usually used to explain social change and social movements were not so evident. The challenges were significantly *intra*-group, not *inter*-group. Calls for accountability came from *within* the countries whose governments were responsible for deciding to invade. The challenge from Arab leaders was, by comparison, muted. The questioning of senior pro-war leaders was often from *within* the political parties of those leaders, and there was certainly no clear left–right divide. The other familiar stereotype that did not fit was the idea that this was a Marxian-style, masses versus the powerful, social movement. Although public protest was considerable, so too were challenges from other power elites. This seemed to demonstrate the globalizing nature of the accountability ethos – it no longer respects the traditions of narrow nationalist interests, political parties, or social class.

It was becoming more difficult for leaders to construct 'sides' across national boundaries, or even along party political lines, as a basis for political violence. Even Blair recognized this when he said, 'The problem with Iraq is that you ended up with an alliance of people on the left and the right saying the same thing.'[194] The use of the word 'problem' is curious. Many see the decline in party power as a positive democratic trend, particularly if it reduces the risk of war. Bush's rhetorical challenge to the world, 'You are either for us or against us', was quickly dropped, as his advisers presumably realized that people across the world were for truth and against deceit.

Could the accountability movement eventually bring about the end of international war, as the world has known it? In March 2004, Desmond da Silva started work as deputy prosecutor at the new Sierra Leone special court. He answered criticism that some of those charged had been fighting to restore the legitimate government by saying, 'You can fight on the side of the angels and nevertheless commit crimes against humanity.'[195] Has the global public now gained a mindset that was previously the preserve of the judiciary? It seems that the conduct of any leader is now to be judged impartially against objective democratic criteria, irrespective of the status, charisma or group allegiance of the perpetrator.

In the context of history, these events seem even more remarkable. By 2004, the public enemies appeared to be the unaccountable leaders on all sides, principally Bush, bin Laden, Blair and Saddam Hussein. Protesters in Baghdad in April 2005 were carrying posters of Bush, Blair and Saddam, side by side. It is as if in the 1940s, the peoples of the world had collectively put Churchill, Hitler, Roosevelt, Stalin and Hirohito simultaneously on public trial for their wartime conduct. But is there something incomprehensible about what happened in 2003–04, or should our incredulity be about what happened after the Second World War? Perhaps the aberration is that accountable leaders from all sides did not go on trial at Nuremberg or Tokyo, for wrongs such as the A-bombing of Hiroshima and Nagasaki, the firebombing of Dresden and of Japanese cities, which killed nearly two million civilians, and the slaughter of the Okinawa population. It is not hard to see these events in terms of terrorism, war crimes and attempted genocide.

It is perhaps less surprising that sixty years later the public collectively adopts an equitable and truly judicial approach to the wrongdoings of all leaders in war, in contrast to the nationalistic sides and victors' justice of previous eras. The new public mood to judge leaders according to their conduct, not their national power base, was reflected in a comment by the moderate Chechen leader, Akhmed Zakayev, when he stated, 'I am anti-Putin, anti-Bin Laden, anti-Bush, anti all of those who are trying to push humanity to the edge of catastrophe today.'[196]

> A change seen across the democratic world is the decline in the effectiveness of command and control governance methods. The image of a pyramid with orders flowing down from above, faithfully implemented by officials and accepted by a deferential public, was always at odds with reality. But it really is at odds now. The British public is less deferential than ever.
>
> Paul Whitely, Professor of Government, University of Essex[197]

The explanations

It is probable that future analyses will focus on four areas of explanation about these events. From one perspective, they may be seen as a logical and proper, if imperfect, development of global leadership accountability, which tested the evolving doctrines of humanitarian intervention and regime change. It could be claimed that US and British leaders simply followed the precedents of regime change in Nazi Germany and Japan half a century earlier, and that the intent was little different to that in relation to Central and Southern Europe during the 1990s, and concerning Liberia and Sierra Leone a little later. This, of course, begs a second question about the legality of the action. The third and contrasting view is that US and UK initiatives from 2001 onwards were motivated by something more than simple accountability and national security interests. They reflected leadership self-interest and a number of attractive outcomes for those in power. The fourth and more benign perspective is simply that leaders have human limitations and failings like everyone else, but that these failings cause them to become trapped in a 'cumulative lock-in' – a train of events which they could not reverse – and so the only option was to deceive the public. But this deceit became the catalyst for the massive challenge.

Humanitarian intervention and regime change

Within the first perspective (and writing with considerable prescience before the invasion of Iraq and the failure to discover WMDs), Gwyn Prins asked why the British and US leaders were relying on WMDs as the rationale for invasion rather than the straightforward removal of a despot. He places his argument within the frame of global leadership accountability – 'this most positive of trends':

> at a certain point, tyrants lose their moral right to rule. Pathological governors who deliberately starve, torture or bomb with chemical weapons their own people, as Saddam did the Iraqi Kurds of Halabja in March 1988, and the Marsh Arabs later, cannot hide behind the UN Charter's non-intervention clause ... when all other means are exhausted, the citizen is justified in rebelling ... It is this right that lays a duty of support upon those of us who rejoice in the rise of human rights: this most positive of trends in global politics since the end of the cold war.[198]

This does, of course, raise the question: why did George Bush Senior not pursue Saddam Hussein in 1990 as the arguments about his despotism were stronger at that time and there was a greater international consensus? Prins continues:

> 'Regime change' is not a perverse preoccupation of ugly Americans. The UN's International Commission on Intervention and State Sovereignty earlier this year provided detailed guidance to show where the 'high and narrow' threshold of 'a shock to the conscience of mankind' is crossed and what to do.

A report by a UN Commission is not quite international law, but historian and author of *The short twentieth century*, Eric Hobsbawm, provided a similar assessment: 'There is a genuine case to be made that there are governments that are so bad that their disappearance will be a net gain for the world.' He continues with a cautious note: 'But this can never justify the danger of creating a world power that is not interested in a world that it does not understand, but is capable of intervening decisively with armed force whenever anybody does anything that Washington does not like.'[199]

More critical analyses of events were being provided by academics such as Noam Chomsky, who claimed that that the US-led military action was a 'preventive', not 'preemptive', invasion. He argued that a preventive war was the supreme crime that was condemned at Nuremberg. He also pointed out that it is wrong to see 'humanitarian intervention' as a product of a new 1990s Western ethic. He reminds us that India's invasion of East Pakistan in 1971 and Vietnam's invasion of Cambodia in 1978 both put an end to crimes by despotic regimes.[200]

From other perspectives, it was argued that the invasion of Serbia in 1999 had also been without UN permission, and this seemed to have established a new precedent in the wake of the failure to help in Rwanda – that humanitarian need could justify immediate intervention. However, in a report from Human Rights Watch, its director Ken Roth concluded that the invasion of Iraq could not be considered a humanitarian intervention because, although the regime had certainly committed atrocities in the past, there was no evidence they were continuing in 2003. He explained:

> 'Better late than never' is not a justification for humanitarian intervention, which should be countenanced only to stop mass murder, not to punish its perpetrators, desirable as punishment is in such circumstances.[201]

Writers such as Yahai Said were talking of Saddam's 'waning regime' as a 'post-totalitarian' state.[202] And in contrast, Bush and Blair did little to inspire intervention in the genocidal activities backed by the Sudanese government a few months later, in which hundreds of thousands of civilians had been brutally killed, nor in equally problematic circumstances in countries like Burma and Turkmenistan.

There seems little question that the invasions of both Afghanistan and Iraq can be placed, in part, within the general context of an era of global accountability, in this case instigated by peers rather than public. In his inaugural speech in January 2005, Bush seemed to include leadership accountability as part of his foreign policy:

> All who live in tyranny and hopelessness can know: the United States will not ignore your oppression, or excuse your oppressors. When you stand for your liberty, we will stand with you.[203]

He talked of 'ending tyranny in our world'. Perhaps he had noticed the strength of the new leadership accountability movement, through personal experience. Peer accountability has a long tradition in the history of ensuring proper conduct by power elites, but the line that distinguishes the enforcement of accountability from unlawful aggression is that the former must be rule-based in some way, and usually in relation to rules that have been mutually agreed at some point by all parties including those who find themselves the subject of enforcement. So what were the views of the legal arguments for the US-led military action in Iraq?

The legal context

In terms of national law, in the US, the president had used the Constitution and 1973 War Powers Act to get the permission of Congress to invade Iraq. In contrast, the British public learned that the prime minister had absolute personal power to take the country to war, under a little-understood constitutional device called the Royal Prerogative. This customary power dates from at least the seventeenth century, and means that the UK is unlike other European countries, for example Germany, and many younger democracies such as Turkey. Constitutionally, the British parliamentary debate based on the 'dossier' was little more than a courtesy. Later, just before the election, the chancellor Gordon Brown promised new legislation to reduce the power of a prime minister and to make all such military action subject to approval by parliament. Blair had presented his dossier to parliament as itself an innovatory attempt at accountable decision-making, even though this was then seen as less than honest. But the ultimate outcome may be a new and well-overdue standard of accountability for war in Britain.

Blair assured the British public that the UN would approve an invasion, but attempts in September 2002 to get such approval were not successful.[204] Germany and France opposed an immediate invasion without a further Security Council resolution. But, contrary to British and US spin, that did not preclude intervention in the future. American and British leaders then provided a *post hoc* argument that existing UN Security Council resolutions 687, 678 and 1441 *together* provided the necessary legitimacy. But they did not explain why, if this were true, they had tried to get a further resolution. The US and British claim that Iraq had not complied with the ceasefire conditions of UN Resolution 687 (1991), after the Gulf War, was subsequently shown to be wrong and known to be uncertain at the time. It was questioned whether the resolution authorizing the removal of the Iraqi military from Kuwait,

678 (1990), could be 'revived' to apply to the proposed invasion of Iraq because it related to a different coalition and was for different purposes at a different time.[205] Resolution 1441, in November 2002, was described by the US State Department, on its website,[206] as 'strengthening the weapons inspection regime for Iraq and giving Baghdad, in the words of the resolution, "a final opportunity to comply with its disarmament obligations" '. The last clause of the resolution reads:

> 13. Recalls, in that context, that the Council has repeatedly warned Iraq that it will face serious consequences as a result of its continued violations of its obligations.

Although a justification for the invasion was therefore not clear from the State Department's own introduction to the resolution, and not directly proposed by the resolution itself, this viewed together with resolutions 687 and 678 was later taken by the US and British leaders as providing permission for full-scale military invasion and occupation.

The legality of the war was widely questioned by many national and international authorities,[207] including a former British permanent representative to the UN, Sir Crispin Tickell,[208] and the British QC Michael Mansfield, who stated that 'the consensus of legal opinion in Britain since the war clearly takes the view that it was illegal'.[209] One British Foreign Office legal adviser, Elizabeth Wilmshurst, had resigned because she disagreed about the advice given to the Cabinet.[210] A leaked UK Foreign Office memorandum evidenced official reservations about the 'automaticity' of the claimed justification for war. It stated, 'It is important to stress that SCR 1441 did not revive the 678 authorisation immediately upon its adoption.'[211] One of Blair's former advisers, Sir Stephen Wall, who was considered 'an ultra-loyalist mandarin', accused Blair of 'departing from the rule of law'.[212] The former development secretary Clare Short claimed later, 'it is clear now there was a date for war so they didn't need Blix to do his job and then come to a second resolution ... they were going to war anyway and they were going to bully and pressure countries to vote for it.'[213] Blix, an international lawyer by training, concluded, 'I don't buy the argument the war was legalised by the Iraqi violation of earlier resolutions.'[214] These views were then affirmed by Kofi Annan who, when asked directly if the war was illegal during a BBC interview in September 2004, replied, 'Yes ... I have indicated it was not in conformity with the UN Charter from our point of view, from the charter point of view, it was illegal.'[215] Opinions that the war was legal were rare,[216] and not widely known among the British public.

In Britain, public and politicians had tried without success to ascertain the full legal advice given by the Attorney General, Lord Goldsmith, to Blair, not just the apparent summary. Had Blair disclosed this immediately, the public view of him might have changed, but he chose not to. It seemed that there was much for the beleaguered Blair to gain from releasing the document, unless it incriminated him. Blair was adamant that he would not publish the advice because, he argued, such advice was always confidential. Others pointed to earlier precedents when similar advice had not been confidential.

Politicians had earlier asked why a specially edited version of the advice for the Cabinet was needed, and it was claimed that Blair had breached his own official code of conduct for ministers which stated that when a summary of legal advice is presented to the Cabinet, 'the complete text of the advice should be attached'. The prime minister has the primary responsibility for upholding the code.[217] But this questioning was muddled by a statement from cabinet secretary Andrew Turnbull who claimed that there was no full version: the 337-word document was the 'definitive statement'. MPs then lodged a complaint with the Bar Council against the Attorney General on the basis that he gave 'definitive advice' about such a serious matter on one page of A4 paper.[218] It was also argued that an attorney general had a duty to advise parliament as a whole, not just prime ministers.[219] And it was discovered that Blair had not formally asked for advice in writing from the Attorney General, as might have been expected concerning such a serious issue.

There then followed an astonishing chain of events fuelled by a new Freedom of Information Act, which the Blair government had proudly introduced a few years earlier. *Channel 4 News* obtained an uncensored version of the resignation letter from Foreign Office lawyer Elizabeth Wilmshurst in which she called the invasion a 'crime of aggression'. From this it seemed evident that the Attorney General had changed his mind from a view before 7 March 2003 that a further UN Security Council resolution was necessary and that an invasion might not be legal, to a view ten days later that the war would be legal.[220] It was noted that foreign minister Jack Straw had described the advice as 'unequivocal'. Blair had told parliament that intelligence evidence was 'extensive, detailed and authoritative'.[221]

Why had the view of the Attorney General gone from balanced caution to absolute certainty in ten days? The only significant event in the interim was that the UN had refused a further resolution affirming the legality of an invasion, and that should have led to greater caution, not greater certainty. A letter from Goldsmith to the Prime Minister's Office, written on 14 March, was also released under the Act. This seemed to place the responsibly for the nature of the legal advice on the prime minister:

> The Attorney General understands that it is unequivocally the Prime Minister's view that Iraq has committed further material breaches as specified in paragraph 4 of resolution 1441, but as this is a judgment for the Prime Minister, the Attorney General would be grateful for this confirmation that this is the case.[222]

The Prime Minister's Office provided the assurance (later shown to be essentially wrong), and Goldsmith then told parliament on 17 March that an invasion would be legal. It appeared that the country's most senior independent legal adviser had based his advice about whether a war would be legal on an unsubstantiated assurance from the principal British advocate for the war, Blair, not on further independent evidence or opinion. The Attorney General had seemingly circumnavigated his own professional role, and changed his view to agree with that of his client.

Then a few days before the election, after part of the advice had been leaked to the press, the full text was put on the website of 10 Downing Street. Across the world people were reading a digital copy of the real document, headed 'Secret'.[223] The press were too concerned with the detail to notice the significance in terms of accountability. Never before had British public opinion forced the release of such a document. Diverse proponents of accountability attacked from all directions. Lord Lester QC asked the Information Commissioner to release the date on which Blair first asked for legal advice, because this could show that he planned to go to war well before he consulted his Cabinet and parliament. Blair had ignored the decision from the Parliamentary Ombusdman that he should comply. Once again, the challenge utilized Blair's own Freedom of Information Act. Another leaked document a few days later, headed 'Confidential', showed that Blair had been given similar legal advice from the Foreign Office much earlier in March 2002. A week before this leak, during a TV interview, he had denied seeing any such advice.[224]

All the advice not only showed a high level of uncertainty about the legality of war, but it also seemed to represent a case for the prosecution of Bush, if not Blair. Concerning the US doctrine of preemptive self-defence, Goldsmith concluded, 'This is not a doctrine which, in my opinion, exists or is recognised in international law.' Goldsmith also concluded that it was for the Security Council, not a national government, to decide if Iraq had breached UN resolutions, as had the earlier advice: 'it is for the Council to assess whether any such breach of those obligations has occurred. The US have a rather different view: they maintain that the assessment of breach is for individual member states. We are not aware of any other state which supports this view.'[225] One of the most significant conclusions was in the final paragraph of Goldsmith's advice: 'regime change cannot be the objective of military action'. Bush had continually presented regime change as the objective. Blair had originally disagreed with this, but then when WMDs had not been found had appeared to rationalize the invasion on the grounds of removing Saddam and his regime: 'I took the view then ... that it was better for this country's security and the security of the world to remove Saddam and put him in prison rather than have him in power.'[226] Earlier, in March 2003, he had said of British troops, 'Their mission: to remove Saddam Hussein from power and disarm Iraq of its weapons of mass destruction.'[227] A few days later families of soldiers who had died started legal challenges against Blair based on the Attorney General's advice, which included a demand for another inquiry, under threat of a judicial review if this was not set up within two weeks. The NGO Military Families Against the War set in motion a case against Blair at the International Criminal Court, claiming that soldiers had been ordered unlawfully to use cluster bombs in civilian areas and destroy essential power supplies.

The complexity of the arguments clouded clear conclusions. But the interest in relation to accountability is the nature of the debate and disclosures. First, whatever their views, politicians, parliaments and people were all arguing on the basis of international law. A decade earlier lawyers and politicians were arguing about whether the term 'international law' even had any credible meaning. The basis for global accountability was now being accepted, if not the detail. Second, the disclosures of secret documents in the UK were mainly through systems set up or previously supported by the Blair government. Like the Nuremberg Tribunal, Blair had created 'dormant precedents', but this time in the form of boomerang precedents. When these documents were being written, those concerned would not have believed that so soon afterwards they would be made available across the world. Third, ICT and the media had facilitated a level of public engagement that had never been seen before, particularly through the letters pages of the newspapers, and here the level of understanding and clarity was often better than that from professional commentators.

> [The Attorney General's] published outline advice did not even mention five key principles of international law.
>
> First, it is up to the UN, not individual member states, to decide how to enforce its regulations.
>
> Second, a war is justified only if it is necessary as a last resort.
>
> Third, states must have no hidden, ulterior motives for going to war: they may only do so for lawful purposes and use only the force necessary to achieve them.
>
> Fourth, there is an overwhelming presumption against war in international law; if in doubt, states must avoid war.
>
> Fifth, the burden of proof is on a state intending to make war to show that it is justified, not on its victim to show why it should not be attacked.
>
> Richard Heller, letter to *The Independent* (written before the disclosure of the full legal advice)[228]

One further legal precedent seems inescapable. The war against Iraq was constructed to implement policy, not to defend or deter an immediate aggressor. Whatever the eventual outcome of formal and informal assessments of American and British leaders since 2001, the assessment, mentioned in Chapter 1, is likely to haunt those concerned:

> the wrong for which leaders are on trial is ... that they started [the war] ... our position is that no grievances or policies will justify resort to aggressive war. It is renounced and condemned as an instrument of policy.

Recall that the writer, Justice Robert H. Jackson, was USA Senior Representative at the 1945 Nuremberg War Crimes Trials, and Chief Prosecutor.

Self-interest

From a more political stance, leadership self-interest was also proposed as the reason for the invasion and occupation. The most obvious argument was simply that leaders like to become famous and leave their mark on history, and a war is an effective way to do that. The need to secure and profit from oil reserves in the Middle East was also a common view. There is now little doubt that cheap oil reserves are in decline.[229] The coincidental benefit of a war to the US oil and arms industries, and to the construction companies that gained a virtual monopoly on rebuilding Iraq and had ongoing links with Bush's Republican Party,[230] were strong complementary explanations. It was also asked why other seemingly despotic regimes have been left out of the 'axis of evil'. Burma was an obvious example, but here the US has major interests in an oil pipeline. The Sudan, Republic of Congo, Turkmenistan and Israel were other examples. Why, it was asked, did Pakistan's admission that the government had supplied nuclear materials to North Korea not provide a reason to include it in the 'axis of evil'?

Arguments were also put that the war was an excuse for increasing budget deficits in the US, which pumped money into people's pockets far quicker than low interest rates or tax cuts might have done – just before an election.[231] Polish economist Michal Kalecki coined the term 'military Keynesianism' in 1943 to describe such economic strategies, and he applied the concept to Nazi Germany. Ronald Reagan apparently used the same strategy under the guise of countering the 'evil empire' (an interesting echo) and supposed communist threats in South America. In that year the US economy grew by 7 per cent and Reagan won a landslide victory. Seeming attempts to impose US-controlled GM crops on Iraq was one of the less obvious aspects to attract concern. An obtuse US/Iraqi law passed in 2004[232] seemed to prevent Iraqi farmers saving certain seeds. The rule was very badly drafted, but there were concerns that one of the seeds that may fall into US control is wild emmer, the ancestor of most of the wheat cultivated in the world today. The likely outcome is that Iraq will be forced to use modern US seed because traditional varieties were largely destroyed during the invasion and occupation, and will have to pay American companies to do that.

A further functional coincidence was that Iraq provided a distraction from the increasing effectiveness of accountability movements from a wide range of protagonists, against Bush, Blair and their peers. It is relevant to recall the political context within which both Bush and Blair came to office. This was the era of the accountability challenges to, and removal of immunity from, other leaders such as Jacques Chirac and Alain Juppé, Chancellor Helmut Kohl, Silvio Berlusconi, General Pinochet, Fujimori and many others across the world. These people were peers and perhaps friends. Berlusconi, for example, had supported the British and UK intervention and was pictured warmly embracing Tony Blair in March 2004,[233] and Blair later stayed at Berlusconi's home while on holiday. This was only shortly after it was announced that Berlusconi's immunity had been removed by the Italian courts and he could be charged for corruption.

On a broader front, civil society organizations had been engaging in innovative and effective accountability protests for a decade against the

WTO, G7/8 and other leadership forums, and against novel environmental risks, for example genetically modified (GM) crops. Blair, with US backing, had supported GMs in much the same way that he supported the invasion of Iraq, and essentially he lost but this failure was masked by Iraq. For Bush, there were additional ghosts from Vietnam, Watergate and the fall of Nixon, the shaming of Clinton, and increasing challenges against Kissinger and US foreign policy in general. He was also being accused of destroying the Kyoto agreement on climate change, and of undermining other international accords such as those about landmines which were starting to put a common global interest above narrow national interests (see Chapter 5). In addition, he would have been very aware that he only held his democratic office because of the vote of one person – the Supreme Court judge who upheld his view that his election was lawful.

Cumulative lock-in

> It is in the nature of a hypothesis when once a man has conceived it, that it assimilates everything to itself, as proper nourishment, and from the first moment of your begetting it, it generally grows stronger by everything you see, hear or understand.
>
> Laurence Sterne, *Tristram Shandy*[234]

Whether or not the war was ethically and legally sustainable, or based on self-interest, one factor is undeniable: US and British leaders made many decisions that seemed strategically unintelligent. This proposes a further explanation, that leaders simply became trapped by a chain of events – a 'cumulative lock-in'. The problem of 'lock-in' is commonly exemplified by the QWERTY keyboard. The letters were originally arranged like this to reduce, not increase, the speed of typing, because the keys of the original typewriters jammed if used too fast. A modern PC does not have this problem, but we are locked into the QWERTY keyboard, because we have all learned to type with this arrangement of letters. Lock-ins are common in a complex world.

Cumulative lock-in can be seen to arise from a string of interrelated factors which create a situation whereby turning back becomes increasingly more difficult. Paul O'Neill, former US secretary of the Treasury, recalls the rigid style of Bush and him saying, 'I won't negotiate with myself.' ONeill continues:

> once the President had taken a position, it was set in concrete and no one should expect to revisit its rationale ... in the weeks following 9/11 Bush had decided to go to war against Iraq. Having made the decision, there was no turning back.[235]

Unfortunately the traditional view of 'strong leadership' is one of someone who will pursue their vision, whatever the obstacles and subsequent objections. But in the modern world, that is clearly a problematic ideology. The central choice for any leader is whether decisions are based on intuition and belief, or are evidence-based and accountable and open to assessment and revision. This latter cybernetic leadership style is the preferred approach in most basic management textbooks. If decisions are made in other ways, managers and leaders are likely to get locked into a degenerative spiral which, as the post-9/11 events seem to show, eventually can only be sustained by deceit which then engenders significant challenges (Figure 2.1). Iraq provides an obvious case study, but it is interesting to compare this with US intervention in Vietnam, from 1962 to 1975, as assessed by one of its main architects Robert McNamara in his book *In retrospect: the tragedy and lessons of Vietnam*.[236] The former Oxfam director-general, Brian Walker, known for his decision to defy the blockade on Cambodia and send humanitarian aid in 1979, has brought the astonishing similarities between Iraq and Vietnam to public attention in *The anatomy of war*.[237]

President Johnson ... made the fateful choices that locked the United States onto a path of massive military intervention in Vietnam, an intervention that ultimately destroyed his presidency ... (p. 173)

Perhaps [Johnson] saw clearly that the decision about changing the war's direction rested with him – and it was a decision he could not bring himself to take. (p. 42)

Robert McNamara

One reason Kennedy and Johnson administrations failed to take an orderly rational approach ... was the staggering variety and complexity of other issues we faced. Simply put, we faced a blizzard of problems, there were only twenty four hours in a day, and we often did not think straight ... (p. 4)

Our policies and programmes in Indochina had evolved in ways we had neither anticipated nor intended ... (p. 41)

We failed then – as we have since – to recognize the limitations of modern, high technology military equipment, forces, and doctrine ... (Conclusion 5)

Robert McNamara

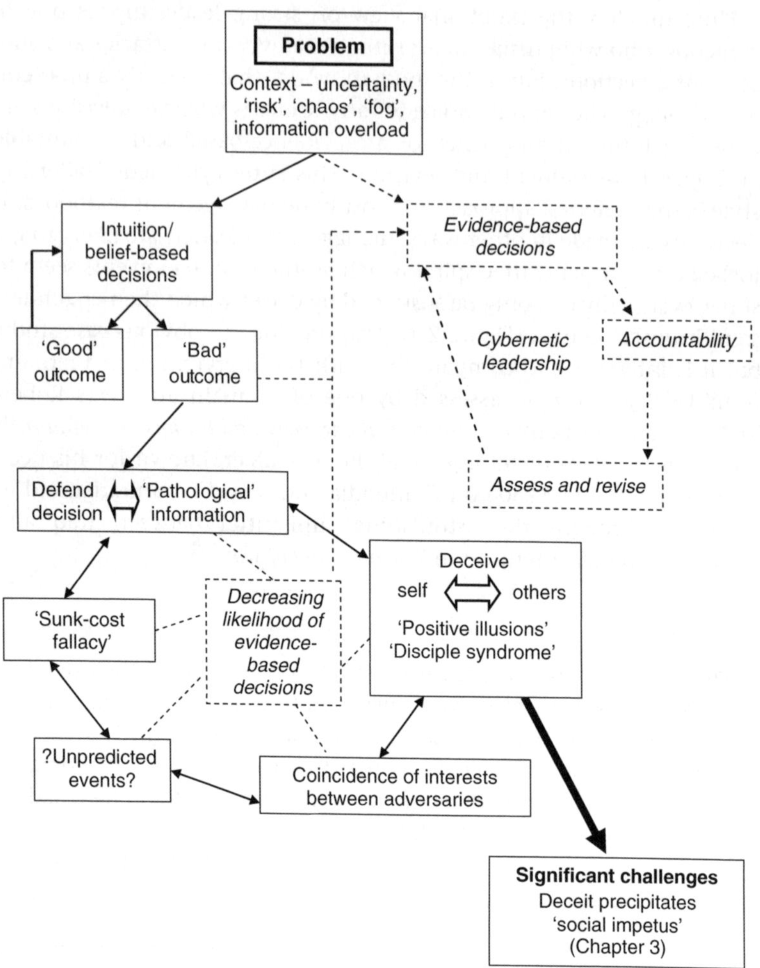

Figure 2.1   Cumulative lock-in

The context of 9/11, and many modern problems, is the complexity, 'chaos' and unpredictability of the modern world, particularly war.[238] As Ulrich Beck has argued convincingly, we now live in an uncertain world – a 'risk society'.[239] This is compounded by the defining problem of the ICT age – information overload. This problem is reflected in the title of the film about Robert McNamara based on *In retrospect – The fog of war.* The unacknowledged limitations of the human mind to comprehend what is happening on a complex global scale underlie many of the new security threats.[240] At a meeting of British experts before the Iraq invasion, one participant reported, 'I was staggered at Blair's apparent naivety, at his inability to engage with complexities.'[241]

In this context of an unpredictable and confusing world, simplistic *intuitive/belief-based* decision-making is an attractive option. So the roots of cumulative lock-in are probably biological, and the way our brain has evolved to make decisions. Recent neuroscience provides a relevant insight. Benjamin Libet's experiments show that most of our day-to-day actions seem to be initiated unconsciously *before* we consciously make a decision to act.[242] This area of experimental psychology has since been popularized by Jonathan Ree in his book *Blink*.[243] It is not quite clear how this might relate to all forms of decision-making, but the notion that political and other leaders often make intuitive decisions and then make their arguments fit their intuition seems plausible. Of course, we could not function without taking intuitive decisions in daily life, but it is questionable whether this is the best way to decide to take a country to war. From the meeting of experts, called by Blair ostensively to inform his decision about an invasion, one participant, Toby Dodge, said of Blair, 'It seemed as if he was just going through the motions. I think he had made up his mind already.'[244] The head of MI6, Richard Dearlove, claimed that 'intelligence and facts were being fixed around policy'.[245] It was reported that Bush and Blair had an understanding about 'regime change' in Iraq as early as March 2002.[246] Blair had seemingly overlooked that he worked within a cabinet government and did not have authority to give personal assurances of this nature, and so his only option was to return home and argue a case for war. The degree to which these two leaders relied on intuition will probably remain a mystery, but it is certainly clear that the decisions were not based on verifiable evidence because subsequent events showed that there was little such evidence, only opinion.

Johnson had made the goal in Vietnam crystal clear. 'Win the war!' … He never deviated from that objective. But we could never show him how to win at an acceptable cost or an acceptable risk. (p. 155)

Robert McNamara

Intuitive decisions are likely to be influenced by social factors, principally personal beliefs or ideologies, which make the decisions appear self-legitimizing. The firm Christian-based beliefs of Bush and Blair were presented by both as justifying their actions, and not least for Bush was the Old Testament notion of retribution. Blair was accused by his former foreign secretary Robin Cook of basing his policy on 'missionary zeal', which seemed reflected in Blair's curious use of the phrase, 'I only know what I believe'.[247] When he addressed the US Congress in 2003 his words were: 'With every fibre of instinct, of conviction, I believe that we are right.'[248] Blair answered sophisticated arguments for not invading, at the meeting of experts, by saying 'But he [Saddam] is evil, isn't he?' One participant recalled that 'it seemed highly personal: an evil Saddam versus Blair–Bush'.[249] Recall that Bush claimed, 'A lot of my foreign policy is driven by the fact that I truly believe that freedom is a gift from the Almighty to every person, and that America has a responsibility to take a lead in the world, to help people be free.'[250] In *With God on their side*, Esther Kaplan provides considerable evidence of the faith-based ideology of the US leaders, and reports that Bush had once said, 'God told me to strike at al-Qaeda and I struck them, and then he instructed me to strike at Saddam, which I did'.[251] Zimbabwe's President Mugabe was one of many to challenge this approach when he stated at the UN General Assembly in 2004, 'We are now being coerced to accept and believe that a new political-cum-religious doctrine has arisen, namely that there is but one political God, George W. Bush, and Tony Blair is his prophet.'[252] Greg Thielmann, a former intelligence analyst, termed the US use of information 'faith-based intelligence gathering'.[253] Of course, the decisions of Saddam Hussein and the (unrelated) al-Qaida activists also appeared to be justified similarly. If intuitive/belief-based decisions seem to create 'good' outcomes, then leaders will probably continue in this mode, with few challenges. But when outcomes appear 'bad', a downward spiral of events is likely to be set in motion, and the inevitable deception eventually precipitates significant challenges from public and peers.

This is likely to be compounded by the type of formal education experienced by elites, which can reinforce the intuition/belief-based approach to decision-making, because it can create the ability to *defend* positions that cannot be sustained without verifiable evidence. Many British and US leaders had experienced a traditional Oxbridge or Ivy League education. This tradition produces elites who can argue their case effectively, and checking facts is often secondary. A scholar is held to account for not winning, less often for being wrong. Centuries ago, a doctorate at Oxford or Cambridge was gained through candidates defending a claim that was presented to them by examiners, for example the Earth is flat, or the Earth is round. For a long time it was assumed (probably correctly) that people who were wealthy and had an elite education were more likely to be right about political and social matters than others in the population, so the skills of argument and persuasion were paramount for leaders. The ethos continues, for example in the adversarial style of contemporary Oxbridge Union debates, and traditional doctoral oral exams. To this day, candidates 'defend' their theses at oral exams. The aim is to create elites who win by strong argument, not who can explain complicated uncertain evidence and question and evolve their own views. This is compounded by the difficulty for busy high-powered leaders to engage in formal lifelong learning.[254] When Blair came to power, he could not use a word processor. He had been too busy to learn. Hans Blix complained that the failures of the American and British leaders stemmed from 'a deficit of critical thinking',[255] and Nelson Mandela termed Bush 'a leader who cannot think properly'.[256]

What I do know is that we received no thoughtful analysis of the problem and no pros and cons regarding alternative ways to deal with it ... (Preface)

We failed to analyse our assumptions critically, then or later. The foundations of our decision making were gravely flawed ... (p. 39)

Robert McNamara

This sets up what management trainers describe as the 'declaim and defend' model, and the need to defend and argue without verifiable evidence sets the scene for distorted use of *'pathological' information*. As Park explains in relation to science, a 'pathological' analysis occurs when fractional pieces of statistical and other evidence are given immense importance because they happen to fit a prevailing analytical framework.[257] Attractive theories are built on virtually non-existent evidence. This is compounded by the nature of risk communication in organizations. An expert on decision-making, Lawrence Phillips, points out how phrases such as 'we believe' can be interpreted by analysts as indicating anything between 20 and 90 per cent certainty. He elaborates in relation to an organization such as a government department: 'As verbal phrases of uncertainty are reported upward, the uncertainty decreases for events people want to happen, and increases for events they don't want to happen.'[258] It seems that in the US this was paralleled by so-called 'cherry picking' and 'stove piping'. The Office of Special Plans in the Pentagon apparently took selective intelligence information and sent it direct to the presidential office without the normal checking by analysts.[259] In the UK and US, the public inquiries revealed the extensive degree to which caveats and cautionary notes had been removed from early drafts of policy documents. The inevitable result will be a false and over-optimistic view of progress.

There was such determination to do something, anything, to stop the communists that discouraging reports were often ignored …

The reports – including my own – on the military situation were often too optimistic … (p. 48)

Like many people, the U.S. commanders also indulged … in wishful thinking. (p. 70)

Robert McNamara

The outcome of pathological information is that leaders probably start to *deceive* themselves, and then inevitably they have to deceive others. In *Overconfidence and war*, Dominic Johnson takes an evolutionary view of how leaders arise, which explains one element as self-deceit. His 'positive illusions theory' holds that they come to power through a key adaptive psychological trait, overconfidence. The result is a decision-making style reflecting overestimation of the strength of one's supporters, underestimation of the opposition, and neglect of intelligence.[260] John Gray explained his view of Blair's conduct, which probably applies to many leaders who become trapped by their beliefs:

It is not so much that he is economical with the truth but that he has no conception of it. For him, truth is whatever serves the cause. Deception is justified if it advances the cause of good – then it is not deception, but the expression of a higher truth.[261]

As a psychologist might, former permanent secretary at the UK Ministry of Defence, Sir Michael Quinlan, concluded that Blair's conduct entailed 'denial'.[262] The evidence about deceit permeates this whole chapter, and was a central public perception of how leaders responded to events surrounding 9/11 (above). The importance of this is explained further in the next chapter. Human beings have a strong instinctive reaction to deceit, which fuels the 'social impetus' to challenge the cheats.

> All of this occurred without adequate public disclosure or debate, planting the seeds of an eventually debilitating credibility gap ... (p. 174)
>
> We misjudged ... the geopolitical intentions of our adversaries and we exaggerated the dangers to the United States of their actions. (Conclusion 1)
>
> We failed to draw Congress and the American people into a full and frank debate ... (Conclusion 6)
>
> Robert McNamara

A culture of deception is likely to be reinforced as close associates are deceived into supporting their leader, or are themselves locked in to decisions that they would otherwise question by their leader. 'Disciple syndrome' emerges. A close circle of followers creates the impression for a leader that belief-based decisions are self-evident truths. The disciples may become even greater adherents to mistaken ideologies, as they complete with one another for the favours of the leader and promote evolved and perhaps even more misleading versions of the justifications for the decisions. The two-page legal advice given to the British parliament by the Attorney General seemed to reflect a disciple view.

> This recommendation for what, in effect, constituted a revolutionary change in U.S. policy rested on an exposition of two and a half pages, with little analysis or supporting rationale. (p. 114)
>
> Robert McNamara

A further factor appears as a paradox, *coincidences of interest* particularly between adversaries. Arguably, weapons of mass destruction became so central to the propaganda surrounding Iraq because this suited Saddam and Bush and Blair. The Iraqi regime wanted to present itself as strong to deter attack, and the US and British leaders wanted an excuse to attack. This is probably why so much of the unreliable evidence put forward by the US and Britain was found to have stemmed from Iraqis who either wanted to support Saddam or were fooled by him. It also suited both Bush and bin Laden to see Saddam and his regime destroyed. This, together with the alienation of Muslims from the West, was probably a welcome 'mass effect' from 9/11 for al-Qaida. More broadly, bin Laden and Bush then got themselves into a position where they needed one another to sustain their positions. Bin Laden, and others such as Abu Musab al-Zarqawi, would probably have remained unknown mystics without Bush, and Bush needed 'terrorist' leaders to rationalize a 'war on terrorism'. A 'terrorist leader' who apparently could be contained but never caught was ideal for the US. And, of course, the US and Iraq leaders were firmly against the setting up of the International Criminal Court which might hold them all to account.

The other compounding factor is psycho-social – leaders become trapped by a *sunk-cost fallacy* ('Concord fallacy').[263] Within endeavours that require front-loaded investment, economic or in terms of personal credibility, there can come a point at which the actors will not stop a project, even if all rational evidence proposes that continuing will entail greater tangible costs than benefits. Leaders and decision-makers enter a state of denial and 'throw good money after bad' because 'now there's no turning back'. The building of Concord was a seminal example. At a certain point, the main losses from abandoning the Concord project would have been political reputations, but the financial losses from continuing were considerable. Unsurprisingly, this idea has also been applied to the war in Vietnam. Lyndon Johnson continued to send troops well after he had concluded that the war was pointless and could not be won.

Unpredicted events further complicate these dynamics. No British leader could have foreseen the suicide of David Kelly and resultant inquiry which disclosed the evidence showing the degree to which the infamous 'dossier' had been manipulated. 'Dormant precedents', identified in the previous chapter, can provide surprises. It is unlikely that Blair foresaw that his own Freedom of Information Act would become the means for public and parliament to demand and force the full release of the legal advice that he had been given, and to disclose that the view of the Attorney General had changed within a few days. The lock-in increases, the chances to reassess and revise decisions become increasingly remote, and so further deceit becomes virtually the only option.

This concept of cumulative lock-in seems to fit other social problems, for example being sucked into criminality or drug dependency. But the broader question about Iraq concerns what leadership theory terms the 'nominal fallacy' – who was really in control?[264] Were the high-profile senior leaders of the US and Britain trapped into this downward spiral by the covert activities of other power elites, such as directors of oil and arms companies, or were they trapped in a mess of their own making? Either way, their situation provides important lessons for all leaders, and the Iraq invasion is probably not an isolated example of these dynamics.

Understanding the nature of cumulative lock-in not only provides a useful lesson for leaders, it also suggests another dimension for the accountability movement in the future, prevention. Modern leaders need to be able to make U-turns, and if this is done for good reason it should be applauded and not criticized as is common at present. The broader lesson for leaders is that they need to develop a context for their actions which permits their decisions to be more like those of a driver of a sophisticated car, and less like those of a rabbit caught in its headlights. We should not need to wait for twenty years for personal reappraisal, as with Robert McNamara.

Wars usually start because of a coincidence of interests – a range of complementary factors that could function to benefit one or more leaderships on all sides of a conflict. The same is probably true of events following 9/11. World leaders probably did sense the ethos of the global accountability movement, and wanted to show leadership in this area rather than being forced into action by civil society movements, as had happened concerning Pinochet and other despots. But they did not seem to consider the public perception of the legality of their actions, which immediately made them appear little better than those they were challenging. They were probably not unaware of the personal benefits of a war, which included not only financial and political rewards but also the chance to construct novel forms of immunity for themselves from the growing accountability movement. But probably the most significant dynamics were human failings and the inevitable pattern of cumulative lock-in that ensued. The popular belief that 'power corrupts, and absolute power corrupts absolutely' reflects the fact that corruption is founded on deceit. Perhaps the only difference between leaders and the rest of us is that we don't have the power to be corrupt, and so generally we avoid getting trapped into the self-destructive degenerative spirals that have characterized leadership throughout history.

Retributive accountability

The violence on all sides was motivated by retribution, albeit falsely rationalized by US leaders in relation to the link between the 9/11 attacks and Iraq. Was it a coincidence that on 11 September 1922 the League of Nations proclaimed Britain's mandate over Palestine, and the Arabs declared a day of mourning? Was it coincidence that the Madrid train bombings were on 11 March? Were the twin towers of the World Trade Center the only 9/11 targets, or were the attackers equally pleased about the demolition of a smaller third tower, about which we heard very little? It contained a CIA department. Those responsible could have achieved equal publicity by targeting the Statue of Liberty or the UN tower. They could have caused even more devastation through hitting a nuclear power station or chemical installation, but the message would have been less obvious. The lesson for world leaders is that they may think they can make themselves secure through extensive and expensive personal protection, but if they are seen as unaccountable they will inevitably be attacked indirectly through vulnerable entities that are symbolically linked to them.

Retribution was also clearly part of the rationale for the US-led response. When discussing the threat posed by Iraq, in 2002, George Bush had stated, 'After all, this is the guy who tried to kill my dad.'[265] It was perceived that Bush wanted to finish off the Gulf War that his father had started. The US Attorney General said he wanted people to 'find and kill bin Laden'.[266] The highest legal adviser in America seemed to be inciting an extrajudicial killing in another nation.

In a candid analysis of the role that global injustice may have played in fuelling the attacks of 9/11 Chalmers Johnson, the author of a book called *Blowback*, assessed the reaction to America's 'imperial projects'. He argued:

> For if it is acknowledged that blowback played a part in the Sept. 11 calamity, then some people holding high elected, appointed or administrative office in the U.S. government are at least partly responsible for the deaths of several thousand of their fellow American citizens.[267]

The proposed ethic may appear far-fetched at the present time, but the idea of provocation is well-established in domestic law. The argument was not that provocation justifies mass murder. It was that the rational strategy against the globalization of violence from non-state actors is to defuse hatred and reduce the perception of abuse of power by the governments of wealthy nations.

Bush, Blair and other Western politicians tried to play down the spiral of retribution,[268,269] but the non-state actors made it clear that they were motivated by US-led military action. Even the British Joint Intelligence Committee (JIC) had warned Blair that an invasion of Iraq would increase insecurity in Britain, and a report from the International Institute for Strategic Studies (IISS) concluded that there was 'no doubt' that the occupation of Iraq had 'strengthened rather than weakened al-Qaida'.[270] The invasion and occupation of Iraq were followed by attacks on US and British targets, in Iraq and elsewhere, which included Riyadh, Pakistan and Istanbul. Australia and Italy suffered similar attacks, which were linked to their involvement with the US. As Japan sent its 'self-defence' troops to Iraq, two home-made bombs exploded near the defence ministry in Tokyo, and the country was put on an unprecedented high level security alert. In June 2004, the Bush administration was forced to reverse a claim that its 'war on terror' was working because the number of terrorist attacks was the lowest for 34 years. It was found that the original State Department statistics were wrong: 2003 had been one of the worst years on record.[271]

In March 2004, another country that had firmly supported Bush and Blair, Spain, suffered a major bomb attack at Madrid station, which killed 200 people a few days before a general election. A taped message apparently from the military spokesman of al-Qaida claimed:

> We declare our responsibility for what happened in Madrid exactly two-and-half years after the attacks on New York and Washington. It is our response to your collaboration with the criminals Bush and his allies. This is a response to the crimes that you have caused in the World, and specifically in Iraq and Afghanistan, and there will be more … If you don't stop your injustices, more and more blood will flow and these attacks will seem very small compared to what can occur in what you call terrorism.[272]

The significance of the retributive element was made even more evident in another statement, apparently by Osama bin Laden, which offered a truce to Europeans. It used phrases such as 'Stop spilling our blood so we can stop spilling your blood', and 'Reaction comes at the same level as the original action. Our acts are a reaction to your own acts'.[273] The new Spanish prime minister, José Luis Rodriguez Zapatero, appeared aware of retributive accountability when he said, 'Wars such as those which have occurred in Iraq only show hatred, violence and terror to proliferate.'[274] A later statement, seemingly from bin Laden, was more explicit, accusing Bush of

> distortion and confusion ... [he] continues to conceal from you the real reason [for the 9/11 attacks] ... we saw the injustice of the US–Israeli alliance against our people ... these meanings produced an overwhelming feeling to reject injustice and generated a strong determination to punish the unjust ones. While I was looking at those destroyed towers in Lebanon, it occurred to me to punish the unjust one in a similar manner by destroying towers in the United States.[275]

In the wake of the moral indignation that the killings aroused in the West, it is easy to miss the significance of the meticulous way the attacks were explained, as legitimate acts of accountability.

Legitimization became more pertinent following the bombings in London in June 2005. At the time of these attacks, Blair and other British leaders immediately claimed there was no link with British intervention in Iraq. But as they were making these claims an unknown group, the Secret Organisation Group of al-Qaeda, presented a justification on Arabic websites which declared that 'it is time to take revenge against the British Zionist Crusader movement in retaliation for the massacres Britain is committing in Iraq and Afghanistan.' Later a video apparently made by one of the suicide bombers, Mohammed Sidique Khan, and al-Qaeda leader Ayman al-Zawahri appeared which stated 'we repeat the warning that we shall respond to anyone who participates in the aggression against Iraq, Afghanistan and Palestine in kind.' A little later a British recruiter for Hizb ut-Tahrir talked of the way in which young people such as Khan were being attracted to terrorism. He claimed that recruiters will argue, 'it's the Caliphate that will bring the criminals – as in Bush and Blair – to account.'[276] Retributive accountability is a motivating force of modern 'terrorism', as it has been throughout history.

Many of the prevailing explanations for events surrounding 9/11 reflect Samuel Huntington's view of a 'Clash of civilizations'. But there is an alternative perspective. Judaism, Christianity, and Islam can also be seen as evolved versions of common civilisational and monotheistic ideologies, based on the same god, which had roots in the ancient Egyptian religion based around the god Amun-Re. One of the shared tenets of this West Asian belief system is human retribution, which is not so central within Buddhism, Hinduism and the East Asian traditions. Future historians may well describe the current form of global feuding as a clash within a religion – a form of global family feud. Further relevant evidence may emerge as we learn more about the belief-based nature of Bush, Blair and bin Laden's decision making, which seems to have fuelled the cumulative lock-in that channelled their actions. This perspective is likely to have particular resonance with Chinese, Indian and other Asian analysts.

It is important to put aside the horror and appreciate what is new about this form of retributive accountability. The weapons of this style of non-state action are not WMDs. They are, as suggested above, 'instruments of mass effect' which target the human mind and deploy the force of ideas. One of the apparent aims for the 'terrorists' is to influence a more powerful adversary by causing in-group conflict and self-inflicted harm – to turn the enemy against itself. The tactic was evidently successful when the British Houses of Commons and Lords argued in unprecedented and undignified ways in 2005 about new anti-terror legislation, which was to remove civil protections dating back to Magna Carta, and Lord Hoffman had concluded, 'The real threat to the life of the nation … comes not from terrorism but from laws such as these.'[277] New visa regulations and aggressive immigration controls, which deterred thousands of visitors and international students from studying in the US and UK, marked a similar success. Precipitating own goals is now a major strategy of war.

John Gray points out in *Al Qaeda and what it means to be modern* that the defining feature of this particular Islamic tradition is that it is thoroughly up to date.[278] Its men often break with tradition and marry friends' sisters instead of girls favoured by their families. And they mend their own clothes.[279] The movement demonstrates an astonishing awareness of international politics and world media. It is innovative and creative. The other strength is that it has effective leadership, and this is in strong contrast with Muslim leadership of previous eras. There are no clear precedents for bin Laden's leadership, except the old Caliphate. Malise Ruthven describes 'The crisis of modern Islam … as a crisis of authority – political, intellectual, and legal as well as spiritual. A world religion demands leadership. Yet outside the Shi'i minority tradition, a leadership commanding universal support is conspicuously absent.'[280] Bin Laden and al-Qaida filled that vacuum, and they knew how to legitimize their view of accountability on a global scale.

If it continues, the outcome of retributive accountability in the modern world is that the 'winners' will inevitably be those with least to lose, not those with the most power. That dynamic might reflect the perception by suicide bombers that their lives are unimportant, or by a community that its social circumstances are so intractable that taking risks cannot make things worse. In contrast, wealthy people and wealthy nations are defending massive but increasingly vulnerable resources and lifestyles, and are therefore unable to win through simple military power.

Former US secretary of state Madeleine Albright seemed more aware of these dynamics than other American leaders when she told a senate commission, 'Al-Qaeda is an ideological virus. Until the right medicine is found, the virus will continue to spread.'[281] Former British cabinet minister Mo Mowlam, whose experience included responsibility for Northern Ireland, was similarly pragmatic in a TV interview when she said that Western governments should open talks with Osama bin Laden and al-Qaida: 'You have to do that. If you do not, you condemn large parts of the world to war forever.'[282] It is not possible to redress retributive accountability, or even win a 'war against terrorism', by trying to shoot or imprison ideas.

It is interesting to conjecture what world opinion might be if al-Qaida were not an Islamist organization, but just an organized challenge to US hegemony. Is that so improbable? Oliver Roy points out that prospective recruits no longer need to promise to convert to Islam. He elaborates:

> Al-Qaida and its many incarnations is a transnational organisation with only circumstantial links in the Middle East ... We tend to overemphasise the Islamic side of al-Qaida and disregard its global, anti-imperialist dimension and third world agenda. Al-Qaida undoubtedly stands a better chance of survival if it devotes less energy to defending Islam and concentrates on joining the vanguard of movements contesting established order and US domination.[283]

What would be the world reaction if al-Qaida became the main challenge to the efforts of American companies such as Monsanto to control world food production through genetically modified crops and patenting? This would certainly create some novel arguments and modified political alliances. The vision is not so improbable remembering that many of the seeds now being manipulated and patented had their origins in Muslim lands and that the US-imposed laws in occupied Iraq tried to control Iraqi seed use. It is not impossible that al-Qaida or an offshoot could adopt a non-religious political stance based more on claims to global accountability in the future, and even adopt a minimum violence ideology. It might even become the leading environmental campaigner against US intransigence about global warming and other environmental impacts, a new form of global Greenpeace.

Another possible outcome is that 'instruments of mass effect' may create forms of war within which there are comparatively few deaths and injuries in relation to the goals that are achieved. There is already some evidence of a trend across the world that violence is becoming 'de-linked' from war, notably in Europe and North East Asia.[284] Further minimum violence challenges to the US would increase the power of the protagonists, and perhaps elevate them from 'terrorists' to freedom fighters, and then to legitimate actors within new forms of global governance. What will be the judgement of history when future generations, who did not experience the direct horrors, read that the 9/11 attacks killed around 3,000 civilians and did little damage to US infrastructure, but brought about lasting changes in US imperialism; in contrast that the falsely justified US retributive attacks in Iraq killed 100,000 civilians and destroyed a nation and society that was a birthplace of modern civilization, devastated one of the multicultural hubs of the Silk Road region, Afghanistan, and probably increased rather than reduced the 'terrorism' it sought to quell? Which leaders will appear more progressive and more humane in terms of the means that they used to achieve their ends? Which leaders already, to people in particular parts of the world, appear less civilized?

But perhaps the most significant aspect of the events surrounding 9/11 was ignored by media, political and academic commentators, because it appears as a paradox. Bin Laden, al-Qaida, Bush, Blair, those who supported them *and* those who challenged them, all claimed to be aiming for the same outcome – leadership accountability. The missing element was any consensus about the ethical and legal basis for what they were doing, and that is why endeavours were retributive rather than legitimate. Interestingly, it is the African Union (AU) that has set a lead in codifying when intervention against despots is legitimate. Article 4 of the AU Charter creates 'The right of the Union to intervene in a member State pursuant to a decision of the assembly in respect of grave circumstances, namely war crimes, genocide and crimes against humanity'. It seems likely that the ultimate cure for the 'virus' of 'terrorism', whether by non-state or state actors, will be a global consensus about the rules for non-retributive leadership accountability. The alternative seems to be ongoing global feuding.

> The lesson may be that, rather than attempting to bolster traditional systems of state control, adopting a more decentralised model that seeks to distribute power, spread accountability through multiple levels of authority, and provide a forum for non-state grievance articulation, may be the safest course.
>
> Cambridge Security Seminar, 2003[285]

In the spirit of accountability, this chapter was sent to the offices of Prime Minister Tony Blair and President George W. Bush for comment and correction of any factual errors.

Implications

- Most of the protagonists in events surrounding the 9/11 attacks – Bush, Blair, bin Laden, al-Qaida and the anti-war protestors – all had the **same goal** – leadership accountability.
    - Actions became retributive rather than legitimate because they were not based on globally agreed **codes of leadership conduct**.
- The **challenge to the pro-war leaders** was unprecedented.
    - New digitalized ICT and media provide **compressed continuous comparisons** of leadership contradiction, but politicians seem unaware of this new dynamic.
    - Leaders make use of **next step agencies** to distance themselves from accountability, but this opens more routes for legal challenge.
    - National **accountability forums** become networked and global, and make available large amounts of information about political actors.
- **Intra-group accountability** was significant – challenges came from *within* political establishments, parties and leadership elites, and from nationals *within* the countries led by pro-war leaders; less from victim populations.
    - Iraq and similar conflicts are seen more as **wars between leaders** which their populations suffer from rather than being a party to.
    - The challenges concern improper **conduct** by leaders, whoever they are, and not constructed views of 'good' or 'bad' leaders.
    - It becomes difficult to construct **'sides'** based on nationalist, party or group identities and loyalty, and therefore to construct traditional forms of war.

- **Deceit** by pro-war leaders was a central public perception, reinforced by abuses of military power, and as a result:
    - **ideological war/intervention** becomes difficult
    - **legitimate defence** also becomes more difficult
    - the **West loses moral authority** in the world.
- The **Iraq Tribunal** will not hear cases against non-Iraqi perpetrators – a unique restriction on a modern war crimes court.
    - **Creative alternatives** are found – cases are taken to other forums – national courts, EC, the ICC, people's tribunals, other tribunals.
    - The absence of accountability against US and UK leaders and personnel justifies further **retributive accountability** by Iraqis and sympathizers.
    - Eventually, to gain popular support, an Iraq government **changes the rules** to include crimes by non-Iraqis.
- Leaders were trapped by **cumulative lock-in**. They made intuitive/belief-based, not evidence-based, decisions, and became caught in spirals of deceit.
    - **Deceit** is inevitable in this mode of decision-making, and becomes the catalyst for challenges.
    - Leaders should be facilitated to make **U-turns**, and congratulated, not condemned, for reassessing and revising decisions.
- Violence surrounding the 9/11 attacks represents **retributive accountability** by all parties.
    - Highly protected leaders are attacked indirectly and through precipitating **own goals**.
    - The 'winners' of retributive accountability are inevitably those with the **least to lose**, not those with most power.
    - State actors are forced into **diplomatic dialogue** with 'terrorists'.
    - History presents leaders who use '**instruments of mass effect**' as progressive, because this strategy **de-links violence and war**.
    - A consensus about the **rules for leadership accountability** provides a basis to redress 'terrorism' by state and non-state parties.

3
Social Impetus: Deceit, Evolution and ICT

> Let all men know how empty and worthless is the power of kings.
>
> King Canute (Knut), England, *c.*1000 AD

> You are the G8. We are the 6 billion.
>
> Banner at the 2001 Genoa protests

Stories of people power and the fall of powerful people pervade world history. So what is significant about the present circumstance? What supports the claim that this is a unique era of leadership accountability? Certainly the scale and scope of recent events are seen as new, and there have been many ground-breaking precedents and initiatives. But these observations raise a further question that has not been properly considered: why is there such a concern about 'distant others' by 'disinterested others' on a global scale? In some circumstances it is arguable that the conduct of powerful people has an actual or potential impact on the lives of unrelated populations in distant places, but that is relatively rare and there are usually many other abuses of power closer to home which should demand attention. We could explain the response in terms of 'a common feeling of justice', but why does that feeling exist, and why is it seemingly common around the world?

The purpose of this chapter is therefore to develop a general explanatory theory of social impetus in relation to leadership accountability on a global scale ('impetus' being defined as 'The force with which a body moves to and overcomes resistance' (Oxford English Dictionary)). This social response is probably a direct reaction not simply to the harm itself, but to a deeper instinctive feeling of wrongdoing and misuse of power – a reaction to perceived deceit, as is proposed in the previous chapter. Therefore evolutionary theory provides an appropriate starting point for analysis, particularly evolutionary psychology.

Evolutionary explanations

A central understanding of evolutionary psychology is that the human brain has probably not evolved significantly since humans were hunter-gatherers – we still have Stone Age brains.[1] That helps to explain, but not excuse, many human failings including rape, aggression, acquisitiveness and an inability to perceive modern environmental threats.[2] This requires an immediate qualification. The claim is not that we must remain controlled by a Stone Age brain. We have also evolved social mechanisms to escape from our instincts. As Richard Dawkins points out when his book *The selfish gene* is incorrectly criticized for being determinist, every time we use contraceptives we are challenging and modifying our evolutionary instincts. This is possible in a myriad of other ways, from outlawing rape to sophisticated international agreements about climate change. The significance is that these instinctive evolutionary drivers persist and are strong, and understanding them provides a *basis* for analysing social behaviour.

So, are there likely to be direct instinctive evolutionary-based reactions to the forms of harm that are the focus of this book, and do these help to explain the global response? If the harm were close and had a direct effect on our lives, then probably we would instinctively feel wronged. But the response is to the news of harm against, or by, 'distant others', not to actual harm, and for obvious reasons it seems hard to find a convincing evolutionary explanation for this. More specifically, we do not intrinsically dislike the removal of trees, the killing of animals and other environmental 'destruction', unless it is our property that is destroyed. In fact there is probably something in our hunter–gatherer brain that views this as positive, which explains among other things why hunting remains popular as a sport. There is probably not an instinctive aversion to resources moving from one person to another through the use of power relations, provided we do not personally suffer, and there is a big psychological reward if we or our close kin or group gain. There is not even total horror at killings and destruction, provided this affects 'others', as is evidenced by the number of people who avidly watch war movies or TV reports of actual war without reacting against it. Why do 'disinterested others' become involved in trying to right wrongs that do not directly affect them? What are the deeper evolutionary drivers of leadership wrongdoing, and the response to it, which underpin a global phenomenon?

In 1998, E.O. Wilson proposed that in order to make sense of the modern world in the context of evolution, there is a need for 'consilience' – a 'jumping together' of knowledge, across disciplines such as environmental policy, social science, ethics and biology. As the father of socio-biology, and arguably of its subsequent incarnation evolutionary psychology, his approach is rooted in biology and evolutionary theory, and that emerges as a very appropriate foundation for building an explanation for global leadership accountability. This is not surprising. Leadership must be one of the oldest social skills among animals and humans, and there must be instinctive aspects to both leading and responding to leaders.

Wilson identifies some 'basic categories', significant evolutionary traits or instincts, from his work, which can relate very directly to understanding leadership wrongdoing:[3]

- *Kin selection and parental investment* – the favouring of offspring, siblings, relatives. This has been fundamental to the maintenance of traditional power, and underpins many examples of leadership corruption in the present day.
- *Mating strategy* – men and women will have different priorities and perceptions of status and power. The traditional perception that leaders should be dominant men (or act like men) is closely bound up with this aspect. The acquisition of women has been a factor in the wrongful conduct of leaders throughout history. In particular, permitting rape has been a means for military leaders to motivate and reward their soldiers.
- *Status* – the seeking of rank, class, wealth, property, including the acquisition and control over women by men. For obvious reasons, acquiring status appears as one of the most relevant aspects in relation to leadership, and is often the ultimate aim of activities which, along the way, do harm.
- *Territorial expansion and defence* – a 'cultural universal' from the level of tribes to that of nations. Again, the relevance is clear, and this instinct obviously provides a motivation for much political violence.
- *Contractual agreement* – the basis of social organization to achieve common goods, including the capacity to cheat and detect cheating. It is leaders who make (and break) the significant contracts.

The secondary aspect of this last element appears most relevant – the skill to cheat and detect cheating. This is not unique to humans, and has also been observed in other primates.[4] The main argument throughout this chapter is, as suggested in Chapter 2, that leaders usually cannot achieve significant harm without deception of some form, and that human beings have an instinctively strong reaction to this, even at a distance, because detecting cheating is a perception-based rather than sensory ability. Why else did British protestors against the invasion of Iraq think it is worth using banners with slogans such as 'Time for truth' or 'B.Liar'?. This understanding is furthered by research showing that the same traits that make a good liar also make a good leader.[5]

Wilson's typology and similar arguments provide one further insight. The main human rights codes, other international laws and a significant amount of national legislation could be related almost perfectly to these evolutionary understandings. For example, the rights to life and health are intrinsic to the perpetuation of genes and arguably so is the right to education. The importance of kin is reflected in rights to a family life. Gender rights address inequities rooted in mating strategies. Preventing misappropriation reflects power and status. Codes about territory exist from the level of the global commons to nation states to the domestic garden. Contract law crosses all elements. But there is one area of this that is hardly evident in any form within international agreements – the deception of a population by leaders. Yet this too must have evolutionary roots, and it has been a conspicuous problem throughout history. It seems that however altruistic the intent of those who create such codes, they are still among the power elites and therefore disinclined to regulate themselves. This omission has especial relevance concerning domestic law on deception, and this problem will be explained further in Chapter 5.

How leaders 'do' harm

The first duty of a doctor, and arguably for anyone with power, is to 'do no harm'. And leaders rarely 'do' harm. They get other people to do it for them, through issuing orders, manipulating systems and managing information.[5] How then do leaders persuade populations to assist in or acquiesce to doing harm? A starting point to understand this is provided by a framework for analysing the relations between leaders and their populations proposed by a Korean scholar, Yun-Joo Lee. She pieces together the basic elements of traditional leadership theory to show that leaders use a combination of 'hard' (coercive) and 'soft' (empathetic) relations to get their 'resources' (for example administrations and political parties) and 'populations' ('accepting' or 'questioning' followers) to achieve the desired 'aims'.[6] This was understood millennia earlier in Confucian tradition as *Fa* and *Li*, and American theorist Joseph Nye has provided further discussion from a Western perspective.[7] But there is also a third way, distinct from direct coercion or empathy – leaders can deceive. They might fool a population into 'soft' support, or claim that totalitarian forces are so great that they cannot be resisted. It is likely that, beyond very rare situations where there is intrinsic total empathy or totalitarian coercion, leaders *must* deceive to achieve significant harm.

Deceit and cheating

Just as trials *in absentia* and the application of dormant precedents in the form of Magna Carta were evident at the time when the seventeenth-century English monarch Charles I was called to account, so too was the concept of leadership deceit. In 1649, Nicolas Culpeper published *The physical directory*. His ostensive aim was to challenge the power of doctors by making medical knowledge accessible to everyone, through translating an obtuse Latin treatise, *Pharmacopoeia*. But Culpeper's motivation for disclosing the secrets of elite physicians was also political – it was a challenge to their power. On the first page of his book he declaimed:

> God gave tyrants in his wrath, and will take them away in his displeasure ...
>
> The liberty of our common wealth ... is most infringed by three sorts of men: priests, physicians, lawyers.
>
> The one deceives men in matters belonging to their souls.
>
> The other in matters belonging to their bodies.
>
> The third in matters belonging to their estates.[8]

Culpeper identifies the instrument of 'tyranny' as deception. Interestingly, the etymology of 'cheat' stems from a fourteenth-century English word *escheat*. This described property that was forfeited to, or confiscated by, a lord or the king, which often occurred through a fraud or trick. So well before Culpeper's observation, the concept of cheating by power elites was already enshrined in the English language. In modern colloquial Arabic, one of the terms referring to a leader is *Jaimme* (زعيم), which means liar. And the circumstance is intrinsic, but often overlooked, in the word 'mislead'.

Culpeper's selection of 'tyrants' also reflects closely the three sectors of accountability in this book. Corruption readily equates with 'matters belonging to their estates'. If writing now, he would probably have no hesitation in seeing environmental health impacts as 'matters belonging to their bodies'. And to understand the relevance of deception by priests, we simply need to keep in mind that the Church was underpinning the violence employed by the political rulers of his time, as often happens in the present. King Charles had claimed that he was God on Earth and that his elites were ordained by Heaven.

To develop Culpeper's insight, it is useful to consider the distinctions made between 'deception' and 'cheating'. Most dictionary definitions present the terms as synonymous. Basic deception is not just lying. It entails concealment of the truth in order to mislead. But this is not intrinsically wrong. It is how the benign magician makes an honest living, how a well-intentioned psychologist may build up an ailing patient, or how a good teacher will encourage an unhappy student. The distinction between deceit and cheating is that the former *may* cause wrongful harm but the latter intrinsically causes wrongful harm. In England, the legal definition of 'deceive' is 'to induce a person to believe that a thing is true which is false, or a thing false which is true, contrary to that which the person practicing the deceit knows or believes to be the case'.[9]

Cheating also has had legal meaning, but less so at the present time. Under English common law, it was defined as 'A deceitful device for defrauding another of his right contrary to the plain rules of common honesty'.[10] Stuart Green concludes that 'despite its seeming importance, [cheating] is a concept that has been almost completely ignored by moral theorists'.[11] Yet all concepts of fairness and justice are rooted in the notion of cheating. But there is a growing realization that the term 'cheat' is more subtle than its everyday usage suggests, and that it explains many social phenomena. Cheating is often conflated with morality, yet public perception often makes a distinction, and sees cheating as more serious than moral wrongdoing. Why, for example, was the American public more concerned that Bill Clinton apparently deceived the public and courts than that he had sexual relations with a member of his staff? This is a rational prioritization. The moralist puts the icing on the cake of civilization, but the cheat may poison the cake.

Green argues that cheating consists of 'breaking an equitable and fairly enforced rule with the intent to obtain an advantage over some party with whom the rule-breaker is in a co-operative, rule governed relationship' (p. 140). But he does not consider deceit as an element of cheating, perhaps because his view focuses on ends, not means. As discussed later, leadership accountability is usually about means, not ends, and it is the means that often involve deceit.

In everyday perceptions, cheating seems to embody three concepts: *deceit*, a related *loss–gain*, and a breach of reciprocity-based *norms or codes*. It is the combination of the three happenings that defines the cheat. A magician might *deceive* through a card trick, so clearly cheating must entail more. The magician may deceive, and even gain through a fee, but no one loses, so that is not cheating either. In many card games, deception permits people to win and lose, but reciprocal rules legitimize the process and it is therefore not seen as cheating. Someone who cheats at cards deceives and achieves a gain at the expense of someone else, but in a way that is contrary to reciprocal rules.

Means and ends

One of the most common areas of leadership deceit is to muddle ends and means. In general, harm occurs through means, not ends. Genocide is one of the few examples of harm presented as a specific 'end'. Killing civilians, unlawful prison camps, appropriating wealth, and environmental destruction have all been utilized recently as the means to achieve other purportedly good ends. These particular examples were employed by both the Iraqi and American leaderships around the period of the invasion of Iraq, and leaders on all sides claimed that they were perpetrated in the pursuit of rightful ends. Neither Saddam Hussein nor George Bush stated a direct aim to kill thousands of innocent people, or to cause environmental damage and health impacts. Outside war, most environmental damage occurs in the pursuit of other goals, usually the fulfilment of essential or non-essential production needs. Even corrupt leaders who misappropriate large sums of public money, and so make it unavailable for hospitals and other public services, are usually doing this as a means to another end – personal power and security. They are not setting out to destroy public services.

Niccolo Machiavelli was a political theorist of the Florentine republic. His infamy stems from his book *The Prince* (1532) in which he argues that all means are permissible to create a stable state. He maintained that even opportunist or devious means are acceptable to achieve politically desirable ends. It is not surprising that leaders often cloud the distinction between means and ends when adopting a Machiavellian strategy. But is the distinction between means and ends so clear, or is the dichotomy often constructed by power elites as part of their perception management? A bomb might be a means for a political or military leader, but it is an end for the civilians that it kills. Rarely do leaders construct an 'end' such as 'killing and incapacitating the enemy', or 'destroying a city'. Those might be termed 'military objectives', but not ends.

The means–ends distinction is, of course, central to the legal claim that an act of violence was in self-defence, or that a harmful act may be necessary to prevent a greater harm, or to utilitarian views which can be related to day-to-day decisions such as forced land purchase and removals to permit a public good such as a railway to be built. But these examples all concern tangible and immediate means and ends in the form of estimable costs or benefits, for example a loss to a few hundred people who may be forced to move house versus the benefit of a new railway to a whole population. Ends framed in terms of an abstract vision, such as 'liberty' or 'security', are categorically different. Perhaps the deepest deceit of Machiavelli was not just to create the ethic that 'the ends justify the means'. It was to set up the rhetorical means for leaders to make questionable distinctions between the two elements, to achieve selfish ends.

One of the familiar means–ends deceit strategies between opposing leaders is to focus on the means of the opposition, which may cause limited harm to a few, and ignore ends which may be morally correct in the views of many. And they do the opposite in terms of their own misdeeds. Immediately following the bombing of trains at Madrid station in 2004, the foreign minister Ana Palacio claimed, 'Terrorism does not serve any cause.'[12] The statement is demonstrably false. Terrorism always serves a cause, and is always defined in law in terms of achieving an end, usually political influence. The two organizations first suspected of involvement in the bombing, Eta and al-Qaida, have clear ends. The aims of Eta are even embodied in its name, which is a Basque language acronym for 'Basque Homeland and Freedom'. Al-Qaida then issued a statement claiming responsibility, which gave clear reasons for the action.

Under the heading 'failure of statesmanship', John Rawls not only suggests a note of caution about the unqualified application of utilitarian ends-justifies-means logic. He also reminds us of the obvious example of the result of a view of world leadership which valued some lives more than others in order to create the ends–means argument:

> The United States was not justified in fire-bombing Japanese cities; and during the discussion among allied leaders in June and July 1945 prior to the use of the atomic bomb on Hiroshima and Nagasaki, the weight of practical means–end reasoning carried the day, overwhelming the qualms of those who felt that limits were being crossed.
>
> Dropping the bombs, it was claimed, was justified in order to hasten the end of the war. It is clear that Truman and most other allied leaders thought it would do that and thereby save the lives of

American soldiers. Japanese lives, military and civilian, presumably counted for less.[13]

When the means–ends argument is failing, the next trick is to present the means as ends, as demonstrated by the infamous logic of a US commander about a Vietnamese village, 'We had to destroy it in order to save it.'[14]

Another aspect of the means–ends deceit is therefore to create a false 'vision' of ends, for example the claim that the West could easily bring democracy to Iraq through military means. Texts on leadership and management provide copious advice about 'vision', which is seen as a positive skill. But this view of vision conflates notions of 'aim' and 'plan' with 'prediction', and authors do not point out that a vision will usually involve deceit if accompanied by any inference that the vision will certainly be achieved. A common trick is to be clear about the vision, but not about when it might be fulfilled. If the vision is not achieved or is harmful, the leader will 'move on', and construct a new vision of ends before the deceit is recognized. There is a distinction between having an aim and a plan to achieve that aim, and presenting a vision as a certainty to justify the use of particular questionable means. Martin Luther King was honest enough to claim that he had a 'dream', not a vision.

Why populations react

If it is accepted that deceit and cheating underpin much of the harm caused by leaders, the probable reason why populations respond would seem very apparent to anyone with an awareness of current evolutionary psychology. As mentioned earlier, the idea that human beings have an instinct to detect and challenge cheating – that we have an inbuilt 'cheater-detector' – is now well-understood both theoretically and empirically, and stems from the work of Cosmides and Tooby.[15]

E.O. Wilson explains the key points in relation to our perception of harmful leadership. Morality is not fundamentally a social construction, as was commonly assumed. It is in the same category as sex drive, a basic evolutionary survival mechanism, which continues to be instinctive and strong in the modern mind:

> Moral reasoning is not a cultural artefact invented for convenience. It is and always has been the vital glue of society, the means by which transactions are guided by ethical precepts, and every one of its members is expected to follow moral leadership and ethics-based tribal

law. The propensity does not have to be beaten into us. Evidence exists instead of an instinct to behave ethically, or at least to insist on ethical behaviour in others.[16]

Wilson continues with an explanation of why we challenge wrongdoing that is perceived as cheating.

> Psychologists, for example, have discovered a hereditary tendency to detect cheaters and to respond to them with intense moral outrage. People by and large are natural geniuses at spotting deception in others, and equally brilliant in constructing deceptions of their own ... Even the tyrant is sterling in pose, invoking patriotism and economic necessity to justify his misdeeds.[17]

The final sentence goes back to the earlier point, that leadership harm is usually associated with means, not ends. Whatever else they do, despots usually claim a high moral goal, and they probably realize that this is the basis for deceiving their followers.

Cheating is significant because it represents a latent, unpredictable and uncertain threat, and leaders have played on the fear of the unknown since they invented gods and demons to be their allies. But there is a further point. When an individual is deceived, there is an implication that the deceiver is more clever than the deceived. This hits our status instinct. Not only can cheats potentially acquire more resources, they also diminish the status of those they cheat, and this is likely to fuel the reaction to cheating. As Iraq showed, the reaction is likely to come not just from populations, but also from other elites, who will want to distance themselves from deception. And, probably more importantly, they do not want their status reduced by appearing to have been fooled by a cheat.

The significance of cheating finds support from emergent research in diverse areas. One study about risk perception found that a hazard is perceived as far more serious by the public if there has been an attempt by power elites to hide it.[18] In the area of health education, another study found that people were more likely to give up smoking if they were shown evidence of the 'deceitful and manipulative' behaviour of tobacco companies than through being told factually about the health problems.[19] This all suggests that educating people about cheating by power elites could become more common in the future, in many areas, but also that deception could be used positively to enhance the pubic awareness of the new 'invisible' risks such as global warming. In settings where risks are outside our evolutionary perceptions, such as motorways where our Stone Age brain does not perceive high speeds accurately, deception is sometimes used to good effect, for example by using optical illusions to make drivers slow down when approaching a hazard.[20]

Within social science, the corollary to deception and cheating, trust, has been examined at length, for example by Francis Fukuyama[21] and Anthony Giddens.[22] Trust is, as the social theorists and Wilson suggest, the 'glue' that holds society together. The image of glue is also reflected in the title of a seminal book about causation by J.L. Mackie, *The cement of the universe*.[23] The coincidence is not accidental. Trust and social causation are related. If A falsely tells B that C has a gun and will shoot B, and B shoots C in self-defence, the social *cause* of the sad outcome is the abuse of *trust*. When we make predictions to plan or strategize, we use our trusted understandings of causation. This insight further strengthens the centrality of our cheater-detector as a survival skill. Deceit destroys that which connects individuals and holds humanity together. Leadership deceit is the solvent of society. If the 'glue' and the 'cement' do not hold, daily planning and strategy become impossible for populations, the present cannot be managed in relation to the future, and our social world falls apart into Kafkaesque chaos of live-for-the-minute selfish survival. And instinctively we all know this.

Why now? The significance of ICT

From the 1990s the exponential change in the effectiveness of all accountability initiatives was brought about by cheap ICT, the growth of effective media and their deployment by civil society.[24] Perhaps the most striking evidence of this comes from analysis of the private notes of Vladimiro Montesinos, Fujimori's head of intelligence in Peru, by John McMillan at Stanford University. He found that the 'typical bribe paid to a television-channel owner was about a hundred times higher than that paid to a politician, which was somewhat higher than that paid to a judge. One single television channel's bribe was five times larger than the total of the opposition politician's bribes.'[25] Examples of the practical application of information technology accompany almost every contemporary report of leadership accountability. Mobile phones are becoming central. The display of people power that precipitated the overthrow of Estrada was orchestrated by texting. The message from the Co-ordinated Multi-Sectoral Opposition – *Full mblsm tady Edsa* – brought thousands to rally around Manila's Edsa Shrine, the memorial to the previous people power movement.[26] Estrada's security services were taken by surprise. His first source of information about these events was his family TV.

In Yugoslavia, the Belgrade radio station B92 precipitated the fall of Milosevic. It is no coincidence that the popular uprising started in the provinces – that was where B92 was still able to reach after its programmes within Belgrade were jammed. When closed by the Serb authorities it continued on its website *OpenNet*, which at one point was achieving a million hits each day. This was used by VOA and the BBC, via Amsterdam, which relayed the news back into Serbia. This all proved more problematic to the authorities than the radio station, which was soon permitted to start broadcasting again. Yugoslavia provided the classic ICT revolution. The end of the old regime effectively came when the government radio and TV station RTS were stormed and taken over by the public.

When the Spanish government had tried to deceive the public into believing that Eta was responsible for the Madrid train bombing, in March 2004, ICT also fuelled the public response. Ignacio Ramonet explains:

> In the face of this official disinformation ... Ordinary people transmitted their doubts via email, internet chatrooms and cell phones; there were millions of text messages. Within a few hours ... an effective anti-lie and counter-information network was established, mobilising hundreds of thousands of people whose votes assured the victory of the Socialist Worker's party ... One of the morals of this tale is that people are extremely sensitive to attempts at manipulating the media. In Spain and elsewhere people do not like to be misled. Many people agree that the media tendency to deceive is one of the great problems of our time.
>
> The Popular Party had gone too far in exploiting its control of information, both spreading lies to justify its commitment to the war in Iraq and in concealing its responsibility for the ecological catastrophe of the sinking of the oil tanker Prestige. Presumably it thought that ... one more lie would pass unnoticed. But when the Spaniards rose in protest, the government fell.[27]

This represents a clear example of how the synergism between ICT and human instinct can construct a public 'cheater-detector' at a speed that no government could control.

But it would be simplistic to argue that accountability stems merely from a greater access to information, because information can contain as many falsehoods as truth, and information overload can stifle as well as support. There are six distinct aspects – the first three are technical and the second three perceptual:

- *surveillance* – awareness and recognition of wrongdoing
- *information management* – efficient recording and exchanging of evidence and analysis
- *time–space compression* – an instant here-and-now perception of events
- a *self-perception* of being part of an accountability movement
- a perception of mass *immunity* from retaliation by power elites
- a perception of effective *sanctions* against leaders who do harm.

The outcome of this is a cybernetic feedback system, much as Weiner proposed in 1949, but on a global scale.[28]

Michel Foucault's *Discipline and punish* provided the history of *surveillance* of the powerless by the powerful.[29] The scope has been broadened by ICT – now, the people are watching the powerful and the powerful are watching the powerful. New technologies increase the possibility for covert surveillance of impropriety. Fujimori's downfall followed the broadcast on cable TV of a short video which allegedly showed Peru's security chief, Vladimiro Montesinos, handing over $15,000 to an opposition congressman, Luis Alberto Kouri, in return for defection to Fujimori's Peru 2000 party. The video of Montesinos soon found its way onto websites, and a transcript appeared on *BBC News Online*. Similarly, the Indian investigative website tehelka.com brought down a minister and government officials within days, through putting the story, together with secretly filmed video clips of officials asking for bribes, online. Governments too have seen the potential to encourage accountability through ICT. Before the invasion of Iraq, the US Congress-supported satellite Liberty TV beamed into the country, and aided the training of Iraqis to use digital cameras, laptops and satellite phones to generate footage of leadership impropriety.

Information management and exchange through cheap information and communications technology have been the key to the efficacy of a globalizing civil society. Simple devices such as email petitions have brought a new scale and scope to public advocacy. EarthAction has created a network of 1,800 international NGOs, which called for a UN that can 'Make global decision-making more publicly accountable.'[30] Sites such as the Independent Media Centre circumvent media censorship and selection. And 'Centre' is misleading. New software such as Active permits individuals to upload content without central oversight, and new websites can be set up in a few hours from anywhere in the world. The initiative was built on the belief in the link between democratic accountability and universally available free software.[31]

The third technical element is *time–space compression* of information, which Marshall McLuhan traces back to electricity. This, he argues, provided the means for the 'instant synchronisation of numerous operations [which] ended the old mechanical pattern of setting up operations in lineal sequence ... what emerges is a total field of inclusive awareness'.[32] The simultaneous existence of varying information creates the possibility for comparison, and from comparison comes knowledge. In addition, through evolutionary instinct we are more likely to respond to the immediacy of wrongdoing, and ICT diminishes the delay and distance of the deeds of despots. The new virtual proximity of wrongdoing by world leaders engenders anger and a response in the global public, just as wrongdoing by a local shopkeeper would. But perhaps the most significant aspect of time–space compression is that it builds a collective historical memory. It is not simply that information from anywhere can be used quickly. It is also that the collective memory of a population can extend backwards in time and hold people to account for wrongdoings many decades earlier. A striking aspect of the evidence in Chapter 1 is the advanced age of many of those who are being brought to account and the long time lapse between the deed and the redress.

These changes in ICT are seen as building an age of 'digital governance'. Within this, Vikas Nath identifies 'wider domain models' which make information more accessible, 'critical flow models' such as tehelka.com which expose malpractice, and more sophisticated 'interactive service' models which allow the public to track administrative procedures or contribute to decision-making.[33] South Korea exemplifies Nath's typology. The 'wider domain' of public electronic access to information is probably greater than in any other country because most houses are networked by cable. The traditional media frequently quote the views of the 'netizens' – Korea's citizen opinion websites – which are taken very seriously and can have strong influence.[34] 'Critical flow' includes the publication of exam results. This obviates the temptation for university staff to accept bribes for amending marks, which was a major problem in the country. Korea's past kings placed a gong (*Sin-Mun-Go*) at the gate of the palace, and anyone with a grievance could use this to petition the king directly. In modern form, this 'interactive flow' includes a *Sin-Mun-Go* section on the president's website. One of the first actions of newly elected President Roh, in 2003, was to email five million netizens, in response to their concerns. Roh was known as the first leader to understand the internet. He was elected because of this skill, which permitted him to bypass the traditional party structures in the direct presidential election.

Writings about the deeds of despots, impropriety and occasional redress have existed for centuries, but until now they have only entered the public domain as isolated records well after the events happened, and even then usually only as dreary written accounts unlikely to engender a widespread emotional response. But now the immediacy and imagery of modern information provide an instant self-perpetuating motivation for the populace to challenge the wrongdoing of leaders. The new proximity of precedent makes possible the creation of new real-time global ethics, which are recognized as legitimate and relevant by courts, politicians, human rights activists and offenders almost simultaneously.

The first perceptual element is the *self-perception* of being part of an accountability movement among people who experience these phenomena. Bem's original premise about self-perception is that people come to know their internal states 'partially by inferring them from observations of their own behaviour and/or the circumstances in which this behaviour occurs'.[35] For example, politicians who observe themselves enthusiastically applauding a particular speech may infer that this is because they agree with that speech and are therefore ideologically a member of that political group. But 'circumstances' also play a part. Those who find themselves spontaneously applauding an unknown speaker will perceive this as greater agreement than if they are routinely applauding a colleague whom they know they wish to please. When there are no obvious alternative circumstantial explanations for particular behaviour, self-perception mechanisms will be strongest and individuals will draw self-influencing conclusions from self-observation.

The significance of self-perception theory is that it sets up 'the conditions for attitude change ... if attitudes are determined by behaviour rather than the other way around, then modification of behaviour will produce concomitant modification of attitude'.[36] It seems possible that the old perceptions of leadership accountability are being changed because ICT is creating a 'virtual context' in which seemingly passive observers perceive themselves as being part of an accountability movement. People watching a football match on TV may cheer when a goal is scored, and perceive themselves as supporters and part of the success. Similarly, people watching the public condemnation or arrest of a

despot are likely to feel elation and a sense that they are part of that success. The perception change among people who have access to modern
communications is not just that errant leaders anywhere can and should
be accountable, but that they as individuals sitting in their living rooms
watching their TVs can be part of the action.

It is probably not just that people can perceive themselves as part of
an accountability movement, but that they also perceive this movement
as having democratic legitimacy. Real-time information exchange permits aggregate global ethics to emerge and evolve instantaneously. And
arguably this represents a novel form of legitimacy, precisely because it
does not stem from a single ideology or group interest, but from unrelated sources that have formed the same, yet perhaps differently rea-
soned, ethical conclusion, independently. It is arguably the purest form
of democracy – government by the people – yet to be achieved.

ICT has also reversed the perception and reality of *immunity*. Now it is
the masses that are protected, not the miscreants, which creates exponential power for the accountability movement. People in one country
can target an errant leader in another, donate to accountability NGOs,
assist through collecting and disseminating evidence, help to plan
strategies, involve others, urge their own and other governments to take
action, all with no fear of ending up in prison. In the fourteenth century, the bishops of the Catholic Church burned children at the stake.
Three-quarters of the so-called 'heretics' who were murdered by the
Church in Britain were women. Now Catholic leaders are called to
account by the children and women they have abused, and imprisoned.

Finally ICT also provides a new form of *sanction* – global naming and
shaming. This might simply be the knowledge that a particular politician has failed to answer a question or disclose a document, or has been
forced to make an apology. Or it might entail TV viewers throughout the
world seeing a powerful person sentenced formally by a court, and
driven off to prison. Gone are the days when an errant leader could quietly pay a token fine and then join elite circles in another part of the
world.

This completes the circle and takes us back to the first aspect of how
ICT enhances and facilitates accountability – from surveillance to information exchange and so on. A psychologist would probably describe
this as 'knowledge of results'. From the perspective of cybernetics it is
'feedback loop'.[37] But whatever the terminology, what is happening is
now happening on a global scale.

One further relevant aspect is the difference between how elites and
populations can process information in the contemporary world, and

the info-digestive capacity of elites and populations. Governments now collect information on a massive scale, especially within their intelligence departments. Corporations are similar. It is no secret that elites cannot now cope with the volume of information that they receive – 'information overload' is a common theme.[38] There is a funnel effect in the relations between leaders and populations, and the neck of the funnel, the region inhabited by up-system power elites, is often choked. Put another way, individual or collective human intelligence works like the human gut – it needs to digest information, throw out the waste and keep the nutrients. If it just consumes and stores information, it becomes clogged.

In contrast, the global population is the other end of the funnel. The amount of information that an elite group can produce is limited, but the digestive system of populations now has an exponential capacity, and therefore it functions with increasing efficiency. Every germ of information from governments is transmitted to a near infinite global info-gut that can eliminate the waste and select and use the nutrients on a massive scale. In *The wisdom of crowds*, James Surowiecki argues that the masses have better judgement than individuals and elites, if that judgement can be harnessed in some way,[39] although this is probably most effective in relation to problems for which the best solution is an aggregate of widespread and informed opinion.[40] But, most importantly, if forced into conflict instead of cooperation, there seems no question who will win – an exponentially info-nourished global population, or an increasingly info-constipated elite.

A social impetus–trends theory

The explanation for the impetus of the present leadership accountability movement seems therefore to arise from a synergism between three simple phenomena:

1. To 'do' harm on a significant scale leaders *must deceive/cheat*, and clouding ends–means arguments is a central aspect.
2. Instinctively, *human beings react strongly to deception/cheating*, even if it is done by 'distant others', because 'cheater-detection' is an intellectual rather than a sensory perceptive skill.
3. *ICT* makes the deception, and the reaction to deception, visible and immediate, through
   - surveillance
   - information management

- time–space compression
- activist self-perception
- perception of immunity
- perception of effective sanctions

which creates a positive *feedback loop* on a global scale.

The seeds of the reaction to leadership harm seem to be planted within the way that the harm is done, and ICT provides the nutrients for them to grow. The fact that leaders must deceive to 'do' significant harm seems to build in a social self-correcting mechanism. Perhaps if that were not so, the world would have been overrun by despots a long time ago.

The old twentieth-century elite theorists contribute a relevant insight specifically about leadership. They argued that the power of traditional political elites stems, paradoxically, from them being a minority.[41] This enabled the elites to negotiate, agree and take action effectively and quickly, in a way that the unwieldy masses could not achieve. Information technology is changing that. Now, the masses can mobilize as effectively as the elites, but with the added power and legitimacy of being a majority. In the light of these understandings of the modern world, it would be more astonishing if global leadership accountability did not happen than that it does. In the future, successful leaders are likely to be those who understand how the evolutionary drivers and ICT networks have turned the masses into the power elites. They will not be charismatic conjurors who just appear to win trust through short-term deception.

A broader proposal arises from this argument, that many forms of social change in the industrial world – impetus and trends (and the overlap between these) – can be understood globally in terms of synergism between the 'basic categories' of our evolutionary psyche (Wilson, above) and technological change, within social, economic and physical contexts (Figure 3.1). This possibility has attracted surprisingly little academic attention, except in the world of commercial advertising. There is no logical reason why virtual-reality women draped over a new car should increase sales, except for a resonance between 'status' and 'mating strategy' and the technology.

Seemingly paradoxical global phenomena may be explained through the relationships between our evolutionary psyche and technology, for example the declining birth rate in countries such as Japan, South Korea, Russia and parts of Europe. The decline is made possible by

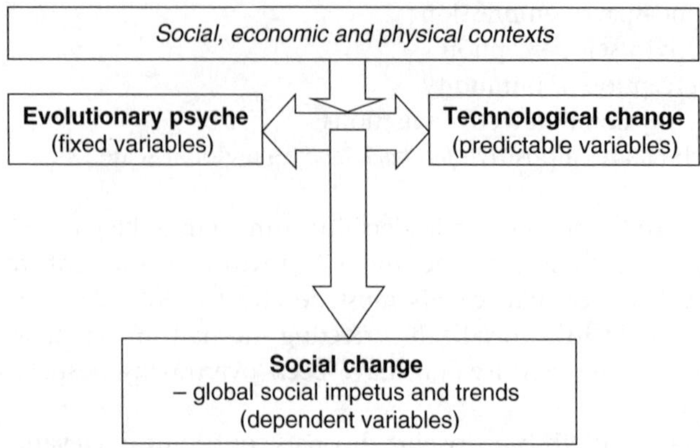

Figure 3.1   A global social impetus–trends theory

modern contraception, the technological change, but seems also to reflect complex relationships between women's 'status', which can now come through employment, not just parenthood, and a 'mating strategy' which can be fulfilled without creating children. The 'kin' factor might appear to contradict the argument. But what we are seeing around the world seems to suggest that we are not directly programmed to want to *produce* offspring, but more to nurture and favour them once they arrive. The desire for a family may be reinforced by a positive anticipatory self-perception of being a nurturing parent, and social and economic contexts. But if those factors are absent there is no direct instinct to want children. Evolution did not need to make the creation of children a strong psychological desire, because the desire for mating automatically achieved that end. To perpetuate the species, there was no need for us to want children, just to want sex – until now.

The attraction of this 'social impetus–trends theory' is its simplicity (Figure 3.1). The dependent variable (social change – impetus–trend) arises from the synergism between a fixed independent variable (evolutionary psyche) and a reasonably predictable independent variable and common context (technological change). There might be developments in our understanding of our evolutionary psyche, but the basics will not change unless scientists can create designer brains. Technological change may appear astonishing, but it follows the laws of the natural sciences and by the time it has broad global impact the technical characteristics of any innovation are usually well-understood.

Global intelligence

The notion of a global world is not just a political, economic and technological concept. Advances in science, particularly biology, are providing parallel views of the planet as a single entity, reflecting James Lovelock's original Gaia hypothesis. Among others, Howard Bloom now talks of the interconnectedness of a planetary intelligence, using the term the 'global brain'.[42] Similarly Alison Jolly predicts a networked planet operating in the future as a 'superorganism',[43] and M. Leslie argues that the mapping of the human genome permits us to perceive the whole ecosystem as a single genome.[44] Bloom's vision is not the obvious one based only on contemporary ICT. He argues that primarily it is our common evolutionary roots that bring species together as a collective intelligence. The specifics and apparent implications of such visions are easy to criticize, but the fundamental dynamics are rational – brains work in much the same way throughout the world, and for human beings ICT can create joined-up-thinking on a planetary scale.

This outcome for leaders is a new form of global legitimacy, but this gives rise to another significant dynamic. Leadership styles that are belief-based are likely to be perceived less favourably than those that are evidence-based. Beliefs, whether right or wrong, are rarely shared across a global population, and will always be construed as deception or cheating somewhere. Paradoxically, this presents entities such as al-Qaida and the Christian belief-based political leaders in America and Britain with common dilemmas when they try to gain global moral authority. It is the 'managerial elites', discussed in Chapter 5, with minimal belief-based encumbrances that are likely to attract global legitimacy, because they will appear to be the least problematic option to the global brain's cheater-detector.

So where might we look for the evidence-based leadership of the future – leadership that may not be honoured and revered, but also will not be seen as being based on deception? North East Asia is the most likely region. Now evolving from an obsession with belief-based Confucian traditions and a belief-based communist system, this region is now organizing its power elites around knowledge, technical efficiency and a god of progress and economic wealth that is loved or despised in equal measure around the globe. These new Eastern managerial elites may not seem to be doing their job very well at present, but neither are they constructing their power on the basis of beliefs that might be perceived in other parts of the world as deceptive. As argued in Chapter 5, the possible shift in moral authority from West to East is indicated in a range of other ways.

The implications of this new 'global brain' are not so hard to grasp, but they seem currently to be missed by many of the world's leaders. Power elites are now not just being questioned by a few individuals, a committee of inquiry, a supranational NGO, or an international justice system. They are not, as they seem to think, just trying to counter a passing fashion or a few irritating campaigners. They now have to answer to an emergent global intelligence.

Unlike the English Viking ruler, famed for trying to hold back the sea, the present-day King Canutes are not just trying to defy the laws of tidal flow. They are trying to counter a biological driver honed to its current strength by millions of years of evolution, together with the laws of physics which are even older, in the form of ICT, on a planetary scale. Contrary to popular myth, when Canute tried to turn back the incoming tide he was not trying to display his power. He was trying to show his people that he had limitations, and that there were forces greater than him. Perhaps the greatest deception of most errant leaders is, as argued in the previous chapter, the self-deception about the strength of their power. This is the deception that will inevitably bring about their downfall.

Implications

- Much leadership harm stems from the human **evolutionary psyche**: favouring kin, mating (sex), status, territoriality, breaking contracts (deceit).
    - The reaction is also evolutionary – the human **'cheater-detector'**.

- To achieve harm, leaders inevitably use **deceitful 'hard' and 'soft' relations** between themselves and populations.
    - Leaders cloud otherwise useful (utilitarian) distinctions between **means and ends**, often by presenting ends that are not assessable as clear costs and benefits (for example 'liberty').

- The **social impetus** driving leadership accountability arises because:
    - leaders must **deceive** to do significant harm
    - humans **react instinctively** against deceit
    - **ICT** makes the harm, the deceit and the response immediate and visible, which creates a **global feedback loop**.

- Global social change can be understood through a simple **social impetus–trends theory**, which identifies synergisms between the human evolutionary psyche and technology.

- **Belief-based** leadership is more difficult on a global level, because beliefs (religious or other) are inevitably seen as deceitful somewhere in the world.
    - Leaders who are not associated with a belief system are seen as more **legitimate** by the world population.
    - Leaders in **North East Asia** fulfil this 'management elite' persona.

4
Personalizing Protest: Global Civil Society

Agreements between democratic – or at least sovereign – governments were once regarded as legitimate by definition. In many cases citizens took little interest. In some, they came to be excluded in a way that would not be defensible in national politics. This approach is no longer tenable. Many different groups are now asking for direct voices at the diplomatic table. In the campaigns on landmines and debt, non-governmental actors became major drivers for agreement, raising the political temperature and coordinating action across borders. At Seattle and Prague we saw what happens when groups do not believe they are being heard.

Peter Hain, Minister of State at the
UK Foreign and Commonwealth Office, 2001[1]

The tyrants who have been running our world from the beginning of so-called 'civilization' know that the jig is nearly up. People are waking up like never before and communicating on a global level.

Ken O'Keefe, former US marine and current activist[2]

Civil society organizations have clearly had a significant role in the impetus of global leadership accountability. In 'The paradigms of people power', anthropologist Nancy Lindisfarne claims that groups such as those challenging the WTO and G8 'have no historical precedent in terms of size, style and political determination'.[3] They are also unprecedented because many now challenge specific named leaders, not just an institution or organization. Protest is being personalized.

Interestingly, notions of a public sphere in the West seem to have started as a reaction against despotism in eighteenth-century Europe and America.[4] As mentioned in earlier chapters, the fall of Charles I was part of that movement. In *Civil society*, Michael Edwards concludes that 'The concept of a "public" – a whole polity that cares about the common good and has the capacity to deliberate about it democratically – is central to civil society thinking.'[5] Mary Kaldor extended these ideas to a global scale in her *Global civil society*.[6] Using occupied Baghdad as an analogy, she talks of how people inhabiting a 'red zone' – a 'hetero-geneous, complex world full of energy, activity, ideas and debate but also violence, frustration and extremism – try to influence elites in the green zone'.[7]

The perspective in this book is slightly different. While it may be possible to identify a few specific actors within a global leadership accountability movement, which cooperate to achieve a particular goal, mostly they are operating independently with a common but uncoor-dinated sense of purpose. There is no 'whole polity', nor do elites and the populace necessarily operate in 'zones' that represent the people versus the powerful. The Koreans and Japanese protesting against Bush and Blair's invasion of Iraq were acting in accord with the views of elites such as the Pope, Mandela and the Archbishop of Canterbury, and there is no evidence of any collaboration. Outside this book, no one has even considered leadership accountability concerning political vio-lence, corruption and environmental harm holistically. The argument from the previous chapter is that the common sense of purpose arises more because of our common evolutionary psyche and the dislike of deceit, and a new common technological context, than through planned interaction. The civil society movements are like spiders spin-ning their individual webs on branches provided by the formal inter-national and national accountability initiatives. But from the perspective of the prey, the overall effect is like a carefully planned and coordinated hunt. The difference is that its strategies and strengths are harder to predict.

This chapter argues that the new accountability NGOs are distinct from their older counterparts, who were essentially providing public services, and from the protest movements of the twentieth century which were issue-based but rarely personalized their protest. The new organizations are developing novel strategies and social sanctions, often coordinated, and have moved from targeting errant organizations and institutions to challenging named elites. Another emergent aspect is a global senior citizenry of e-enabled retired activists with a lot of time and motivation to pursue goals that eluded them earlier. But although civil society action has been a significant aspect of the era of accountability, this chapter ends with a question that is often overlooked by these organizations: to what degree should the current impetus be encouraged? Or should it, in the words of an old Scottish adage, 'hasten slowly'? As political analysts conclude, and the harm done by the occupation of Iraq demonstrated, the aim should be 'smart accountability' which avoids collateral damage to social institutions and whole populations.

The accountability NGOs

Jeremi Suri describes an important landmark in global accountability in *Power and protest* – the emergence of the protest movements, which he sees as a response to a particular era in the evolution of global leadership.[8] He explains that during the 1960s:

> In place of the charismatic politics that characterized the early part of the decade, leaders now practiced profoundly conservative politics ... [Détente] further isolated policymakers from their publics. In this way détente contributed to the pervasive skepticism of our 'postmodern' age.
>
> ... young men and women grew visibly more violent in nearly every society. Adopting the 'language of dissent' popularized by a series of authors, students accused their elders of hypocrisy and corruption. Leaders were delegitimized by their own rhetoric ... Studying the 1960s and détente in global terms reveals how ideas, institutions, and personalities transcended national boundaries before the internet.

Suri identified the expanding higher education institutions as providing the '*infrastructure*', while 'prominent iconoclasts – writers as well as musicians and artists – supplied the *language*'. This is certainly a plausible explanation for the era of protest in the 1960s, but contemporary leadership accountability is a distinct development of this. Protest involved building a new ethical consensus, solidarity and a feeling of people power, but the 1960s did not see powerful people being asked to account as individuals for their actions and sanctioned if their account was not acceptable, as has happened subsequently. Now, the discourse is personalized: tyrant, despot, dictator, bully, cheat, liar.

The recent wave of challenges to those who abuse their power from a globalizing civil society and the media has been widely documented, and the names of the key organizations are very familiar.[9,10,11] Human Rights Watch, Amnesty, Indict and Redress inspired and assisted action against war and political criminals. The NGO Stopwar targeted political leaders more specifically in its campaigning. This accountability movement has been complemented by professional organizations such as the International Bar Association, and the Coalition for International Justice, which supports the war tribunals. US-based Judicial Watch filed a complaint with Europol and Interpol against Jacques Chirac for the 'illegal proliferation of nuclear technology'.[12] Transparency International (TI) and Corporatewatch have introduced a range of innovative initiatives to counter political and economic corruption, and are a central source of information and inspiration. In 2004 TI focused on political corruption, providing a list of the 'Graft Top Ten', which was topped by Suharto, Marcos and Mobutu. The nobribes.org website of the Anti-Corruption Network for Transition Economies facilitates information exchange across the former Warsaw Pact countries.[13] The Canadian organization Probe International looks globally at corruption, particularly between rich and poor nation leaders.

Access to the international forums requires resources and specialist expertise that are usually available only to the UN organizations, governments, or large civil society organizations. Guides such as *The Pinochet precedent: how victims can pursue human rights criminals abroad*[14] from Human Rights Watch, and the IWGIA *Human rights and indigenous peoples*[15] provide a clear understanding of possibilities and process. But these generally relate to high-profile cases, and the function of such publications is probably more to legitimize and build public support for high-level global accountability than to provide the tools for individuals or small NGOs to redress personal or local concerns. *The torture reporting handbook*, available through Redress, is an example of a guide that aims more specifically to facilitate individual action.[16] Books such as *Holding governments to account: public expenditure analysis for advocacy*, from the Save the Children Fund, provide similar support concerning corruption.[17]

Initiatives are not entirely from NGOs. When not collaborating with governments, the commercial sector can also be seen as part of civil society. Ethical codes have proliferated within business. Organizations such as the Turkish Ethics Value Foundation (TEDMER) encourage different industries to work together to overcome corruption. The St Petersburg Centre for Business Ethics provides training programmes, and is specifically working with the construction industry. In South Korea, commercial leaders started to organize themselves in March 2002 to scrutinize the campaign promises of election candidates and expose contributions to illegal campaign funds.[18] The motivation is, of course, commercial self-interest, but such initiatives probably strengthen accountability through increasing plurality and the balance of power within elites. The academic world also contributes. British scientists are setting up the International Forensic Centre of Excellence for the Investigation of Genocide (Inforce), which will provide a much needed evidence base for establishing the circumstances of mass killings.

Politicians and public have become very aware of the new global civil society organizations. Protests such as those against the WTO and its director-general Mike Moore in Seattle in 1999 and in Prague in 2000 made clear that world leaders and summits such as the G7/8 could no longer meet and make decisions without world interest.[19] History will probably recall these events less in terms of 'anti-capitalism' or 'anti-globalization' and more in terms of up-system accountability. But some of this initial personalization of protest may have been rough justice, for example against Mike Moore. In a private interview after these events he was proud of his background as a social worker and trade union activist, and was surprisingly enthusiastic about accountability movements:

> the good thing is … that when a corporation does something, has an oil spill, is unkind and brutal to the environment, or suppresses workers – someone with a camera is out in front of them. Somebody goes along to Stockholm or a shareholders' meeting and gets up, and suddenly someone is protesting. Look, they are not perfect. These guys are not angels! But they are exposed to a scrutiny now they never had before, and this is a good thing …
>
> You find a new generation and you talk to the kids at school – they are tougher than we are. They are not going to buy these products, they are going to do boycotts, there is going to be informal industrial action and environmental action. And corporations don't understand this – and do work on this and have staff working on this – they are going to take real hits.[20]

Even before becoming director-general of the WTO he had written; 'Citizens of individual countries will not, and should not, accept any form of international regulation or institution over which they have little control.'[21]

A more global display of civil society concern occurred on 15 February 2003 when millions of protestors around the world simultaneously demonstrated against the proposed invasion of Iraq by the US and UK. But another small initiative at this time appeared significant. A group of British development NGOs placed full-page advertisements in the press thanking Tony Blair and his chancellor Gordon Brown for their initiatives to reduce debt in, and increase aid to, the less developed countries. This appeared strange because Blair was very unpopular at that point because of the Iraq war. But it perhaps indicates a new and effective strategy of condemning and rewarding the conduct of specific leaders, rather than attacking or applauding them as personalities.

Other innovative cases demonstrated the global–local reach of civil society influence. Safiya Huseini, a Nigerian woman who faced a Sharia court's sentence of stoning to death in March 2002 is perhaps the most remarkable example. The case was widely publicized, the Nigerian government received a deluge of criticism from around the world, and the sentence was overturned. Then in August, a Pakistani woman who had been sentenced to be gang-raped by a Punjab village council, as a punishment for her brother's alleged affair with a woman of higher status, attracted similar world attention which forced the Pakistani courts to intervene and charge those concerned. Even the accountability of traditional judges in remote parts of the world is now within the influence of a globalized civil society.

At the UN Millennium Summit, its co-chair President Tarja Halonen of Finland proposed: 'The 21st century must be a Citizen's Century'.[22] Recognition and support for the trend is coming from surprising sources. In 2005, talking about the India–Pakistan peace process, President Musharraf concluded, 'People's wishes and aspirations have overtaken their leader's and their government's.'[23] Shareholder action has moved on from anti-capitalism activists buying a few shares and disrupting board meetings. In 2003, shareholders in GlaxoSmithKline, Britain's biggest drugs company, voted against large pay-offs for inefficient senior executives at a London meeting. The general secretary of the Amicus Union, which had supported the shareholder action, called the event 'a new era of corporate accountability'.[24] In parallel, the British Trades Union Congress (TUC) started a global campaign to target the 'platinum parachutes for failure' that senior executives commonly received.[25]

A Western-dominated media can create a misleading impression that civil society is a Western phenomenon. China's biggest civil court action against corrupt government officials was pursued by 2,200 families from Sichuan in 1997.[26] During President Mugabe's visit to the UN Millennium Summit, Zimbabwean activists used the eighteenth-century Alien Tort Claims Act to summons him in relation to intimidation during the elections. Similarly, the impeachment of Nigeria's senate president had been instigated by pressure from trade unions. In November 2000, Swaziland's pro-democracy movement presented an ultimatum to King Mswati III, the Commonwealth's last absolute monarchy, in the form of the Nelspruit Declaration.

By October 2000, the media were talking of 'the Belgrade Effect', as popular uprising against unaccountable leaders spread, apparently inspired by the fall of Milosevic, for example in response to the annulling of election results and illegitimate claim to power by General Gui in Ivory Coast.[27] The impeachment and final ousting of Philippines president Joseph Estrada, in January 2001, followed pressure from numerous notable public bodies, including the head of the Catholic Church, Cardinal Sin. The media were quick to point out that this echoed Cori Aquino's 'People power' movement of 1986, which brought down the then dictator, Ferdinand Marcos.[28] And parallels were again drawn with events in Belgrade. The eventual demise of Madagascat's president, Didier Ratsiraka, in July 2002, after thirty years in power, continued the trend of people power victories, as did Georgia's Rose Revolution, Ukraine's Orange Revolution and the more violent Tulip Revolution in Kyrgyzstan. Civil society organizations were not only concerned with the obvious despots. In July 2002, the US anti-corruption pressure group Judicial Watch had filed a case against US vice-president Dick Cheney, in relation to the overvaluation of the oil company Halliburton in the 1990s.

One of the most interesting civil society actors was George Soros. By 2004, he had made it clear that he wanted to bring about the demise of President George Bush. He declared, 'America under Bush is a danger to the world'. One of his concerns was that by 2004, 68 per cent of the US population still believed that al-Qaida was linked to Saddam Hussein and that he was linked with the September 11 attacks in the US. Soros financed political opposition, and set up a grassroots organization called MoveOn.org. His aim was 'to defend the principle of open society in America'. The countries in which he wanted to improve the accountability of heads of state was interesting – Zimbabwe, Libya, Burma, Turkmenistan and the United States.[29]

The credibility of the civil society accountability movement is starting to be shown through its own history. One of the first demonstrations to attract violent state resistance was at the University of British Columbia in 1997. In 2001, an inquiry concluded that political pressure had been wrongly put on the police to quell demonstrations. More significantly, the world's press recalled that one of the less well-known targets of the 1997 demonstrations was, by 2001, the shamed leader of Indonesia, General Suharto.[30] In the same week, police chiefs in Genoa were sacked for the oppressive use of police force at the G7/8 meeting in 2004, and 28 Italian police officers were charged with lying, slander and complicity to seriously harm demonstrators.

Strategies and social sanctions

Civil society strategies and social sanctions are not a second-best accountability system. They are an integral part of the whole picture. Just as the national courts are likely to have effect on a broader scale than the international courts, social sanctions will work on a wider scale than any court system. In essence, social sanctions have been the accountability mechanism of our evolutionary history, well before formal justice systems were conceived.

Innovative approaches appear almost daily, but generally fall within the following headings:

Strategies
- Questioning and dialogue
- Evidence-gathering and advocacy
- Whistle-blowing

Sanctions
- Naming and shaming
- Public apology
- Hearings *in absentia*

The efficacy of these strategies is greater in combination, and the orchestration of joined-up accountability by civil society organizations is increasingly evident.[31] Critics of these initiatives, like the critics of the international measures, argue that they are arbitrary and random because the norms of wrongdoing and sanctions should be codified and foreseeable. But, as argued in Chapter 1, within bounds an element of uncertainty encourages a precautionary principle among those with power.

Questioning and dialogue

Amnesty was the pioneer of letter-writing as a means of achieving change and up-system accountability. Letters could do little more than ask questions and register an opinion, but they had effect. Techniques have kept pace with new technology. Now supporters sign online petitions, and lodge their emails and mobile phone numbers so that they can be mobilized quickly and simultaneously. It is quite common that a specific, well-orchestrated campaign will render the fax machine of a particular government department unusable for days.

Some organizations are moving beyond simply using correspondence to register a point of view and are demanding answers. For more progressive correspondents, the initial letter is just a start. They want replies, not least because the replies often build an effective media story or court case, or provide evidence of information that is disingenuous in the context of time. Comparing answers to the same question from different senior figures can identify contradictions and conflict, and provide a lever for change. Advice on writing more broadly to achieve accountability, in books like *Writing for change*, is creating a more effective 'questioning community' in countries such as Canada.[32] Organizations are also coordinating endeavours in increasingly effective ways. Before the WTO Seattle meeting, Friends of the Earth produced online *The world trade system: an activists guide*. It provided a well-researched briefing, and advised writing letters to heads of state, parliamentary representatives and the press. A 'tool kit' gave advice on writing letters and press releases, and how the media works.[33] Following the invasion and occupation of Iraq, sites such as www.MoveOn.org and www.dumpblair.co.uk encouraged the public to use democratic means to hold US and UK leaders to account. The US site www.PetitionOnline.com provides free online hosting of public petitions for responsible public advocacy, internationally. More than 15 million signatures have been collected for thousands of petitions.

There is now a move forwards from expressing moral indignation about wrongdoing towards 'solution-oriented' dialogues, as pioneered by the UK NGO Forum for the Future. In general, leaders know the problems but are more likely to respond if they are made aware of a potential solution. Books such as *Everyone's guide to achieving change: a step-by-step approach to dialogue with decision-makers*, from the Oxford Research Group, are based on sound empirical understandings and a wealth of experience (Figure 4.1).[34]

Step 1: Three principles – Change happens through individuals, dialogue is different from lobbying, think in new ways.

Step 2: Identify the right decision-makers – Research and understand relevant organizational structures.

Step 3: Be aware of assumptions – Decision-makers operate on the basis of deep-rooted beliefs – what are they – how can they be changed?

Step 4: Make contact – Use letters to get face-to-face meetings. Demonstrate knowledge and serious intent, avoid aggression, gain the interest of the decision-maker.

Step 5: Manage anger – Genuine anger can be effective, but counterproductive if it creates fear and resentment. Match means to ends.

Step 6: Plan alternative strategies – Predict a range of scenarios, and formulate appropriate responses to them.

Step 7: Non-confrontational communication – Develop a dialogue, not monologue.

Step 8: Prepare for meetings – What is to be achieved? What are the questions? What should be said first, etc?

Step 9: Follow-ups – Be ready for media interest and other publicity.

Step 10: Change is possible – Don't be overwhelmed by the magnitude of world problems.

Figure 4.1   Achieving change – dialogue with decision-makers

Source: *Everyone's Guide to achieving change: a step-by-step approach to dialogue with decision-makers.* Oxford Research Group: Oxford (2000) (51 Plantation Road, Oxford OX2 6JE, UK).

Evidence-gathering and advocacy

Countless websites now gather evidence of the *prima facie* wrongdoings of power elites and argue for action. For many years the Simon Wiesenthal Center in Israel has been amassing evidence about Nazi war crimes, and advocates and supports prosecutions. It publishes a league table of the success rate of 18 countries in bringing war criminals to justice. In the US, the Centre for Public Integrity investigates and analyses public services and government accountability, making its findings widely available to the public.[35] The Massachusetts Institute of Technology (MIT) is creating sites on which the public can post information about the activities of government organizations, officials and the judiciary. An existing site http://opengov.media.mit.edu encourages the public to list basic information about leaders, such as their business links and sources of funding. The new site will be called Government Information Awareness (GIA). It will work in much the same way as CIA databases. Anyone can search for patterns of suspicious behaviour. It will avoid the problem of legal action from false information being posted by borrowing a trick form the Napster software that created music file-sharing. Information will be distributed around the internet.

Another innovative approach is to gain evidence through the scrutiny of public speeches, broadcasts, biographies and other books by powerful people who may have been responsible for wrongdoing. In May 2001, Human Rights Watch demanded an inquiry into possible war crimes in Vietnam, following discovery of a comment by former US senator Bob Kerrey that he had been present when villagers in the Mekong Delta were killed in cold blood by a special military police unit in 1969. A week later, Human Rights Watch also wrote to French president Jacques Chirac pointing out that the book, *Special Services, Algeria 1955–1957*, being promoted in Paris by General Paul Aussaresses, included descriptions of his own participation in the torture of Algerian activists, including Liberation Front leader Larbi Ben M'Hidi. The general was then summonsed. Although the special amnesties given to him by the French parliament protected him from prosecution for the actual deeds, they did not give him immunity for condoning crimes in a book. This strategy relies on the recognition of a simple human failing of despots – the desire to boast about how they have used their power.

Other websites provide formal evidence and legal argument about the conduct of wayward leaders which can establish the basis for court cases. The Balkan Institute in Washington DC provides a site for *War crimes and individual responsibility: a prima facie case for the indictment of Slobodan Milosevic*.[36] This type of initiative influences public opinion and generates support for the advocates of accountability. It can also save considerable expenditure for the prosecution services of low-income countries, which do not have the technology and expertise to build a convincing case against despots who have near infinite resources. Perhaps most significantly, a global audience can critically test the legal arguments, and additional evidence and argument can be collected – virtually for free. Of course, this level of public debate can also help the lawyers who are defending a despot, because they have time to consider and plan their response. But the overall result, even if there is an acquittal, is better justice. In the long term that is more important than conviction, if the global public is to continue to support international tribunals and national courts that are assuming international jurisdiction.

The creative use of the internet evolves almost daily. In the UK, a handful of individuals set up writetothem.com which, given a post-code, will name the relevant MP, MEP or local councillors, and provide advice about writing, petitions and lobbying. It also provides data on how many faxes have had replies, the MPs' speeches, attendance record in parliament and declared interests. Many other innovative strategies are emerging. One proposal is to mobilize 'shadow MPs'. The public life of each parliamentarian would be tracked by a volunteer, who would gather evidence of wayward conduct – and hopefully sometimes commend good conduct. A home page might display regular bulletins, which would provide an instant ongoing source of stories for journalists. As with many of the other initiatives, the difficulty for activists using this strategy would be to tread the fine line between accountability and harassment.

Whistle-blowing

During the 1990s it was realized that a number of disasters in Europe which caused significant loss of life could have been prevented if ordinary employees had been able to inform a higher authority of the misdeeds of senior managers. The result, in the UK, was an innovatory whistle-blowers' NGO, Public Concern at Work.[37] This acts as a confidential agent between an employee who fears recrimination and senior managers or officials beyond the employee's direct line management who are likely to respond to a complaint. The National Health Service then introduced a special phone-line to increase the reporting, by junior staff, of fraud and corruption.[38] In the US, the National Whistleblower Centre provides a similar service.[39] In the UK, these initiatives culminated in the Public Interest Disclosure Act 1998, which protects genuine whistle-blowers.

This approach is reflected elsewhere, for example the Vulnerable Persons Protection Act 1992 in Alberta, which requires the reporting of abuse by care professionals and protects them provided they act in good faith. An important principle in legislation of this nature is that subordinates can report over the head of an immediate line manager, because that manager may be the cause of the problem or have an interest in deterring any reports. Within organizations, official 'chain' reporting routes are often line management structures. One missing link in the chain prevents the report reaching appropriate authorities, and the missing link is often the person who is acting improperly.[40]

'Whistle-blowing' assists accountability through improving information flow within administrations.[41] The idea was formalized in the UN Declaration of Basic Principles of Justice for Victims of Crime and Abuse of Power (VCAP). States are 'to promote disclosure of relevant information to expose official and corporate conduct to public scrutiny'[42] As a governmental example, the UK Civil Service Code requires that:

> Where a civil servant believes he or she is being required to act in a way that:
>
> is illegal, improper, or unethical;
>
> is in breach of constitutional convention or a professional code;
>
> may involve possible maladministration;
>
> or is otherwise inconsistent with this Code;
>
> he or she should report the matter.[43]

They should also 'report to the appropriate authorities evidence of criminal or unlawful activity by others'. The latent implication of this is that, although complaints about a breach of the code cannot be made officially by the public, if anyone tells *any* civil servant of a suspected wrongdoing by another civil servant, they must report it further. If they did not, they would be in breach of their own code. That should, of course, include the civil servants administrating the work of the civil service commissioners who hear complaints, but they dispute that reasoning and block complaints directly from the public.[44] Civil society organizations are likely soon to blow the whistle on such contradictions, if the staff do not.

Whether or not people have an express duty to report wrongdoing by others is a contentious moral issue. In the 1980s, a publicity campaign in the US, encouraging the public to report drug-users, ended up with children reporting their parents. The overtones of Nazi Germany and the excesses of communism quickly led to the withdrawal of the campaign. While the encouragement of public reporting may well reduce abuse of power by leaders, it is probably undesirable to make public reporting mandatory. But the ethical context is different within an organization where there are clear lines of responsibility and often a duty of care to the public or clients. It therefore seems reasonable to argue that, within organizations, everyone has a duty to report wrongdoing to an appropriate higher authority, and this can easily be achieved, for example through employment contracts.

The 'on notice' principle is common to many legal systems, and similarly improves accountability through information. The principle is very simple. When a hazard has been identified, the responsible people or authorities are made aware formally, in writing and perhaps publicly, of a potential for harm. If actual harm subsequently occurs, the sanctions against those responsible are then more severe, and compensation awards greater, because it is clear that the cause could have been avoided. This is one of the main strategies of the 'whistle-blower' agencies.

Naming and shaming

'Naming and shaming' individuals or organizations that are otherwise hard to bring to account operates in countless ways. In some post-communist countries in Central and Eastern Europe, transitional governments have made police records open to the public, which created the possibility for press and public approbation of petty officials involved in oppressive regimes but avoided more disruptive sanctions. More informally, websites such as mybosssucks.com permit a global shaming of poor managers, and bad university lecturers are shamed on teacherreviews.com, although the basis for such sites is more commercial advertising than justice. CorruptIndia.com fuses NGO and commercial tactics. It invites nominations for the 'top ten' corrupt people, departments and states. It encourages reporting and gives rewards (Figure 4.2). This will be supported by satellite 'Corruption TV'. In March 2001 the Indian news site tehelka.com ('making waves') presented video evidence of corrupt dealings which brought down six senior politicians (Figure 4.2).[45]

An innovative approach was utilized by the UK Commission for Racial Equality before the elections in 2001 – a web pledge.[46] The Commission wrote an 'Election Compact', which included Principles for Good Practice and Conduct during the elections. Party leaders and politicians were asked to sign up to various undertakings including the avoidance of activities 'likely to generate hostility or division between people of different racial, national or religious groups'. A list of signatories was published, and so too was the list of those who had not signed or had refused to sign – much to the delight of journalists in search of an instant election story. Politicians from both main parties were resentful of the efficacy of the initiative and complained bitterly. They seemed to forget that the Commission is a government agency which was set up by the Conservative Party, retained by Labour and publicly supported by both.

CorruptIndia.com

bluntly telling the truth

Valuable quotes	Ten most corrupt people	Ten most corrupt departments	Corruption index of states	Complaints	Rewards

HOME

India celebrates its Independence Day every year on 15th August. Independence from what and for whom? From the nagging persistence of poverty and social justice? From the unfair system and corrupt practices? From the clutches of political leaders who mislead people with false slogans and insincere promises. How come our independence has been hijacked by corrupt people who have made majority of the honest people impotent. Have we really become impotent? If impotency is not to overwhelm us, we must take the right initiative to move forward in weeding out corruption. At this critical juncture, we should give clear and candid message : either govern and deliver the goods or get lost!

HELP US CATCH SOME CORRUPT PEOPLE AND WIN REWARDS

Source: Adapted from www.corruptindia.com

INDIA'S PREMIER ONLINE GALLERY

tehelka.com

NEWS, VIEWS, ALL THE JUICE

OPERATION WEST END

A story of how the suitcase people are compromising Indian defence

Tehelka blows the cover off the unholy nexus of politicians, senior defence personnel and ubiquitous fixers who infiltrate and infest every defense deal. Floating a fictitious company flogging non-existent thermal imaging binoculars, the Tehelka Investigative Team encountered and cracked the closely guarded bastion of manufacturers, agents and their military and political patrons running up to the highest offices in the land…

Investigated & written by
ANIRUDDHA BAHAL & MATHEW SAMUEL

This is the story of how we did it.

**COMPLETE TRANSCRIPTS OF THE FILM
ROGUES GALLERY: CAST OF CHARACTERS**

Source: Adapted from www.tehelka.com/investgation/ investigation1.htm

Figure 4.2   Indian websites

Civil Association of Wave 21: 'Expel Political Misfits'
Now large number of voters does not support any party. There is no particular candidate you wish to vote for. We hate the politics that does not change for millions of years. Then, you give the incompetent politicians a benefit to use such situation that the people put some distance from the politics, so they could abuse their authority in hidings. And again, we hate such corrupt politics and go away from politicians who could bring only chilly bad news to us. This is a vicious circle we had never seen …

Let's participate in the movement 'Expel Political Misfits' to drive out the unworthy politicians and candidates from Nagatacho!

Standards for your reference to cast Minus Vote for unwanted politicians/candidates

Basic rules for damnation
Record of corruption, tax evasion, and illegal act in election

Neglect of parliamentary activity? Frequency to attend the diet, number of questions, tendering law proposals

Keywords to consider which menace our lives and living

Against peace: militarists, those who look down upon other peoples and nations

Against human rights: discrimination, repression

Against national environment; pollution, contaminating soil, water, air, producing garbage, priority for development

Against social welfare and pushing policies for that: ignoring weak people, advocating discrimination

Those who misrepresent history and wish to destroy democratic education:

Responsibility of war, war compensation, abduction for labor, entertainment women, education to produce 'Emperor's loyal subjects'

Figure 4.3   Wave 21 – 'Expel the Political Misfits', Japan
Source: A gift from Korea, *Asia Week*, 9 June, 2000.

Naming and shaming is a very attractive strategy for small-scale accountability organizations, which depend on high-impact low-cost techniques. In Japan, there has been growing public unease about 'heritable power' within government – 122 of the 500 members of the lower house are the offspring of other MPs. One response has been the 'Expel Political Misfits' website where people can publicly mark their discontent about particular MPs[47] (Figure 4.3). The initiative is basic, but not just a crude attempt at personal spite. It provides an ethical basis for complaints in the form of 'Basic rules for damnation' which are very pertinent in contemporary Japan. The idea was borrowed from Korea where a similar approach led to 59 of 86 named politicians failing to regain their seats.

Humour provides a complementary and sometimes safer approach. For thousands of years – in the West, certainly since the ancient Greeks – satire and political cartoons have covertly or overtly named and shamed those who abuse power. Cartoons offered a measure of immunity from recriminations, for example during the time of the monopolists in England (Figure 4.4). New IT is providing new possibilities. The website for 'Kim Jong II's North Korea Fan Club' is one of many examples. Texting creates a significant new forum. The overthrow of President Estrada in 2001 was fuelled by jokes about the president communicated cheaply, and without fear of recrimination, across the 7,100 Philippine islands in a manner that had not been possible a few years earlier.[48]

Although attractive for its effectiveness at gaining a measure of redress against otherwise unimpeachable power elites, the increasing ease of naming and shaming through global IT gives rise to the question of the accountability of those who make use of this strategy. It is a very easy channel of power for unbalanced individuals or citizen despots. It also creates a very attractive option for national security agencies wishing to discredit civil society organizations or individuals through presenting them as vindictive or themselves unaccountable.

Public apology

As an extension of naming and shaming, public apology is one of the main remedies available to organizations and agencies enforcing peer accountability, particularly among politicians. The UK Parliamentary Commissioner, Elizabeth Filkin, considers this a major punishment – 'they do not like it at all' – and the underhand endeavours of some British MPs to remove her from her post seem evidence of her success.[49] The eventual outcome can be failure at an election or difficulty in finding further senior appointments. If apology is accompanied by ritual, as in its Japanese form of bowing until the head touches the floor – *dogeza* – the efficacy is probably even greater.

Retrospective apology is also increasing. In 1995 the Japanese prime minister formally apologized for wartime abuse of the Korean 'comfort women', and then later for atrocities committed during the occupation of Korea. In 2000 the Pope apologized for centuries of sin by the Catholic Church – 'Even if we are not personally responsible, all of us carry the weight of the errors and the sins of our predecessors. To recognize the deviations of the past also helps to stir our consciences regarding the compromises of the future.'[50] The admission of the Guatemalan president Alfonso Portillo, in August 2000, that the state had committed crimes against humanity during the 36-year civil war, surprised even the

Figure 4.4   The fate of the monopolists

The English 'Monopolists' were commercial elites who corruptly inflated the price of food, and were eventually brought to account by the public at the end of the eighteenth century. Traditionally, the devil played the violin or 'fiddle' which is also English slang for cheating. 'Dance' refers to the involuntary movements of hanged men. Villages had a central 'green' where people met, public punishments were carried out, and the 'fête' (pronounced like 'fate') happened.

Source: November 10, 1795, London. Published by W. Holland, No. 50 Oxford St. [Author's private collection.]

human rights activists who had been fighting for justice.[51] In July 2001, Polish president Kwasniewski apologized for the massacre of Jews in the village of Jedwabne, sixty years ago. A month later, the new Indonesian president, Megawati Sukarnputri, apologized to people in the provinces of Aceh and Irian Jaya for human rights abuses by previous governments: 'We apologize to our brothers who have long suffered as a result of inappropriate national policies.'[52] At the 2001 UN conference on racism, in Durban, European nations agreed a formal apology for slavery as a crime against humanity. Even the IRA joined the trend in July 2002, when it apologized for the killings of 'non-combatants' during the previous thirty years. Then in 2003, the Fijian prime minister presided over an apology to the family of a missionary who had been killed and eaten by his people 136 years ago.

Former British foreign secretary Douglas Hurd considers retrospective apology to be 'humbug', on the grounds that an individual cannot apologize for the errors of a past counterpart.[53] But is it the intergenerational logic of this new ethic that is uncomfortable to leaders, or the idea that at some future point someone might be apologizing on their behalf, to the detriment of their reputation and the shame of their descendants? If the precept of intergenerational justice is accepted – a responsibility to future generations – why not a responsibility *for* past generations? If saying sorry is so meaningless, why does the likelihood of American leaders apologizing for America's war-related misdeeds, as Japanese leaders have done, seem so remote? If the argument is simply that present generations can have no responsibility for the acts of previous generations, then Mr Hurd should be vociferous among those calling for third world debt to be dropped, because this is essentially an international form of intergenerational bonded labour.

In *On apology* Aaron Lazare provides an analysis which shows that saying sorry is far from an empty gesture, and has a long and relevant history.[54] The absolution from guilt through death is mainly a Western-style abdication of responsibility. Traditions such as those in East Asia and India embody a more tangible link between living generations and their forebears. The Western-dominated view seems to forget that individuals are responsible not only for their physical acts, but also for their ideas. Genes and memes do not die at the same moment, so neither perhaps should accountability and the need for apology. And cultural aspects apart, what is wrong with an apology if it causes no harm and helps to heal old wounds?

Hearings *in absentia*

There are obvious reasons to be cautious about the formal trials *in absentia* outlined in the first chapter, but the constraints need not apply so strictly to other forums that have no power to impose a punishment. Civil society organizations have created very effective accountability forums, often called people's tribunals, which record evidence, pass judgment, and if appropriate name and shame. These include the International People's Tribunal, the Indian People's Tribunal and the African Court of Women. The Permanent People's Tribunal[55] (PPT), which was set up in 1979 following the Bertrand Russell tribunal on Vietnam and South America, visits many countries and hears evidence and provides judgments in intractable cases such as that concerning the Union Carbide/Bhopal disaster. The proposed International Roma Court, which would hear cases of racism and genocide against Roma people, might act similarly.[56]

The outcome of these tribunals is far from meaningless in terms of accountability. It creates a sound record of evidence which is publicly tested by adversarial lawyers to standards well beyond any academic debate, and viable declarations of principle.[57] And they have influence on those whose actions are being held to account. In France, the Elf oil corporation attempted to close down PPT proceedings about alleged corruption, through an unsuccessful court case.[58]

On a more populist level, in 1999, President Clinton's visit to Athens was preceded by a mock trial of him in the city centre, concerning the NATO bombing of Belgrade and his 'crimes' against Yugoslav citizens. Although this had none of the rigour of the PPT, and the verdict was a foregone conclusion, the symbolism was very strong particularly in a country that would claim to be the cradle of Western justice. One outcome was security measures for the presidential visit that virtually closed down the centre of Athens. Few Athenians would not have known the reason for the inconvenience, and many would have been supportive of the action.

The idea of symbolic trials is gaining legitimacy. A few months after the Athens trial, in December 2000, a mock international war crimes trial in Tokyo found the late Emperor Hirohito guilty of forcing foreign women to work as sex slaves. It concluded that 'Superiors can be responsible for the acts of their subordinates if they had known or should have known that these acts had been committed', and that Japan should pay compensation. More than 450 people attended the hearing, and legitimacy was considerably enhanced by the status of the head of the four judges, Gabrielle McDonald, a former president of the UN's Yugoslavia war crimes tribunal.

The idea of judgment *in absentia* also extends beyond death, and represents another aspect of deterring despots from trying to time out justice. Historical records have often been employed to create a balance of power between the powerful and the people. In ancient Sparta, in the second century BC, the sentence of *damnatio memoriae* could be passed against high officials after their death. The names of those considered guilty of a major wrongdoing against the community were erased from every library record, portraits were destroyed and statues were disfigured. In Korea the idea was more sophisticated. An independent historian recorded every aspect of a monarch's formal life. On the death of the ruler, the record was assessed, and the king was formally named at that point. A king only became a proper king after his death if he had behaved well. Historical judgment in the present day was evident when, in 2004, the Budapest council removed Stalin from its list of 'honorary citizens'. The resolution stated: 'Stalin committed horrible crimes against humanity, against Europe, Hungary, the Hungarian people as well as Budapest and it citizens.'[59] Such events may seem to have little significance, but they are all part of the broader pattern of leadership accountability and the message that populations are sending to miscreant leaders.

Trial by text provides another perspective. The justification for books like Christopher Hitchens's, *The trial of Henry Kissinger* is much the same as that underpinning other *in absentia* hearings. Again, new ICT is the key, because it greatly enhances the ability of lone researchers to amass an impressive array of concrete evidence quickly and at minimal cost. The resultant type of analysis was previously only possible through the combined efforts of numerous historians long after the event. The evidence amassed may well be used in formal hearings later. The challenge posed to those accused is straightforward. If the charges are wrong, sue. And in Britain, even in court, guilt can be inferred from silence.

Literature has played a similar role. In 1902, Joseph Conrad's *The heart of darkness* awakened world opinion to Belgian King Leopold II's responsibility for the death of between five and ten million Congolese people. Leopold had claimed in 1876 that Congo was his private fiefdom. In recent times, leaders themselves have joined the trend. In his book *In retrospect* and later in the film *The fog of war*, former US Defense Secretary Robert McNamara provided compelling analysis of his own failings and weaknesses. He concludes that perhaps the greatest lesson for leaders is that they can probably never comprehend war: 'war is so complex that it's beyond the ability of the human mind to comprehend all the variables – our judgment, our understanding are not adequate … It means that national leaders should be much more cautious in the way they draw their conclusions.' He concluded, 'Every leader has a responsibility to look at his career and draw lessons from it.'[60] He might have added, 'or historians will'.

How long before we see a *damnatio memoriae* website or an intergenerational version of the Japanese 'Political Misfits' home page? Specific criteria might be observed for extension of accountability beyond death, for example that an individual evaded justice during his or her lifetime or that new evidence has become available. Accountability *in absentia*, especially after death, may appear not to address the deterrent function of justice. But leaders are often very interested that their reputation should be held in good esteem for posterity, and are likely to be concerned about their future family. The behaviour of wayward leaders may occasionally be moderated by the likelihood of bequeathing moral negative equity to their descendants.

There are powers greater than man. You cannot escape the judgment of history.

Dmitri Shostakovich, Symphony No. 11

If we are wrong … I am confident history will forgive.
British Prime Minister, Tony Blair, Speech to the
US Congress, July 2003

Hasten slowly

The increasing strength of civil society organizations should obviously be viewed with a note of caution. While the questioning of abuse of power appears welcome, arguably it sometimes does not have a legitimate basis in the traditional understanding of that notion.[61] It sometimes reflects the rough justice of opportunism and the ethics of expediency. If civil society is to hold world leaders to account, how do its own leaders demonstrate legitimacy when they are arguably less representative of the global population than those they criticize?

Civil society needs to be conspicuously operating within reciprocal global standards, if it is to keep its moral high ground. At present, the global ethics gap appears to be plugged by relatively benign agencies. But history shows that dictators, fundamentalists and violent cults such as the Aum in Japan can also exploit moral vacuums. The call by WTO director Mike Moore for civil society organizations to accept a code of conduct is unsurprising but not unreasonable. He has proposed that they should reject violence, and have transparent rules governing membership, financing and decision-making. Their funding by foundations and charitable mechanisms should be dependent on compliance.[62]

Sympathies become more confused when a globalizing civil society appears in the guise of pan-European direct action from farmers, fishermen or truck drivers describing themselves as the 'crusade' of the 'People's Fuel Lobby', and are utilizing tactics such as blockading fuel depots to force governments to reduce fuel tax.[63] Decisions for politicians in this circumstance are not easy. They must balance the freedom of one sector of civil society to have unlimited cheap fuel against greater harm such as climate change, which can be moderated by increasing fuel taxes. If one country concedes, that provides a strong lever for the short-term populist argument elsewhere.

Overenthusiastic advocacy can also provide the opportunity for questionable leaders to play the accountability card and other political dirty tricks, and honest leaders may be the easiest targets in some circumstances. Rightly or wrongly, there are many leaders who maintain their innocence after court cases. In instances such as that of Thai prime minister Thaksin Shinawatra, leaders have been acquitted following indictments. In this example, the indictment happened a few weeks before an election, and seems to have been politically motivated.

In China, the 'strike hard' campaign has engendered large-scale executions – in a three-month period 2,960 people were sentenced to death. According to Amnesty, prosecutors were urged not to 'get entangled in the detail' to achieve 'quick approval, quick arrest, quick trial and quick results'.[64] Similarly, Amnesty was concerned that, in 2004, evidence used against Pasteur Bizimungu, Rwanda's first post-genocide president, who was sentenced to 15 years in prison for creating a militia and inciting ethnic violence, had been obtained under torture. The accountability card can also be played in a manner that seems not to be unreasonable, but with implications that are obviously not in line with prevailing global ethics. For example, during the presidential elections in April 2002, French National Front leader Jean-Marie Le Pen claimed that he would end the 'decadent and corrupt system' of Chirac's era.[65]

Those who instigate and implement anti-corruption measures inevitably become targets for revenge. China's justice minister, Gao Changli, who instigated the anti-corruption purge, was seemingly caught in his own net at the end of 2000.[66] Similarly, Clodosvaldo, a Russian put in charge of Venezuala's anti-corruption campaign, faced the possibility of appearing in court in relation to embezzlement involving senior military officers. US attempts to undermine the popular Venezuelan president, Chavez, in 2002, through installing a pro-American candidate who would probably open up the country's nationalized oil industry, was fortunately overcome by public protest and support of the new democracy by the military. But we nearly witnessed a return to a 1970s-style puppet government. In Russia, parliamentarian and journalist Olga Kitova was charged with slander and interference in a criminal investigation, following articles she wrote about official corruption.[67]

Another example of the abuse of the new leadership accountability ethos was the campaign by the South Korean opposition party, the Grand National Party (GNP), against the unification minister Lim Dong-won in 2001. The GNP accused Lim of a technical breach of the law, which prohibits praising communist North Korea. Efforts to engage in constructive dialogue with the North are hard if the minister who has the responsibility for improving North–South relations cannot display an element of courtesy towards the communist regime. And the need for the so-called 'sunshine' policy to succeed should put it above party politics. A similar circumstance surrounded the impeachment of Present Roh in 2004. He was seen as one of the most honest and open Korean leaders of the past half-century. The opposition party utilized a legal technicality which, if enforced to the letter, would make open political discussion very hard for any serving president because they could never make a positive comment about any political party. A constitutional court then overturned the impeachment and Roh was reinstated.

Broader political intrigues can also be wrapped in the mantle of accountability. In one week, in April 2002, there were reports that the US government had apparently tried to play the accountability card three times. In the first instance, the US State Department ousted the director-general of the Organization for the Prohibition of Chemical Weapons (OPCW), Jose Bustani, on the grounds of his 'management style'. Bustani's achievements included increasing the number of signatories to the Chemical Weapons Convention from 87 to 145 in five years. He was also encouraging Iraq to join the OPCW, and getting close to an agreement to inspect Iraq's weapons. This would have removed the excuse for US military action against Iraq. And politics aside, this is another example of the US not following rules that it has previously agreed to. Under the Convention, member states must 'not seek to influence' OPCW staff.[68] US officials also insisted on the investigation of Swedish diplomat Hans Blix, who headed the UN team to investigate Iraq's weapons programme. Again, this seemed to be motivated by the US desire to demonstrate that Saddam Hussien would not permit investigations. The 'failure' of investigations could then legitimize military intervention, but Blix was likely to succeed.[69] Then the next day, the chair of the International Panel on Climate Change (IPCC), Robert Watson, was removed following US pressure. This reflected the views of the ExxonMobil oil company.[70] One of the future roles for civil society will be to 'police the police' and challenge the misuse of the accountability card.

Smart accountability

The main lesson from the evolving history of leadership accountability over the past fifty years is that to be effective it must be focused on the most significant actors and avoid collateral damage. This awareness is not new. When the English King Charles I was beheaded in 1649, the contemporary rationale was explicitly to avoid the need to bring down the judiciary and other state institutions – to achieve leadership change but avoid 'regime change'. There is an Arabic saying, 'When you hit the chief, all the followers will take note.' In Korea, a similar sentiment embodies ideas of corruption and environment, 'If upstream is clean, downstream will be clean.' US defense secretary Rumsfeld reflected the sentiment when he was asked, in relation to Iraq, how you stop a column of ants advancing. His answer was, 'Tread on the first dozen.'

In an assessment of the trials of military leaders in Greece, Argentina and South Korea, Terence Roehrig concludes that long-term success is more likely if accountability initiatives clearly target senior individuals and therefore do not threaten the whole of a nation's military and other state structures. This was the case in South Korea and Greece, but less so in Argentina. In South Korea, 'authorities were able to keep the trials limited and the public seemed largely content to prosecute only the highest leaders'. Similarly in Greece 'the government also went to great lengths to demonstrate their intention to limit the scope of the prosecutions'.[71] In Greece 126 were charged and 86 convicted, while in South Korea 15 of the 16 charged were convicted. But in Argentina, nine junta and 3,000 military personnel were charged, yet only five junta personnel were convicted and all soldiers convicted were pardoned. From the perspective of modern restorative justice, holding only the most senior leaders to account now fulfils the major social functions of preserving the complex and vulnerable machinery of the modern state and avoiding anarchy and civil conflict.

The idea of limiting direct accountability to the most senior leaders seems to have been the undeclared strategy of the US and British regimes when they invaded and occupied Iraq in 2003. Writing very soon after these events, Milan Rai argues convincingly that

> it is more appropriate to describe US policy as one of 'leadership change' rather than 'regime change' ... What is clear and unambiguous is that Washington and London had no intention of forcing a real 'regime change' on Iraq, and, when the regime dissolved during the war of 2003, the US and UK attempted to rebuild that regime, with limited results ... A war supposedly for 'regime change' actually ended with the restoration of leading fascists to power.[72]

Although the original intention might have been to remove a few significant despots and leave the rest of the state machinery with the capacity to function, the Iraqi regime was 'changed', or rather destroyed, by the invading and occupying forces. Of the many consequences, a well-run and effective education system ended up in the hands of an American company called Creative Associates International, one of the best higher education systems in the Middle East collapsed, the police and domestic security forces were unable to function effectively because of local resistance, and previously efficient hospitals became warehouses for people dying from simple preventable conditions. The US-led intervention in Iraq showed that over-hasty leadership accountability can easily become unwanted regime change.

But even the principle of limiting accountability to the key figures should be viewed with caution. In 2004, British MP Dominic Grieve argued the case for assassination as a means to remove dangerous power elites without doing further harm.[73] He cited the example of the assassination by Israeli forces of Hammas leader Sheik Yassin, which had been condemned by the UN and many world leaders including senior British ministers. It is easy to see the attraction of such a strategy. It is less easy to see how a global consensus could be formed about who should be removed in this way. Until we see the existence of a world court that might have the legitimacy to order this form of judicial sentence or at least permission to employ 'reasonable force' on a global scale to make an arrest, and a codification of the standards of conduct expected of leaders as international law, it seems unworkable.

Future history will doubtless demonstrate further examples of the pre-science of people power movements, of mass oppression, of civil society movements acting without a sound evidence base, and of unlawful assassinations. An increase in accountability rhetoric raises many ethical questions about that concept and practice of accountability, especially by unrepresentative public groups. Two central questions are addressed by David Crocker. In an article called 'Reckoning with past wrongs', he asks: what is 'success' in terms of accountability initiatives? And do the ends always justify the means?[74] To these could be added: how do we challenge evil acts rather than so-called evil people? These questions perhaps present the main future role for civil society organizations – to develop the ethics of accountability processes, and to police the police. As events surrounding the invasion of Iraq show, this accountability of accountability embraces challenging extremism and scapegoating, and ensuring that self-declared accountability forums do not obfuscate and cover up for miscreant power elites.

Implications

- Global civil society is increasingly **personalizing protest**. Separate entities:
    - are **mutually reinforcing but rarely collaborate**, and their resultant diversity and unpredictability is a strength.
    - embody **multiple loyalties** – supporters have different national interests, political allegiances, social classes and other group alliances.
    - include an emergent **global senior citizenry**, retired activists making full use of ICT.

- **Strategies** include
    - questioning and dialogue
    - evidence-gathering and advocacy
    - whistle-blowing

    and **social sanctions** include
    - naming and shaming
    - public apology
    - hearings *in absentia*.

Organizations increasingly **coordinate** these approaches.
* Ensuring the **legitimacy** of civil society endeavours is crucial, which will entail shifting from direct action towards the **accountability of accountability**:
    - encouraging **smart accountability** – well-focused action against the most significant elites
    - '**policing the police**' – ensuring that force is not used politically or retributively by any power elites
    - **commending good acts of leadership**, particularly sensible U-turns.

5
Prognoses: Changing Relationships

> While in the past, political leaders could get away with [bad]
> behaviour, we have now moved into a revolutionary new
> world. All over the planet executive and bureaucratic hierar-
> chies are being challenged by increasingly empowered and
> informed electorates, as well as by e-enabled protest. Voters
> want service and ongoing accountability, not dictation and top
> down arrogance. And if they cannot get it they will employ
> ways other than through voting and party politics to satisfy
> their needs.
>
> Lord Howell of Guildford,
> Opposition Spokesman on Foreign Affairs, UK[1]

It seems clear that there is a strong and growing response to the personal
abuse of power, through both governmental and civil society initiatives.
And it is hard to think of a historical parallel within which political
elites and populations have worked towards a broad common goal so
determinedly, albeit usually without direct cooperation. But agreement
about specific goals has not been unified, because of an absence of a
consensus about the standards that can reasonably be expected of leaders operating at a global level. That raises an obvious question: how will
leadership accountability develop, and what might be the broader
global outcomes? There are three relevant areas. First, who will influence
change, what are the issues that will be of concern in the near future and
who is identifying them? Then, on an individual level, what are the
personal implications of recent and future trends for future leaders, and
how will leadership conduct be judged internationally? Third, at the level
of institutions, what might be the implications for democratic systems, in
particular voting systems? The unifying idea is straightforward: power

relationships between leaders and those they perceive as followers will change.

Future concerns

The concerns of journalists may appear to be trial by media, but they provide an obvious indicator of future world interests. Although media professionals appear to be bound up with current events, they are also demonstrating long memories and great enthusiasm to pursue people who abused their power many years ago. The focus for historians is travelling in the opposite direction, and they are extending their interests into very recent history. Their particular contribution is to uncover abuses of power that did not receive attention because they were against victims in 'enemy' nations, or perpetrated by temporary allies, when the atrocities happened. As the interests of journalists and historians meet and influence one another, the time gaps through which despots have commonly escaped identification are being closed.

Journalists

John Pilger echoes a classic phrase when talking of the role of journalists in the modern world – 'to call power to account'. He elaborates: 'when power moves into unaccountability, that's where journalists excavate true meaning'.[2] As a journalist with an acute sense of colonial history, Robert Fisk focuses unsurprisingly on atrocities in the Middle East.[3] He cites the killings in Sabra and Chatila, Lebanon, for which the Belgian courts wanted to interview Ariel Sharon. Fisk reminds us that the same year, 1982, saw the massacre of 6,000 people in Hama, Syria, for which the president's brother Rifaat Assad is answerable. Rifaat now lives in a large villa in Spain. A year later, Saddam Hussein's army gassed a train carrying hundreds of war-wounded Iranians – a clear war crime, but at the time Saddam was seen to be fighting for Western interests and the atrocities were ignored. (Fisk's views were written before the US invasion of Iraq.) The Palestinian town of Jenin has since been added to the list, following the refusal of the Israeli government to permit an immediate investigation by a UN fact-finding mission into killings and destruction by the military there in April 2002. In July the Palestinian envoy to the UN then demanded that Israel be taken to the newly constituted ICC for killing 15 people in an air strike on Gaza. Fisk also suggests that US politicians and military personnel may have been complicit in crimes against humanity in Afghanistan[4] and, of course, Iraq.

In the East, Kim-Jong IL, the 'dear leader' of North Korea, is a constant concern and source of fascination, but not just because of his human rights record and seemingly bizarre behaviour. Despite his reputation as a recluse, he and his aides also seem to have a very acute sense of international politics. One of his self-evaluations sums up why Western leaders are wary of him: 'I know I'm an object of criticism in the world, but if I am being talked about, I must be doing the right things.'[5] North Korea could well become the pivot around which North East Asia reframes its place in the world, not least in the form of a unified Korea with a nuclear capability and a new sense of East Asian regional identity that will almost certainly challenge American hegemony.

Events in Central Asia are less well-known but of growing interest to the press. President Niyazov of Turkmenistan took office as head of the Communist Party during 1985, and became 'president for life' in 1999. In neo-Stalinist tradition he has renamed the days of the week and months after himself and his family, and has published a 'moral guide' which is required reading in schools and a prerequisite of getting a driving licence. Paradoxically for a communist, he presents himself as a god-figure. One of his poems reads, 'I am the Turkmen spirit reborn to bring you to a golden age ... I am your saviour.'[6] Like Kim Jong-IL, Niyazov is challenged by human rights groups who are concerned about media control, torture, disappearances, arbitrary detention and forced labour. He has also banned opera, ballet, circuses and music. Libraries and schools in rural areas have been closed. Attention is also turning to dictators such as Karimov in Uzbekistan.[7] A report for the Afghanistan Justice Project, *The candidates and the past: the legacy of war crimes and the political transition in Afghanistan*, gave historical method current relevance by identifying alleged war criminals among the warlords who were likely to become part of the new government.[8]

In relation to Africa, the American journalist Bill Berkeley claims that during the Cold War, US Democratic and Republican administrations 'often overlooked, excused, rationalized, and bankrolled wanton repression, injustice, corruption and economic mismanagement by unelected leaders who were willing to oppose Moscow.' In his book, *The graves are not yet full*, he elaborates: 'Call it "tribalism", call it "nationalism", call it "fundamentalism" – the role of political leaders in fomenting civil conflicts has been the paramount civil rights issue of the post-Cold War era.' And he concludes, 'It takes leadership, operating in a context of political upheaval and insecurity – and impunity – to translate hostility and suspicion into violent conflict.'[9] His arguments echo the basic realization that underpinned the original war crime tribunals – wars can only come about through the actions of power elites. The next step is for African journalists themselves to look more critically at political interference in their own countries, and to question their own leaders more quickly.

Online journalism is providing another dimension, because of the relative freedom for writers and the wide impact. Writing in the online version of the Argentine newspaper *Clarin*, Carlos Fuentes presents a view from the Americas. He argues that US foreign policy decisions are responsible for crimes against humanity in Vietnam, Chile, Uruguay, Argentina, El Salvador, Guatemala, Iraq and the Balkans.[10] In December 2003, the work of a doctoral student at Colorado University, about US war crimes in Vietnam and increasing admission by war veterans, seems indicative of an ongoing and growing future interest by young and old alike. Government records show that atrocities were far more common than is believed, and it is evident that US soldiers were often ordered to carry out these acts.[11]

Journalists have focused not only on individuals, but also on broader institutional concerns. Writing in *New Scientist*, Alan Trounson points out that new technologies will raise new challenges. For example, the Genetics Policy Institute has asked for a ruling from the International Court of Justice as to whether reproductive cloning might be a crime against humanity. A precedent was set by the Nuremberg Code of Ethics of 1947, which came in the wake of Nazi experiments in the concentration camps.[12] The development of the accountability institutions in relation to corporate crime is another issue. Nuri Albala argues that there is concern about the lack of an international legal definition of economic crimes, and of a forum similar to the ICC, which could hear cases of corporate crime by transnational companies and their leaders. This is excluded from the remit of the ICC, and national governments are so bound up with transnational companies that they are unlikely to pursue cases through the International Court of Justice (ICJ).[13] In general, corporate law regulates companies, not executives.

But across the world, the US seems likely to be the main focus of attention from all directions. Foreign policy and related atrocities are central concerns, but there are likely to be others. Sir Crispin Tickell provides the obvious list of issues that are attracting the attention of the media and academics alike:

- the withdrawal from the Anti-Ballistic Missile Treaty
- the failure to ratify the Biodiversity Convention or to accept the Biosafety Protocol
- the refusal to join the International Criminal Court

- the failure to ratify the UN Convention on the Rights of the Child
- the refusal to accept the new protocol to the Biological and Toxic Weapons Convention
- the withdrawal from the Kyoto Protocol[14]

Indications in the US press suggest that in the near future we may see US leaders such as George Bush, who openly admit responsibility for reversing environmental regulation that is in the global interest, called to account by other nations, and probably US citizens, for related environmental impacts.[15]

Press reports also remind us that the challenge to US leaders also comes from inside the US establishment. A class action filed against the CIA by its own employees, for 'abuse of power' by senior managers, suggests that the challenge to wayward leadership is not only coming from outside the US. It is claimed that, among other things, managers blamed mid- and low-level staff for covering up mistakes that led to the bombing of China's embassy in Belgrade in 1999.[16] Chomsky reminds us of the degree to which US leaders have actively supported despots. In addition to Saddam Hussein, he mentions Ferdinand Marcos, 'Baby Doc' Duvalier and Nicolae Ceausescu as examples who were eventually overthrown by democratic movements in their own countries.[17] Others include Suharto, Mobutu Sese Seko, Teodoro Obiang of Equatorial Guinea, and the South Korean dictators.

Henry Kissinger poses a specific interest for the accountability journalists. Documents released from the US National Security Archive in 2003 indicate that Kissinger approved the Argentinian military junta's brutal efforts to eliminate opposition.[18] Writing about the murder of General Rene Schneider in Chile, Christopher Hitchens claimed, 'We can say with safety that [Kissinger] is prima facie guilty of direct collusion in the murder of a democratic officer in a democratic country.'[19] The phrase 'prima facie guilty' might seem an oxymoron, but a book by Hitchens, *The trial of Henry Kissinger*, detailed other 'prima facie' crimes that in his opinion 'should be placed on a proper bill of indictment'. These include the 'deliberate mass killing of civilian populations in Indochina', 'deliberate collusion in mass murder, and later in assassination in Bangladesh', and 'the personal suborning and planning of murder, of a senior constitutional officer in a democratic nation – Chile.'[20] At the time that Hitchens's book was published, Kissinger presented his perspective in the academic journal *Foreign Affairs*. He wrote warning about the dangers of universal jurisdiction – 'Historically the dictatorship of the virtuous has often led to inquisitions and even witch hunts.'[21] He is, of course, correct, but it has also led to the overthrow of despots, such as Saddam Hussein.

Hitchens's views were shared by others. While in Paris, in May 2001, Kissinger was summonsed by Judge Roger Le Loire to answer questions about Operation Condor and five 'missing' French citizens. Kissinger fled overnight, but in New York he received similar summonses from Spain and Argentina.[22] Hitchens also provided evidence concerning the death of Charles Horman, an American film-maker, during Pinochet's regime.[23] A month later, the Chilean judge who indicted Pinochet made it known that he wanted to question Kissinger about the killing of Horman.[24] Then in September, the family of General Schneider filed a lawsuit against Kissinger claiming damages of $3 million for 'summary execution', assault and civil rights violations.[25] When Kissinger visited Britain in April 2002, activist Peter Tatchell applied for a warrant on the basis that he had allegedly 'commissioned, aided and abetted and procured war crimes in Vietnam, Laos and Cambodia', between 1969 and 1977.[26] Whether or not such actions succeed is probably secondary to the publicity that is achieved, and the discomfort and irritation felt by those who are being called to account. If nothing else, it takes the gloss off the jet-set lifestyle and that is a tangible sanction for international elites. Israel's political leaders now do not travel abroad without advice from international lawyers. In 2005, a retired Israeli general, Doron Almog, had to return home without leaving his plane at Heathrow airport because an arrest warrant had been issued against him concerning alleged war crimes in the Gaza Strip.

Historians

Historians are uncovering abuses of power by former Western leaders which have been buried over the past century for political reasons. The war crimes committed against ethnic Germans in Czechoslovakia, after the end of the Second World War, are being brought to public attention. Atrocities against Germans attracted little sympathy at that time. If terrorism is an evil, how should we now judge Winston Churchill when he talked of 'the bombing of German cities simply for the sake of increasing terror' and Britain's 'acts of terror and wanton destruction'?[27] In Dresden 25,000 civilians died, and that was not the biggest such incident.

Writers are also starting to consider more fully the war crimes committed by Russian troops as they entered Germany at the end of the Second World War. It seems clear now that Beria and Stalin were well aware of the magnitude of rape and other atrocities committed by their troops.[28] From Latvia, Estonia and Lithuania there are similar stories.

Another apparent act of genocide in the first part of the twentieth century, against Armenians in Turkey, is also being revisited. The prevailing view is that this was not systematically organized by Turkish political leaders, but it is hard to explain the scale of the killings without some form of coordination, and it may be found that local leaders and warlords played a significant part, much as in Rwanda and Burundi.

Historians in Belgium are demystifying the atrocities committed in Congo a century ago, under the rule of King Leopold II. There are claims that ten million Congolese were murdered or worked to death, that women were systematically raped, and that amputation of hands was a common punishment. In his book *King Leopold's ghost*, Adam Hochschild compares the situation to the Nazi Holocaust and Stalin's purges. Academics at the country's anthropological museum have started to represent exhibits to create a more global view of Belgium's colonial history. It is interesting to view these trends in the light of the global jurisdiction adopted by Belgian courts for war crimes, which elicited such a strong response from US leaders.

Elsewhere in Europe, French involvement in Algeria is now being questioned. In November 2001, retired French general Paul Aussaresses went on trial for allegedly 'condoning war crimes' in his book *Special Services, Algeria 1955–1957*. In interviews he had admitted ordering torture for 'patriotic' reasons, and he claimed that the French government condoned such acts.[29] As with the Pinochet case, the timescales of accountability are at last becoming commensurate with the power of those concerned to delay and deter justice. Assaresses was 83 when he went on trial. Another event in French history is also resurfacing – the killing of hundreds of Algerian demonstrators, by police and security services, in the 1961 'Battle of Paris'. At the time, the French government claimed that only a handful of people had died, and yet the whole of the French security services was immediately given immunity from prosecution in relation to the event. If only a few people died, and their deaths were lawful or accidental, why the need for such an extraordinary extension of the principle of immunity?

Recent history is also being reviewed in South Korea, where around five million people were displaced by the US-led intervention. During the Korean War, in the non-communist village of No-Geun-Ree, American troops are being blamed for a Vietnam-style massacre of the villagers. Further south, when the invading communists reached the river Nag-Dong-Gang, US troops were apparently ordered to kill everyone who was Korean. These massacres have been hidden from the world, not least because the South Korean government has blocked efforts to achieve redress, but historians such as Bruce Cummings are addressing the omissions. In a South Korean village near Anyang, he records how it was reported in the *New York Times* that, as a result of US attacks, 'the inhabitants ... were caught and kept in the exact postures they held when the napalm struck – a man about to get on his bicycle, fifty boys and girls playing in an orphanage, a housewife, strangely unmarked, holding in her hand a page torn from a Sears-Roebuck catalogue ...'. The US secretary of state Dean Acheson wanted this 'sensational reporting' stopped by the censorship authorities.[30] On the domestic front, disappearances during the 1980s student riots are also now being examined by accountability NGO Jin-Sang-Gyu-Myung ('Discover the truth'), which is trying to trace how and why students died, and what was the involvement of the police.

The accountability ethos is also evident in the North where there are ongoing efforts to establish that US troops used biological weapons in Pyongyang. More napalm was used in North Korea than in Vietnam, and with a more devastating effect because urban populations were more dense. Noam Chomsky reminds us that a more significant event is likely to surface when the North rejoins the world community. In May 1953, a month before the armistice, an 'object lesson in air power to all the Communists in the world' – bombing raids by the US – left the country with no further military targets to bomb. So the US air force then destroyed irrigation dams which supported 75 per cent of the rice production. A US report concluded, 'The Westerner can little conceive the awesome meaning which the loss of this staple commodity has for the Asian – starvation and slow death.'[31] The statement is a clear admission of a war crime, similar to those that German and Japanese leaders had been convicted of perpetrating a few years earlier.

The legendary status of Mao Tse-tung in China is likely to be eroded as a book by Jon Halliday and his Chinese wife Jung Chang (author of *Wild swans*) finds its way into the country. In *Mao: the unknown story*, they expose the myths and deceit that surrounded his conduct.[32] The supposedly heroic crossing of the Dadu river during the Long March is one example. Mao reputedly led his soldiers across the bridge, hanging from the suspension chains and fighting against flames, and then drove off the enemy. But elderly people who lived near the bridge told Halliday and Chang that this simply did not happen. Contemporaneous reports by Mao's men concur with this. It is unlikely that the Chinese government will ever openly denounce Mao, but they are very likely to see such books as doing little that is against the interests of the modern leadership.

The questioning of American conduct is also growing in relation to Japan. The Tokyo war crimes trials did not take account of probable war crimes by US leaders. The trials erred, more than the Nuremberg trials, towards victors' justice. There was no redress for the use of the A-bomb twice, over Hiroshima and Nagasaki, which killed 103,000 people. The firebombing of 67 Japanese cities which killed 1.9 million civilians, including Tokyo in March 1945 which produced the greatest number of casualities in any single incident during the Second World War, were also acts of terrorism. The overt aim was a premeditated attempt to incinerate large numbers of civilians in order to influence Japan's military and political leadership. It was calculated that Japanese houses were built of wood and paper, and it was known that Tokyo had 1,100 firemen, aged between 13 and 17, to protect eight million people. In his film *The fog of war*, former US defense secretary Robert McNamara gave a candid admission that he was 'part of a mechanism that recommended [the firebombing]', and that had the US lost the war, the conclusion would probably have been that he and Major General Curtis E. Le May were 'behaving as war criminals'. In 1945, a military aide to General MacArthur described the firebombing as 'one of the most ruthless and barbaric killings of non-combatants in all history'.[33]

In Japan, the issue is not relegated to history. Each year all schoolchildren mark the date of the A-bombings by making thousands of paper peace cranes. This is, in effect, an ongoing mass protest by the young against the US. There are also ongoing protests in Okinawa against the use of the island as a US military base, violence including sexual offences and rape against local women by US soldiers, and environmental destruction. This is in the context of a growing questioning of why a third of Okinawa's civilian population was killed by invading US forces in 1945.[34] Will the US government ever make an apology to Japanese people, in the spirit of the Japanese government's apology to Koreans for the sexual slavery of thousands of Korean 'comfort women' during the Second World War?

As their interests converge, journalists and historians will increasingly influence one another, and this synergy will influence activists and prosecutors. This outcome is likely to develop a new view of world history which challenges the self-declared moral high ground that the West has claimed to inhabit for the past century. This will be reinforced as people in the victim communities rediscover their own history, and start to feed a non-Western view into the liberal world media.

Of course this process will not always bring the most significant cases to public view, simply the most media-compatible and historically intriguing. But the broader outcome is likely to be, as we saw in relation to the invasion of Iraq, that the future forces of accountability will not represent the traditional loyalties and 'sides' that leaders have taken for granted throughout history. The phenomenon of multiple loyalties has been noted in relation to other areas of globalization, for example global civil society movements, environmental campaigners and internet users. The significance of global accountability is that leaders are only leaders because they have followers, and in the future it will be increasingly difficult to identify and predict who those followers will be.

Leadership integrity and moral authority

> *Kgosi ke kgosi ka batho* – A chief is a chief by the people.
> > (Botswana, Southern Africa)

> It is not the leaders who govern people but it is the people who let the leaders govern them.
> > (Digital Governance home page –
> > www.cddc.vt.edu/digitalgov)

As in the past, future leaders will only be seen as leaders if they maintain their integrity in the eyes of those whose lives they affect. Personal integrity and moral authority have been central to assessments of leadership throughout history, but the relevance is likely to increase in a globalizing world because integrity is the only thing that can bind populations to leaders across the planet. As proposed in Chapter 3, world leaders will now need to maintain their integrity in the eyes of 'distant others' whose lives they do not directly affect, and that is something new. One potential outcome, fuelled by the events described in Chapter 2, is a shift in the relative moral authority of nations from West to East. New forms of accountability indexes suggest this effect, and these can be combined to create a Global Leadership Responsibility Index which could be used to track changes in the future.

John Kane concludes that, through their 'moral authority' or 'moral capital', leaders

> generally form a significant repository of trust for those whose interests they try to represent, or in whom they have inspired some

ideal to be realized ... Genuine respect facilitates the achievement of political goals, while its absence or loss may make it impossibly difficult to gain even trivial ends.[35]

But the principles of leadership integrity and moral authority are not new. There is a traditional Chinese belief that the concern of leadership ethics is not how to make leaders moral, but how to create a realization that the way to be a leader is through displaying moral behaviour.[36] The Chinese words for 'govern' and 'correct' are homophones – *cheng* – and cognate, showing that the concept of governing was related to that of correcting. K'ung-fu-tzu (Confucius) extended this into an argument that leaders should model good conduct: 'To govern (*cheng*) is to correct (*cheng*). If you set an example by being correct, who would dare to remain incorrect.'[37] The ethic is not lost. In a recent private interview, Lee Man Sub, twice speaker of the South Korean Congress, claims: 'I have my own will, and I followed my will. I was never corrupted by other people. That's why I survived 40 years of politics.'[38] His words are well-founded. He survived the most corrupt period of Korean leadership history.

This principle also appears in Western traditions, in Ancient Greece for example. According to Thucydides, Pericles was 'a man clearly above corruption, [who] was enabled, by the respect others had for him and his own wise policy, to hold the multitude in voluntary restraint'.[39] Garry Wills argues that 'the Periclean type of leadership occurs rarely in history, if at all'.[40] That may be true, but the more interesting question is: what is the significance of this ethos for world leadership in the future? John Kane argues strongly that 'moral capital' is now a significant prerequisite of effective leadership.[41] On a global scale, contemporary leaders will certainly have great difficulty in achieving recognition simply through coercion, bribery, trickery, or even charisma. The world is too big, complicated and unpredictable. Their main option is to achieve recognition through integrity which is aided, or not, through the global media and other cybernetic information networks. Perhaps the ancient Chinese and Greek leadership ethic was simply prescient of a globalized world. Or did the idea arise because those ancient leaders saw themselves, and were seen by others, as world leaders?

Leaders recognize the link between integrity and legitimacy in their peers, even across sectoral divides. Albert Einstein concludes of Gandhi that he led 'through the cogent example of a morally superior conduct of life'.[42] It is not surprising that this ethic of good leadership is also central to Indian traditions, and that it fulfils a regulatory function.

Sundeep Waslekar is clear:

> If a ruler does not have attainments and if he does not perform these tasks, he is a despot. He is not accepted as a ruler. Thus, to be a ruler, it is important to behave as virtuous. If not, there is no entitlement to the role of ruler whether one is born in a royal family or elected by a clear majority of the population. This is the main difference between the Western and Bharatiya approaches towards governance.[43]

But, in the context of history, perhaps the ethics of East and West are not so different. Morgenthau provides a very similar conclusion in relation to the conduct between European leaders in the seventeenth and eighteenth centuries, on a 'supranational' level:

> A violation of his moral obligations, as they were recognized by his fellow monarchs for themselves, would set in motion not only his conscience but also the spontaneous reactions of the supranational aristocratic society, which would make him pay for the violation of its mores with loss of prestige; that is loss of power.[44]

The idea also appeared in tangible form in the 1999 UK House of Lords judgment about Pinochet.[45] Lord Browne-Wilson provided a seemingly novel argument which extended rather than refuted the traditional notion that 'leaders have immunity because they are leaders' (immunity *rationae materiae*). Torture could not be a legitimate state function, he argued, and therefore any person responsible for torture could not be considered as a legitimate head of state. From this lordly catch-22 (based, it seems, on a prejudgement of Pinochet's guilt as a torturer), Browne-Wilson concluded that Pinochet did not therefore have immunity.

There are signs that some political leaders are now overtly displaying more integrity in relation to the decisions they make, including decisions about the conduct of their associates. In 2002, South Korean president Kim Dae-jung resigned prior to the Korean elections, and then twice apologized on TV for the corruption scandal surrounding his three sons and close aides. In Confucian tradition he said, 'I am ashamed and feel guilty about not being able to take care of my sons properly.'[46] In the commercial sphere, Pierre Bilger astounded his French colleagues when he turned down a pay-off of £2.87 million from the engineering company Alstrom, which had declined dramatically under his leadership. When he left he said, 'Whatever anyone may say, I have always been careful to respect the principles of corporate governance.'[47] Hopefully, public opinion and history will come to demonstrate respect for leaders of integrity who accept responsibility for mistakes, even though they may not be to blame for the basic wrongdoing.

The corollary to personal responsibility is that leaders who do not take action to address wayward conduct by other leaders, or who fail to support leaders who are wrongly oppressed or, worse, actively support miscreants, are also not worthy to be considered leaders within the international community. The claim by George Bush (Snr) that Mobutu was 'one of our most valued friends [on] the entire continent of Africa' certainly caused people to question his notion of integrity.[48] Similarly, Margaret Thatcher's attempts to protect Pinochet, during the British extradition proceedings in 1999, led to a questioning of her values, and arguably the demise of her standing within the world community. The welcome extended to President Mugabe by President Chirac and Belgian leaders in March 2001 probably had a similar effect. It was left to Gay Rights activist Peter Tatchell to put global ethics into action when he attempted a citizen's arrest of Mugabe under the UN torture convention.[49]

Human rights activists, civil society organizations and the media provide an interesting new dimension, because they now exert real-time influence in the field of leadership accountability. If as a result the global public comes to see civil society leaders as embodying greater integrity than mainstream leaders, it may, in the tradition of the Chinese leadership ethic, come to see them as the legitimate world leadership. Former director of Médecins sans Frontières, Rony Brauman, provides a hint to mainstream leaders when he argues, as an echo of Confucius, 'A state is only a state if it has a constitution that places limits on the power of its leaders.'[50] Of course, civil society influence has been apparent for centuries – people power and social movements are not new. But, as argued in Chapter 3, the exponential increase in ICT provides the new ingredient that could turn civil influence into civil power. And that may not be a desirable outcome, unless it represents a balance of power rather than a force of power. We hope that, instead of increasing violence, civil society will take on a dual role. It will work first to delegitimize improper global leadership, and second to support leaders of integrity, particularly if political leaders fail to do this.

There is a common argument that the increase in leadership accountability will deter good people from seeking responsible jobs, for fear of false accusations. But the counter-argument is probably stronger: that good people will avoid positions of leadership if they are likely to become tainted because leading cadres are seen inevitably to be corrupt. In August 2000, Japan's prime minister, Mori, told the 'Children's Diet' about a survey showing that 'politician' was seen as the 'least attractive profession' by high school students. He concluded, 'I've had to reflect that I should work harder to be trusted by more people. I would be happy if you were to have a dream one day of becoming a parliamentarian.'[51] Similarly, in the commercial sector, research for the Institute of Business Ethics suggests that young British job-seekers are increasingly concerned about the ethical standing of potential employers.[52] The growing interest from the commercial sector in business ethics over the past decade tries to address this trend. Whether better self-regulation can reestablish the integrity of leadership, and therefore a willingness to become a leader, is hard to predict, but that should certainly be one of its objectives.

In the light of these dynamics, contemporary leaders might consider their response in relation to the oppression of leaders of integrity such as Aung San Suu Kyi, and the many others who are unknown – the senior scientists, journalists, academics, trade unionists, and minority and religious representatives. Lin Hua, the leader of 2,000 Chinese scientists who were opposed to the building of the Three Gorges dam, worked and died with barely any international support before he could witness the Chinese leadership revising its stance to agree with his view in 2005. The name Denis Halliday was almost unknown until he resigned from his post as a UN assistant secretary-general in 1998, because of his concern about the impact of sanctions in Iraq. He believed that crimes against humanity had been committed, and as he had direct responsibility for Iraq for 34 years his view was based on sound information.

Good leaders are scarce. Their loss on the world stage, in the context of pressing global problems, is itself harmful. There would be little disagreement that the world would be much poorer had Gandhi or Nelson Mandela ended their days in prison. But it is probably more thanks to civil society than the efforts of their political peers within the international community that they did not. Ken Saro-Wiwa was not so lucky.

On trial also are the Nigerian nation, its present rulers, and all those who assist them. Any nation which can do to the weak and disadvantaged what the Nigerian nation has done to the Ogoni loses a claim to independence and to freedom from outside influence ... The military does not act alone. They are supported by a gaggle of politicians, lawyers, judges, academics, and businessmen, all of them hiding under the claim that they are only doing their duty
Final statement to the Tribunal, 1 September 1995[53]
[Ken Saro-Wiwa was killed by the then leaders of Nigeria on 10 November 1995]

Causing harm through deceiving a population

> If a man steals £100 he is sent to jail, but if he steals a million pounds he is sent to parliament.
>
> George Bernard Shaw

> If a man kills one person, he is sent to prison, if he kills ten, to a prison mental hospital; but if he is responsible for the death of thousands he is crowned emperor, made the Duke of Marlborough, or elected President of the United States.
>
> James Gilligan[54]

The aspect of leadership integrity that was highlighted in Chapters 2 and 3 is deceit, and the public is becoming increasingly aware of this. It is almost impossible for leaders to do significant harm without deception in some form and, if noticed, populations react strongly to this. Detecting and redressing leadership deceit therefore provides the obvious Achilles heel of harmful leadership but, as we saw from events surrounding 9/11, there is a wide gap between a population perceiving that they have been deceived and being able to do something about it. That has been the case throughout history. The assessment of the Balkan Wars in 1912–13, mentioned in Chapter 1, concluded: 'The true culprits are those who mislead public opinion and take advantage of the people's ignorance to raise disquieting rumours ... inciting their country and consequently other countries into enmity.'[55] Recognizing that fact did not prevent the two subsequent world wars. If the world is to move forward from Michels's pessimistic conclusion, mentioned in the Introduction of this book – that 'If laws are passed to control the dominion of the leaders, it is the laws which gradually weaken, and not the leaders'[56] – we should understand why it is so hard to hold leaders to account for deceit through law.

At one level, the answer is self-evident: there are few if any laws that directly redress harm arising from the deceit of populations by power elites. There are many statutes to redress interpersonal deceit, which help to maintain public order and make populations easier to govern, but little to redress up-system infidelity, and in the modern world leaders rarely do harm on an interpersonal level. That gap is, of course, not surprising as leaders make the laws. But exactly how this has come about is less evident.

The legal understanding of 'deceive' in Britain is 'to induce a person to believe that a thing is true which is false, or a thing false which is true, contrary to that which the person practising the deceit knows or believes to be the case' (see Welham VDPP [1961] AC 103). The subtlety of the definition is that it acknowledges that deceit is not only caused by lying or concealing – a person is simply 'induced' to believe something false, and that has a wide meaning. It can cover a spectrum of tricks including concealing information and presenting ambiguous information. In contract law, 'misrepresentation' entails 'a false statement which misrepresents a material fact ... which is made with the intention that the person to whom it is addressed shall act on it' (see UK Misrepresentation Act 1967). An offence can be committed deliberately, through neglect or innocently, if the miscreant has 'no reasonable grounds for believing that statement to be true'. A further clarification by a British law lord, Lord Denning, holds that 'any behaviour, by words or conduct, is sufficient to be misrepresentation if it is such as to mislead the other party. If it conveys a false impression, that is enough' (*Curtis* v *Chemical Cleaning and Dyeing Co. Ltd* [1951] 1 KB 805). This cleverly circumvents the need to codify the multitude of tricks, clouded in the rhetoric of means and ends, which a powerful deceiver can utilize. If there was a misleading act and as a consequence someone was misled, that is sufficient. 'Lie' has no direct meaning in law, yet the state will sanction those who do not 'tell the truth, the whole truth and nothing but the truth', but only in a court setting and if deliberate deceit can be shown.

But there are three barriers to redress, and the first stems from the devil in the detail – the elements that must be evidenced to prove deceit in law:

- a false statement of fact made by one person
- knowingly or recklessly (a 'misrepresentation' can also arise innocently)
- with the intent that it should be acted on by another person who, as a result, suffers damage.[57]

It would seem reasonable to claim that deceit is wrong if *anyone* consequently suffers harm, not just those who 'act' and are deceived, but that is not how law is usually framed. In part this arises because the jurisprudence of causation favours adjacency of cause and effect,[58] but it is probably not just coincidence that this aspect of legal wisdom protects power elites.

Whatever the exactitudes of domestic law, the court of public opinion is able to make the conceptual leaps that are necessary to judge leadership deception, as Bush and Blair discovered. And there is always the chance in a common law country such as Britain that a judge or a jury could make the same conceptual leap. It is not hard to guess how a lawyer might present the case for a common-sense evolution of common law in this instance – 'If A deceives B by saying falsely that C had a gun and might shoot B, and B shoots C in apparent self-defence, is A responsible in any way, even if that false statement is not deliberate? Now view Bush and Blair as "A", parliament and people as "B", and Saddam Hussein and the Iraqi people as "C".'

Another barrier stems from the ethics of cheating, and laws that reflect this. The relevant element here is, as explained in Chapter 2, that the cheat deceives to achieve personal gain with a consequent loss elsewhere – there is a tangible zero-sum relationship. The difficulty this raises in relation to cheating by leaders is that the gain is often the achievement or maintenance of power, for example through a vote or popular support, and that is very difficult to prove. It is hard to demonstrate that particular politicians won an election because they started a war on a false pretext two years earlier. And more tangible gains can be hidden, either in the form of favours or as imperceptible social or professional gains many years later, or in Swiss bank accounts. It is equally hard to show the loss. How could a decline in a nation's commercial activity be shown to be directly caused by the impropriety of political or commercial leaders? Again, beyond card games, it is usually the leaders who make the laws, and laws are often framed in such a way that the loss–gain associated with leadership deceit is not against the rules.

The third barrier is embedded within the legal concept of 'incitement' – a concept that would seemingly be very applicable to harmful leadership, yet is never used for up-system accountability. Even if deception were not proven, a court should have no difficulty in seeing the example above (A,B,C) as 'incitement', an act of urging to a course of criminal action. But that approach often fails because the court's view of incitement is usually at an interpersonal level, the harm resulting from the actions of leaders is often not clearly codified as illegal, or the power elites control the only forums and processes through which the illegality can be demonstrated. One person shooting another is usually unlawful. But the legality of war or other major catastrophes can be constructed politically, and usually this is done by the winning side or those with most power.

Paradoxically then, the codes and concepts that frame deceit, cheating and incitement provide the means to deceive and cheat – for leaders. The barriers arise because:

- To establish an act of *deceit* entails proving that the person who is deceived is the same person who acts on that deceit and suffers the consequential harm, and that is usually not the case with leadership deceit.

- To establish an act of *cheating* entails showing a tangible loss–gain, and the losses–gains associated with leadership cheating are usually intangible.
- To establish an act of *incitement* entails demonstrating that a party was urged to commit a specific crime, and power elites can control whether particular harm is criminal.

It is rarely necessary for current leaders to interfere greatly with the law to achieve these protections. They inhabit a historical pathway of power that has been well-prepared, legally and ethically, by forebears who shared common interests of self-protection.

So broadly, the position in law is that shopkeepers who deceive customers are guilty of 'misrepresentation', even if they do so innocently. Others who cause harm, for example a professional who gives a client wrong advice, may be liable for the consequences of 'deceit', even if the deceit occurred through a reckless not deliberate act. But political leaders who cause harm through careless misrepresentation of information or reckless or deliberate deceit of a whole population are usually legally guilty of nothing. The main exceptions are in a few limited aspects of commercial law. The broader outcome is that this builds a perception that leaders cannot be challenged, and even if channels for legal redress exist in particular circumstances, they are rarely used.

How could laws and ethics evolve to redress this circumstance? Deceit, cheating and incitement all involve the mismanagement of information to influence the perceptions that others have of a situation, often in the form of spin. It is therefore no coincidence that the concepts of deceit and cheating reflect the criteria for 'unreliable information' proposed in *Leaders of integrity*: in an ideal world leaders should 'not, through act or omission, instigate, promote or permit information that is manifestly false, misleading or unsubstantiated, and is purported to be fact, and could cause public hatred, harm or hazard'.[59] If there is falsehood and harm to anyone, whether or not a gain can be proven, and whether or not that harm is interpersonal, should be irrelevant. There is need for a new statutory concept, 'Causing harm by deceiving a population', meaning any definable population such as a cabinet, parliament, army, or national or global population. Why should that appear so improbable? The principle would have useful applicability in many other areas, for example cult leaders who induce mass suicides, other faith-based crime, interference with websites, extremist ideological indoctrination, harmful advertising such as that from tobacco or junk food companies, and misuse of school curriculum and history books.

A precedent has already been set by the Arusha Tribunal when it convicted journalists and media managers for inciting hatred through press and radio, in 2003. The British government already warns teachers not 'to advocate your own personal views on a controversial matter in a way which undermines the ability to young people to think for themselves. If you teach in a school, it could also be against the law.'[60] But political leaders are not precluded from doing the same thing on TV. In 2005, a 55-year-old woman who posted a packet of talcum powder to Tony Blair was charged under new British terrorist laws for 'intending to induce a belief that it was likely to be a noxious substance'.[61] This does not seem far from 'intending to induce a belief that a country was likely to have WMDs'.

There is, of course, nothing new in pointing out that leaders, especially politicians, are perceived as cheats. Like countless other surveys, the 2004 Transparency International 'Corruption barometer' shows that politics is perceived as the most corrupt sphere of public service in most countries. The idea is so common that it has lost its meaning, and we fail to ask why the situation should be allowed to continue.

A global shift in moral authority

The perception of leadership integrity influences the moral authority of whole populations and whole nations. The revelation that 4 per cent of America's Catholic Church leaders had been accused of child sexual abuse over the past half-century certainly undermined the moral high ground of the Catholic Church in America.[62] Similarly, the actions of Osama bin Laden brought into question the standing of moderate Muslims throughout the world, the illegal killings authorized by Israel's political leaders threatened the status of Jewish people everywhere, and commercial corruption such as that at Enron or Shell lowered the moral standing of all large corporations. But this becomes more interesting at the international level, and has received little attention beyond the political and media rhetoric and a concern about the authority of the United Nations.

In former eras, the relative moral authority of nations was largely constructed through the stereotypical views of travellers, such as traders, missionaries, invaders and diplomats. In a world of global media, the views of moral authority are now being constructed through the perceptions that the global public has of the most conspicuous media elites, and in general this means political and commercial leaders. Rightly or wrongly, nations led by leaders who are seen as lacking integrity will have difficulty claiming moral authority, whatever the moral qualities of their populations. Therefore, another long-term outcome of global leadership accountability may be surprising shifts in moral authority, and the most likely axis of moral authority is from West to East.

Western leaders continue to assume the moral authority of their post-Second World War forebears, sustained by the West's seemingly triumphant role in the Cold War. It is worth recalling how US President George Bush presented this in 2004:

> I truly believe that freedom is a gift from the Almighty to every person, and that America has a responsibility to take a lead in the world, to help people be free.[63]

But memories of the Second World War are fading, and from the end of the Cold War a US-led West was no longer the high-profile force for good fighting against the apparent evils of the communist world. As a result, the assumed moral high ground of the West is being questioned, from outside and within. Not least, the claims that the US and UK had spied on the UN and Kofi Annan preceding the Iraq war appeared to put the two founding counties of the UN in breach of rules they had themselves set up, and hypocrisy is a sure way to lose moral authority.

Of many critiques of America, Emmanuel Todd's book *After the Empire: the breakdown of the American system* is one of the most influential. Todd was known for his prescience about the fall of the Soviet Union. In an interview in 2004 he stated:

> Until two years ago, America retained its legitimacy. Before Bush went on that frightful course and started boasting about America's strength, most people were ready to accept a king of continuing peaceful US hegemony. No longer.[64]

He continued, 'If Europe, Russia and Japan were to realize that America is not a superpower, then we would have a new world order overnight.'

Following 9/11, the moral authority of the West was questioned by many other observers. A report from the US International Institute for Strategic Studies concluded that the US cannot now 'assume a high moral position' in the world, and that 'The credibility of America's externally directed human rights message has been damaged.'[65] Later, the UK-based Institute for Public Policy Research reflected this view: 'UK support for the policies of President Bush ... will potentially make it harder for the UK to gain support for human rights initiatives.'[66] Individuals concurred. Among many others, Hans Blix, the UN weapons inspector, was critical of US and British action and claimed that the action 'damaged the credibility of the governments pursuing it'.[67] British Liberal Democrat leader Charles Kennedy agreed that deception surrounding the Iraq war 'inevitably reduces the United Kingdom's standing as an honest broker throughout the world'.[68] The vice-chair of the US Senate Intelligence Committee, Senator Jay Rockefeller, concluded: 'Our credibility is diminished. Our standing in the world has never been lower.'[69] The increasing questioning of the invasion of Iraq was accompanied by the ongoing echoes of the corruption scandals within US companies such as Enron which alone caused $68 billion of capital to evaporate and 5,600 jobs to be lost.

One of the more tangible indicators of a possible loss of trust in the US seemed to be the dramatic decline in the numbers of overseas students applying to study in American universities. Lawrence Summers, president of Harvard University, was prescient of the potential long-term consequences:

> If the next generation of foreign leaders are educated elsewhere, we also will have lost the incalculable benefits derived from their extended exposure to our country and its democratic values.

It was not clear if the 32 per cent decline in applications resulted from visa problems, or a loss of trust in the US. But Danielle Guichard-Ashbrook of MIT had little doubt. She asked, 'Is it because students have tried to apply but had trouble, or is it the perception that the US is not friendly? I think it's more the latter.'[70] By September 2004, the American public seemed to agree with these views. The Globscan group found that, in relation to Bush's foreign policy, 40 per cent of Americans polled said that foreign dislike of the US was a 'big problem' and 30 per cent 'somewhat a problem'.[71] A survey carried out for the World Economic Forum (WEF) in 2003 provided a leadership dimension. 'Leaders of the USA' came bottom in a global survey of trust – only 27 per cent of those polled trusted them. Leaders in Western Europe achieved 36 per cent, and at the top were NGO leaders with 56 per cent and the UN with 42 per cent.[72]

Arguably, a contrasting situation is found in the East. One of the outcomes of global accountability is that there are now clearer distinctions being made between the conduct of the powerful and the people. It is increasingly realized that, over the past century, the *people* of East Asia have constantly been victims of their own and other country's leaders, in ways that are beyond the imagination of most Western observers. Mao's Cultural Revolution, Pol Pot, the Vietnamese and Korean wars were not disagreements between peoples, but between power elites and peoples. People in Japan were victims of both their own Meiji rulers and those of wartime America. People in Korea and China were victims of Japan's leaders, and then of their own. Around the world, there is a growing understanding and sympathy with the people of the East. At the same time, within the region, there is a growing questioning of the US, as was expressed in the mass anti-American rallies in Seoul in 2002.

These 'tiger' countries, old and new, achieved economic development at an astonishing speed. South Korea has moved from being the world's second poorest country in 1945 to eleventh richest, aiming to be sixth in a few years. China is likely to be the world's richest nation by 2041.[73] And through initiatives such as the OPEN anti-corruption project in South Korea and the Discipline Inspection Commission in China, these countries are working to achieve moral development equally quickly.

In 2004, it was announced that the Chinese government had committed itself, in an amendment to the constitution, to provide 'greater respect for and protection of human rights'. This was, for the first time, expressed without the usual caveat about 'rights of subsistence'. Of this Rob Gifford, Beijing correspondent of the National Public Radio (USA), commented, 'The supremacy of the Communist Party has led to officials being untouchable. By saying the law should be above everything, the reformers are hoping to make them more accountable.'[74] Shortly afterwards it was announced that the Chinese government had agreed to an unconditional invitation to the UN Special Rapporteur on Torture and representatives from the UN working group on arbitrary detention to inspect Chinese prisons. The officials could meet and talk with anyone and interviewees would be protected from recriminations. This appeared in stark contrast to the ongoing detentions at Guantanamo Bay and the refusal of the US administration to admit observers into the camp. A few months later, Foreign Ministry spokesman Liu Jianchao talked of a country 'with more accountability and a more open and tolerant civil society'.[75] Then politburo member Luo Gan, who is responsible for internal security, told public officials to address public grievances rather than use force against the rising number of public protests. He claimed that 80 per cent of complaints were reasonable. At the start of 2005, China's State Environmental Protection Agency halted 22 questionable power projects pending environmental impact assessment. China seemed to be demonstrating its new moral credentials when, in November 2004, the government criticized Japan's prime minister for attending the infamous Yasakuni war shrine. That stance would have been laughable a few years earlier.

Soon we may see countries such as South Korea complaining about having to deal with 'corrupt' nations like France and Italy, and China expressing a concern about the global human rights record of Britain and the US. The view of India is an interesting indicator of a significant proportion of the middle ground of world opinion. In October 2004, Indian and Chinese soldiers celebrated China's national day by standing together, for the first time, at the Himalayan border, and the Indian government has started to encourage 'Look East' initiatives. This is not to say that these East Asian countries are currently exemplars of desirable conduct, but that the situation is changing and could change more rapidly in the future.

> When I was at school in the 1980s, we were taught that knowledge and morality will be the essence of development for our generation in the next decade. And because of this, in the coming century, Korea will be a leading country in the world.
>
> Yun-Joo Lee[76]

This prognosis of a shift in relative moral authority also gains a modicum of support from various emergent global indexes. The Corruption Perception Index (CPI) of Transparency International (TI) is based on a survey that asks business people, risk analysts and the general public to score countries on a scale from 10 – highly clean – to 0 – highly corrupt.[77] Overall, countries in East Asia score, and are ranked, much lower than the US. But looking beyond the index as a crude league table and analysing trends suggests a different picture. Over the period 2000–05, the trend within the East Asia 'tiger' region is upwards, but US data suggest a downturn (Figures 5.1 and 5.2). It can be argued that, because the Asian countries are lower down the table, improvement is not surprising, and America is just displaying normal fluctuations associated with being nearer the top. But then if we look at Singapore the trend seems even more striking. By 2004 Singapore (9.3 – 5th) was already well above the US (7.5 – 17th) in score and ranking, despite formerly having had a reputation for corruption, and its upward trajectory is by the same amount as America's downturn (Figure 5.3).

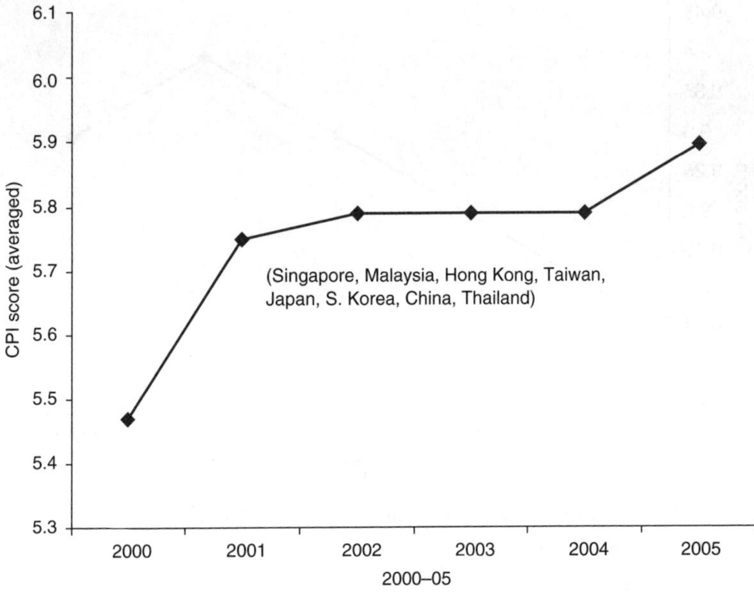

Figure 5.1   Corruption Perceptions Index (CPI) – East Asia 'tiger' countries
Source: www.transparency.org

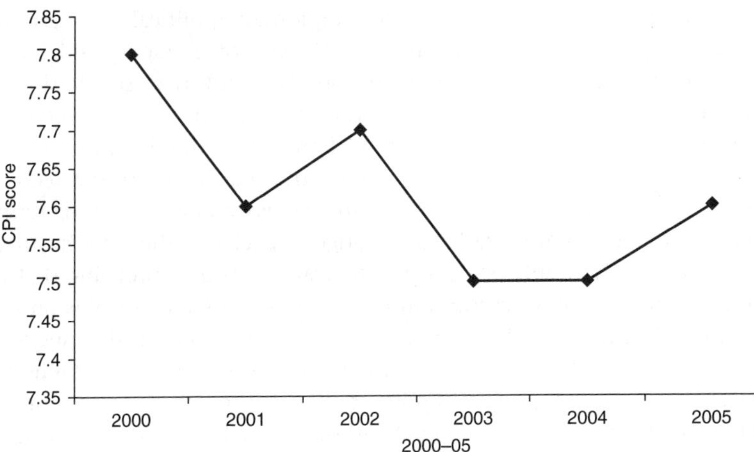

Figure 5.2   Corruption Perceptions Index (CPI) – USA
Source: www.transparency.org

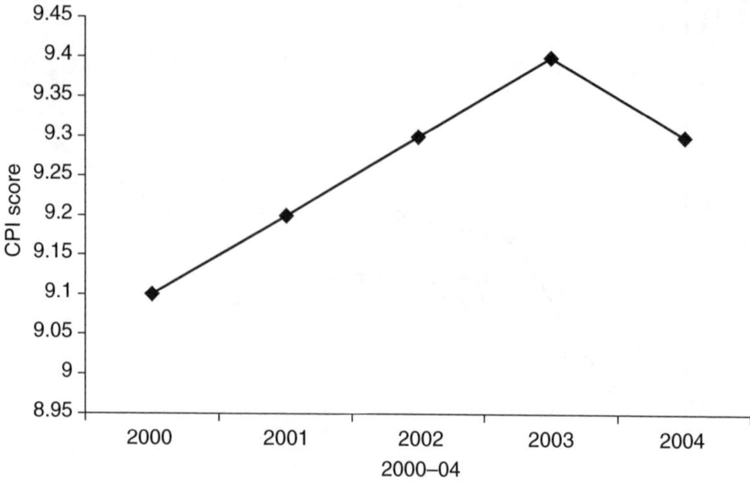

Figure 5.3   Corruption Perceptions Index (CPI) – Singapore
Source: www.transparency.org

TI's Bribe Payers Index (2002) provides a more definite contrast between East Asia and the US. Respondents were asked to identify the three governments most likely to be associated with unfair practice to gain unfair advantage in international trade and investment. This excluded direct bribery but included: diplomatic/political or financial pressure, pricing issues, tied-aid, the threat of reducing aid, tied defence/arms deals, favours/gifts to officials and tied scholarships/ education/healthcare. The position of the US is clear (Figure 5.4), and this was before the world became aware of Enron, and the deceit, coercion and nationalistic favouritism concerning the Iraq invasion and recon-struction. The methodology for the TI indexes is new and their long-term reliability and validity are hard to judge, especially when contrasting large and small countries. And paradoxically, it is also probable that a negative perception of corruption may arise because a country is publi-cizing new anti-corruption measures, as in East Asia. But the data suggest that it will be interesting to follow these indexes in the future. The tech-nical detail is perhaps less important than the perceptions that such indexes reflect or create. The moral authority of nations and the integrity of their leaders arise from such perceptions, not necessarily from reality.

Political violence is harder to quantify because this requires a consen-sus about what constitutes the legitimate use of violence. However, in

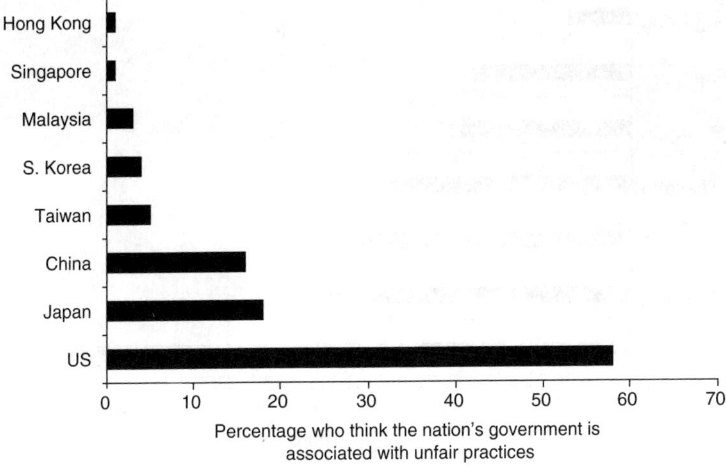

Figure 5.4   Bribe Payers Index (BPI)
Source: www.transparency.org

1999 the *Observer* newspaper created a Human Rights Index utilizing data from Amnesty the United Nations Development Programme (UNDP) and the US State Department.[78] One index (black bars) shows the simple ranking from ten 'headline abuses', and a more sophisticated weighted index (white bars) takes account of the idea that what happens in less wealthy countries can, to some extent, be excused (Figure 5.5). (The weighted index only shows the worst 100 countries, which excludes Hong Kong.) But whichever methodology is used, the ranking remains the same and, in comparison with East Asian tiger countries, the status of the US is above only South Korea and China. But this was in 1999, before the invasion and occupation of Afghanistan and Iraq, the infamous Guantanamo Bay prison camp, the draconian post-September 11 domestic legislation, and the attempt to derail the International Criminal Court.

In the third area, environment, the concept of the 'ecological footprint', developed by Mathis Wackernagel and Larry Onisto, gives an indication of how political leadership may be making an effort, or not, to achieve global environmental responsibility (Figure 5.6). But the index does, of course, also reflect a nation's state of industrial development. Although it is therefore problematic to compare the US with countries such as China, and an average 'tiger' footprint would be meaningless, the US still comes out as more profligate than other rich

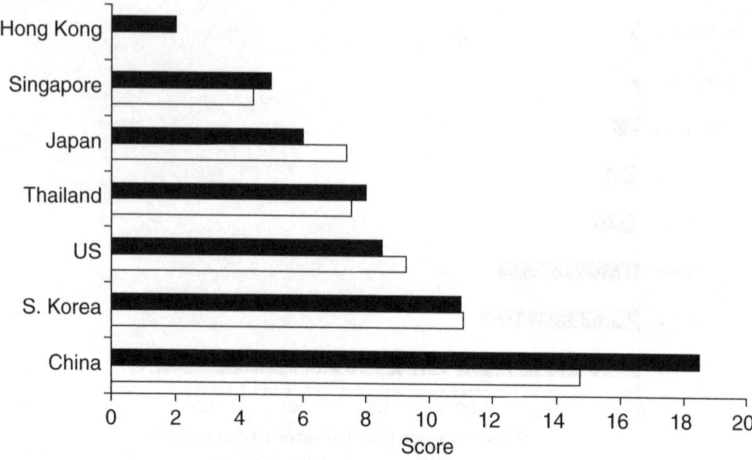

Figure 5.5   Observer Human Rights Index 1999
Source: www.guardian.co.uk/Tables/4_col_tables/0,5737, 94899, 00.html

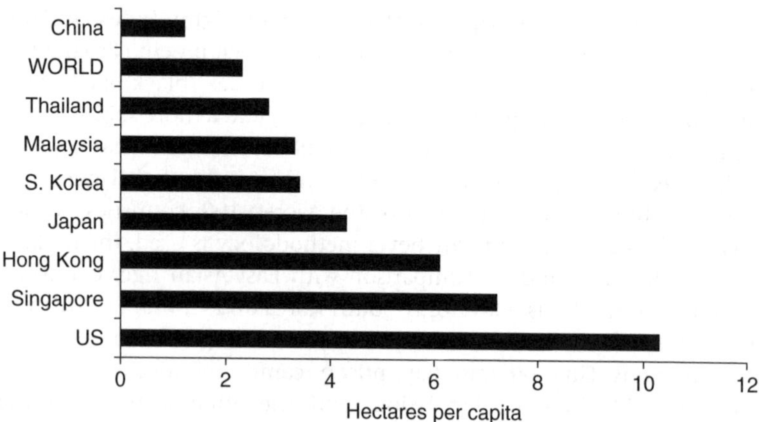

Figure 5.6   Ecological footprint – East Asia and US
Source: www.ecouncil.ac.cr/rio/focus/report/english/footprint/ranking.htm

East Asian nations such as Japan, Singapore and South Korea. Viewing
this, and many similar data, within knowledge of America's attempt to
frustrate the intent of the Kyoto and similar agreements, brings
America's moral authority into question.

Western values underpin most assessments of this nature, but more importantly Western power influences and controls many of the main messages. America has claimed the moral high ground about human rights through the State Department's country reports on human rights. But for five years now, China has issued its own country report about America.[79] The authors point out:

> For a long time, the US State Department has been publishing 'Country Reports on Human Rights Practices' every year. It presumes to be the 'Judge of Human Rights in the World' and ... denounces other countries unreasonably for their human rights status in compliance with its own ideology, values and human rights model. Meanwhile it has turned a blind eye to its own human rights problems ... The human rights record of the U.S. is absolutely not in accord with its position as a world power ... The United States should take its own human rights problems seriously ... and stop its unpopular interference with other countries' internal affairs under the pretext of promoting human rights.[80]

It is hard to find fault with the argument. The style of the Chinese report is similar to the US reports, except for the final section, 'Infringement upon human rights of other nations', which has no parallel in the US reports. The 2003 report points out that the US

> has resorted to the use of force against other countries 40 times since 1990s ... since 1945, the United States has attempted to overthrow more than 40 foreign governments, suppressed over 30 national movements, in which millions of people have lost their precious lives and many more people have been plunged into misery and despair.[81]

The rhetoric is predictable, but it does provide a contrasting contribution to the views about global accountability, and in the long term that is valuable. One further point is worth noting. Through the China website, it is possible to learn of the US reports, and therefore for Chinese people to find and read them. The US site makes no mention of China's contribution.

One of the failings of Western observers is perhaps to underestimate the depth of what East Asia can offer the world in terms of moral authority. The twentieth century is certainly problematic, but the region's previous history and recent strengths are different. The population has a philosophical tradition that is less encumbered by the conflicts and contradictions of religion, and the Confucian legacy has contributed much to global and leadership ethics. As symbols of peace, Japan is the only victim nation of nuclear weapons of mass destruction, and Korea can claim to be one of the few nations that has never aggressively invaded and occupied another country, except for a brief extension of its northern border centuries ago. The region now has considerable strength in ICT, and ICT has underpinned the social impetus that has driven global accountability. Korean 'netizens' provide a model of innovative e-democracy, and tradition and modernity combine. In ancient times, any commoner could petition a Korean emperor by banging a gong at the palace gates. The government's home page continues the tradition. Most East Asian governments now represent forms of managerial elites which are far from perfect but which are more likely to respond to accountability on a pragmatic basis in the future, as discussed further in the next section

The East may therefore be generating a 'pull' on moral authority, and the questionable hegemony of America and its allies is almost certainly creating a 'push' in the perceptions of those in other regions, not least the Middle East. In the context of this, much of what happens in the West could soon be presented as absurd. Consider what would be the Western view if a single East Asian leader took a nation into war in the Middle East, based on a Confucian edict or a Samurai code. Then consider the world view of a British prime minister who can take Britain into war anywhere on the basis of a centuries-old customary power called the Royal Prerogative.

A Global Leadership Responsibility Index

How might global shifts in leadership integrity and moral authority be tracked in the future? Could a Global Leadership Responsibility Index (GLRI) be created? One approach is to link data from indexes like those discussed above, reflecting the three sectors of leadership impact that structure this book, and to add further scores for countries that have supported relevant international agreements. This does not directly assess current leadership because of the long time frames of decision-making and outcomes. It indicates the degree of global responsibility embodied in cumulative policy and decision-making over the past fifty years. Figure 5.7 presents an impression of how an index might be created and the outcomes.

Political violence is the most difficult aspect to assess, because increasingly war is exported to countries other than those of the main protagonists. Data about people displaced as refugees from a particular country

Rank		Violence				Corruption			Environment			
		War	HRcodes	SECcodes	ICC/ICJ	CPI	BPI	CORcodes	Eco.Foot	ESI	ENVcodes	GLRL
1	Sweden	0	10	3	2	9.3	8.4	3	−5.9	7.2	5	**42**
2	Netherlands	0	9	3	2	8.7	7.8	3	−5.3	5.4	5	**38.6**
3	UK	−3	10	3	2	8.6	6.9	3	−6.2	7.5	5	**36.8**
4	Canada	0	9	3	2	8.5	8.1	3	−7.7	6.4	4	**36.3**
5	Belgium	0	10	2	2	7.5	7.8	3	−5.0	4.4	4	**35.7**
6	Germany	0	10	2	1	8.2	6.3	2	−5.3	5.7	5	**34.9**
7	France	−1	10	3	1	7.1	5.5	2	−4.1	5.5	5	**34**
8	Japan	0	8	3	1	6.9	5.3	3	−4.3	5.7	5	**33.6**
9	Spain	−1	9	3	2	7.1	5.8	1	−3.8	4.9	5	**33**
10	Italy	0	11	2	1	4.8	4.1	2	−4.2	5.0	4	**29.7**
11	S. Korea	0	9	1	1	4.5	3.9	3	−3.4	4.3	3	**26.3**
12	China	0	6	2	0	3.4	3.5	2	−1.2	3.9	4	**23.6**
13	Malaysia	0	2	2	0	5.0	4.3	2	−3.3	5.4	4	**21.4**
14	Russian F	−4	8	2	0	2.8	3.2	2	−6.0	5.6	2	**15.6**
15	US	−3	5	2	0	7.5	5.3	3	−10.0	5.3	0	**15.1**
Average		*−0.8*	*8.4*	*2.4*	*1.1*	*6.7*	*5.8*	*2.5*	*−5.1*	*5.5*	*4*	*30.4*
Max.		*−0*	*13*	*3*	*2*	*10*	*10*	*3*	*−0*	*10*	*5*	*56*

Figure 5.7   Global Leadership Responsibility Index (GLRI)
Key

War – conflicts between 1990 and 2002.[a]
HRcodes – Party to human rights (UNHCHR) instruments, 2005.[b]
SECcodes – Party to security codes.[c]
ICC/ICJ – Party to the International Criminal Court. Recognizing 'compulsory jurisdiction' of the International Court of Justice, 2005.
CPI – TI Corruption Perceptions Index, 2004.[d]
BPI – TI Bribe Payers Index, 2002.[e]
CORcodes – Party to anti-corruption codes, 2005.[f]
Eco.Foot. – Ecological Footprint, 1997.[g]
ESI – Environmental Sustainability Index, 2005.[h]
ENVcode – Party to environment codes, 2005.[i]
MAX – the maximum possible score in each column.

Notes on data presentation and standardization

- Countries are selected because full data are available in each area.
- HRcodes, SECcodes, CORcodes, ENVcodes, Covenants, ICC/ICJ, OECD/UN are binary inputs 1 = Yes, 0 = No. Countries score 1 for being full parties, not just signatories, except for the 2003 UN Corruption Convention which only had 22 full parties by 2005.
- CPI, BPI, Eco. Foot are calculations that reflect a 1–10 range. The ESI score divided by 10 to give a 1–10 range.
- Negative impacts are shown as a minus number, i.e. War, Ecological Footprint.

Sources

[a] Smith, D. (2003) Table of wars 1990–2002, in *The atlas of war and peace*. Earthscan: London. Open armed conflict, at least two parties, centrally organized, contested political power or territory, continuity between clashes, minimum 25 battle deaths in 12-month period in context of several hundred. 'Interventions' are omitted.

[b] UNHCHR, Country status, April 2005:

- Convention against Torture and Other Cruel Inhuman or Degrading Treatment or Punishment
- Optional Protocol to the Convention Against Torture and Cruel Inhuman or Degrading Treatment or Punishment
- International Covenant on Civil and Political Rights
- Optional Protocol to the International Covenant on Civil and Political Rights
- Second Optional Protocol to the International Covenant on Civil and Political Rights
- Convention on the Elimination of All Forms of Discrimination against Women
- Optional Protocol to the Convention on the Elimination of All Forms of Discrimination against Women
- International Convention on the Elimination of All Forms of Racial Discrimination
- International Covenant on Economic, Social and Cultural Rights
- International Convention on the Protection of the Rights of All Migrant Workers and Members of Their Families
- Convention on the Rights of the Child
- Optional Protocol to the Convention on the Rights of the Child on the involvement of children in armed conflict
- Optional Protocol to the Convention on the Rights of the Child on the sale of children, child prostitution and child pornography.

[c] Security codes:

- Mine Ban Treaty 1999, status 2005
- Chemical Weapons Convention 1993, status 2003
- Convention ... Suppression of Terrorist Bombings 2001, status 2005
- All Geneva Conventions and Protocols, status 2005.

[d] Transparency International, 2004 Corruption Perceptions Index.
[e] Transparency International, 2002 Bribe Payers Index.
[f] Corruption codes:
  - OECD convention for Combating the Bribery of Foreign Public Officials in International Business Transactions, status 2002
  - Signatory (not party) to the UN Convention against Corruption 2003
  - Regional: Inter-American Convention against Corruption 1996 *or* ADB/OECD Anti-Corruption Plan for Asia and the Pacific 2000 or Council of Europe Criminal Law Convention on Corruption 2002, status 2005.

[g] Wackernagel, M. & Onisto, L. (1997) *Ranking the ecological impact of nations* – www.ecouncil.ac.cr
[h] YCELP (2005) Environmental Sustainability Index – www.yale.edu/esi
[i]
  - The Kyoto Protocol 1998, status 2005
  - Convention on Biological Diversity 1992, status 2005
  - Cartegena Protocol on Biosafety 2000, status 2005
  - Rotterdam Convention … Hazardous Chemicals and Pesticides … 1998, status 2005
  - Stockholm Convention on Persistent Organic Pollutants, status 2005.

may reflect violence by leaders in those countries, but sometimes they reflect intervention by other countries, as in Iraq or Vietnam. National death rates may or may not reflect violence and neglect by national leaders. But data such as the 'Table of Wars' compiled by Dan Smith provide a reasonable start. He does not include all disputes, but selects on criteria that reflect active political violence. For example, the North–South Korea, China–Taiwan and Japan–Russia disputes are excluded, which arguably reflects the responsible conduct of leaders who have essentially 'de-linked' war and violence.[82] A further refinement is to exclude humanitarian 'interventions' that are considered to be responsible by many, if not all, nations. Support for international human rights codes, security conventions and the international justice institutions (ICC and ICJ) provides complementary data indicating a willingness to prevent and redress political violence.

Data concerning corruption are more sophisticated from Transparency International. These can be complemented by support for the OECD and UN Bribery and Corruption Conventions. The Urban Governance Index currently being developed by UN-HABITAT will provide further relevant data. African Union member states have all signed an anti-corruption convention; many Asia-Pacific states are implementing an Asian Development Bank (ADB)/OECD anti-corruption initiative; many American countries have signed the Inter-American Convention against Corruption. The Ecological Footprint and Yale Environmental Sustainability Index provide similar data about environmental responsibility, to which can be added support for the Kyoto Protocol and other environmental agreements.

As with any compilation index, vagaries in specific data are likely to be minimized through aggregation. More importantly, such a compilation reflects the realities and generic nature of leadership. Specific leaders often make major decisions across all these areas, and are therefore balancing and trading off the cost-benefits. For instance, although Sweden is usually seen as exemplary in terms of violence and corruption, its score is reduced by environmental impacts that are higher than in, for example, China which fares well in terms of war but does less well in terms of corruption. Taken together, we get an impression of the level of global responsibility of national leaderships.

The assumption underpinning a GLRI is that leadership, especially political and commercial, has significant responsibility for the outcomes that are indicated by the data. There are many methodological questions, for example the radically different ways in which input data have been created, and whether it is reasonable to equate numerically factors such as a ratification of a convention with a one-point score on the CPI. Data that only reflect national not global interests, such as GDP/GNP, are excluded. Data reflecting the outcomes of GDP/GNP, such as mortality rates and the UNDP development indicators, are not included because these may be outside the influence of national leaders. But despite the obvious reservations, the outcomes of this prototype index seem a plausible reflection of the degree of global responsibility shown by leaders in these countries over recent decades.

The contentious result is, of course, America. Its leaders appear to lack global responsibility mainly because of its environmental impacts, foreign policy and reluctance to support international codes. The latter point was made very evident by the ratifications of the UN covenants. Until 1992, America had ratified neither, but the 'axis of evil' countries – Iraq, Iran, Syria, Afghanistan and North Korea – had ratified both. (In 1992, the US ratified the covenant on Civil and Political Rights.) The pattern of American conduct is that US leaders have often helped to formulate and then signed international agreements, which encourages other countries to adhere, but then they do not ratify. If they do ratify, this is done in a way that prevents US citizens using the codes as a basis for challenge in the US courts – citizens are 'non-self-excluding' and individual petitions are disallowed. So once again there is a perception of deceit. The low position of the US does not arise from a methodological flaw. None of the indicators could reflect jealous, vindictive or sour-grapes perceptions of America. If anything the methodology should give the US an advantage, because it measures participation in the international institutions that were essentially set up and nurtured by American leaders, not least the UN itself. This point is particularly evident through a comparison of US support for the early international agreements (Figure 5.8). The US achieves the highest score. Even if such an index is, for some reason, biased against the big powers, the US still comes lower than China. And this represents another aspect of the argument above, that moral authority could shift from West to East.

Direct democratic accountability

In parallel with possible future influences on leadership integrity and moral authority, the institutional significance of global leadership accountability is likely to have an effect on democratic and other governance systems.[83] Across the world the trend towards direct democratic accountability has been paralleled by a declining public participation in traditional democratic processes. Between 1945 and 1990 participation

	L.of Nations 1919	Chemical War 1925	Geneva Con. 1949	Plant Con. 1951	Total
Belgium	2	1	2	2	7
Canada	2	1	2	2	7
France	2	1	2	2	7
Italy	2	1	2	2	7
UK	2	1	2	2	7
US	2	1	2	2	7
Japan	2	1	1	2	6
Netherlands	1	1	2	2	6
Spain	1	1	2	2	6
Sweden	1	1	2	2	6
China	2	1	2	0	5
Germany	0	1	1	2	4
Russia/Soviet Union	0	1	2	1	4
Malaysia	0	1	1	1	3
S. Korea	0	1	0	0	1

Figure 5.8   Early support for international agreements
Key
L.of Nations – League of Nations, 1919.
Chemical War – Geneva protocol for the prohibition of the use in war of asphyxiating, poisonous or other gases, and of bacteriological methods of warfare, 1925.
Geneva Con. – Geneva Conventions, 1949.
Plant Con. – Internional Plant protection convention, 1951.

in elections increased; since then the turnout figure has fallen from 68 to 64 per cent.[84] Is there a link? Over the past twenty years there have been many plausible explanations for the seeming decline in democratic participation.[85] But until recently little consideration has been given to the possibility that, far from being indifferent to politics, a globalizing public is simply finding other ways of achieving the basic aim of democracy – government by the people. And these ways now appear more immediate and more effective than the ballot box.

Sociologist and former director of the London School of Economics, Lord Tony Giddens, describes one aspect as 'continuous direct democracy',[86] reflecting a new era of constant media and internet questioning. Lord Howell elaborates:

Voters want service and ongoing accountability, not dictation and top down arrogance. And if they cannot get it they will employ ways other than through voting and party politics to satisfy their needs.[87]

The obvious example seems to be global 'anti-capitalism' demonstrations, such as the 'Battle of Seattle'. How do we equate a supposed declining interest in politics with the increasing numbers of young people who are prepared to spend much time and money organizing protests and travelling long distances to demonstrate their concerns at meetings of world leaders? Do they see traditional democracy now as too slow and localized, in the context of the speed and reach of global leadership? The president of the World Bank, James Wolfensohn, seemed aware of the trend when he argued that young people are

> searching for something they can believe in and not finding it in the leadership ... None of us is giving these young people a real, true sense of purpose and a true sense of values, and a true moral case in terms of the issues of development and the issues of social justice.[88]

So is direct democratic accountability an alternative?

Perhaps we are witnessing a mass realization that democracy, in the form of voting, is not the paramount mechanism for political accountability in a globalizing world. It is just one of a range of many options, which happened to be modestly effective in certain regional social contexts at particular periods of history. This idea is not new. Early in the twentieth century, the 'elite theorists' from Pareto and Mosca onwards argued that Western-style democracy gives very little power to the masses.[89] More effective media have changed this to some extent, but the outcome has probably been more to increase public scepticism of politicians than to control them. From a global perspective, it is notable that the US government actively promotes the idea of 'democracy' throughout the world, often tying aid to the improvement of democratic systems. But judging by the US withdrawal from the ICC and similar abdications of global responsibility, US leaders do not wish to promote accountability. Global democracy and global accountability are clearly separate in the minds of US foreign policy-makers, and the distinction now seems to be made in the minds of a globalizing civil society.

Is the global population now becoming distrustful of claims of representative global leadership? Parallels are being drawn between present world leaders at forums such as the G7/8 and previously despotic regimes such as apartheid South Africa in the way in which they claim legitimacy. Like the former South African politicians, members of the G7/8 summits claim that they are elected representatives, but they do not, even together, represent more than a small fraction of a global constituency. They take decisions that can have global implications but, like the South African apartheid leaders, their mandate is from a small privileged sector of those affected by their decisions.

There seems to be a similar questioning as to whether mainstream political parties now provide distinct choices of policy and governance, or are all much the same. ICT has increased the research capacity of political parties, and opinion polls provide convincing (if perhaps not accurate) indications of what the public seems to want, and all shades of the political spectrum respond to this. Opinion research may seem a welcome extension of democracy in practice. But the party analysts now use similar strategies to those employed in market research: ignore extremes and focus attention on the uncertain voters in a population. Aiming advertising at those who always or never buy a product is not worthwhile. Similarly, responding to the unquestioning followers or the constant critics of a party is a waste of resources. As a result, democracy is increasingly driven by the need to respond, or appear to respond, to those who might change their minds. Manifestos and party policy are now largely focused on this small but shifting middle cadre. As a result, democracy becomes government by the uncertain minority, and majorities with progressive views about the need for political change or with a traditionalist belief in caution are probably becoming aware that political parties will now never respond to their arguments through the ballot box.

Democratic voting fulfils two jobs in relation to accountability – selection of leaders and impending sanctions through loss of office, and decision-making. Democratic elections certainly do not have an impeccable record for selecting effective or moral leadership. Hitler, Mussolini and the leaders of apartheid South Africa are the classic examples. Although decision-making by vote usually produces clear-cut decisions, there is no intrinsic reason why a majority view will produce the best decisions. The main function of the voting process is to produce decisions that are accepted by the majority, not decisions that are optimum. Notable organizations such as the OECD opt to arrive at decisions by consensus rather than vote, as traditionally do many forums at all social levels in countries such as Japan.

Voting systems may well decline because many of the risk-related decisions that need to be taken in the future are decisions that are likely to be less good if based on a majority view, for example reducing car use, increasing food prices to reduce obesity in rich countries, and moderating oil consumption.[90] In theory, democracies could end up being ruled by particular groups simply because those groups have a policy of increasing their population. As population increase is not in the broader interests of human survival, this would be a perverse situation. Immigration and cross-border families provide another driver of change. In the US city of Maine, 33 per cent of the population were not born in the US. Non-nationals do not have the right to vote. How will a voting system defend its legitimacy if 51 per cent of constituents do not have the vote?

Managerial elites

A combination of these and other changing circumstances will probably lead to the public believing that who is in power is incidental – 'great men' will be out of favour. The important conditions will be that power elites do their jobs transparently and efficiently, and that they are accountable if they do not. It is sometimes argued that a benign dictatorship can be preferable to a corrupt democracy, if those conditions are met. In Pakistan, there was remarkably little opposition, locally or internationally, to the continued leadership of Pervez Musharraf after 1999. He did not fit the profile of a Western democratic leader, but he was technically competent and able to relate positively to other world leaders. In Africa, President Museveni's one-party democracy in Uganda has been tangibly supported by older democracies such as Britain, through generous aid loans and grants. But it is far from 'democratic' in Western terms.

The legitimacy of leadership in many of the successful developing nations of the past fifty years, such as South Korea and Singapore, has stemmed more from apparent economic success than the traditional Western criteria of good leadership and governance. But in fifty years, the South Korean public has moved quickly, through internal volition, from an apparent acceptance of authoritarian leadership for the sake of economic development to public trials and convictions against some of those leaders for corruption and political violence in 1996. In 2003, the election of Roh Moo-hyun was largely because the young '20–30' generation believed that he would be accountable. One of his first initiatives was to send emails to five million of the country's 'netizens' explaining his policies.

Legitimacy through a combination of technical efficiency and accountability is not a new idea in elite theory. In 1942, James Burnham proposed that future power would be in the hands of 'managerial elites' who were technically efficient but may have no other significant claim to legitimate power.[91] This is sometimes recognized. In the context of protests against the dictatorial style of Haiti's president, Jean-Bertrand

Aristide, an opposition leader, Frandley Denis Julien, said, 'We are in a struggle that is pitting the people against the state. We need institutions. We need leadership. We don't need a charismatic leader to replace Aristide.'[92]

One outcome is that managerial elites might remain in power for long periods simply because, while they remain efficient, there is no particular reason to remove them. President Mubarak of Egypt came to power unexpectedly following the assassination of Sadat in 1979, and was considered a stop-gap leader for six months. He then became known as 'the executive leader', and has held power ever since despite turbulent circumstances. His authoritarian style may be questionable, but there has been no large-scale violence in the country. Even before Mubarak's era, in 1975, George Lenczowski was talking of the 'special case' of the 'organizational elite' in relation to the Middle East, which

> does not conform to this standard [democratic and capitalist] model of qualitative superiority, but rather, secures and maintains its political influence and power as a result of other characteristics ... But whether their predominance depends upon manipulation or the use of force, the ultimate skill is organisational ... Such leadership possesses qualities and attributes which, whether ascriptive or based on merit, inspire trust in a large part of the community. This trust ... does not produce unquestioning approval of the leadership's policies under all circumstances. It merely means that the role played by the dominant group or individual is not considered contrary to the conventional patterns and expectations of the society.[93]

Perhaps those 'patterns and expectations' will soon be that leadership is fully accountable to those who are affected by its decisions, including a global community.

To the notions of management or organizational elites can be added the ongoing argument that Western-style democracy is not suited to all countries. Countries with independent cultural histories, such as China, and those at a fragile stage in development, such as Uganda, may do better with accountable managerial leadership. Non-democratic forms of government can be very successful, but there are no perfect models. The traditionally-based constitutional monarchy in Jordan has produced exemplary post-war leaders who have been supported on domestic and international levels, despite a near impossible task of reconciling Arab and Western demands in order to maintain the economic viability of the country. In contrast, Swaziland's monarchy is a dictatorship constantly criticized, both by its subjects and by the international community.

The elite theorists claimed that pluralist power elites embody greater accountability,[94] and this has perhaps led to a conflation of notions of democracy and plurality in the minds of political commentators. There are democratic leaderships within plural contexts which are seen as increasingly unaccountable – the US provides the obvious example.[95] And conversely, it is perfectly possible to have non-democratic leadership within a plural system which is highly accountable. The leaders with the greatest claim to global legitimacy – those of the UN organizations – are generally not elected. But they are highly competent, are very visible to the international community, and are held to account from every possible direction. Is it coincidence that there have been no significant global demonstrations against the UN and its organizations? (The WTO and World Bank are not UN organizations.) The EU is another example of a managerial elite that is largely accountable through bureaucratic systems rather than elections. Other emergent forms of global governance will almost certainly opt for managerial elites because of the practical problems of implementing voting-based systems of accountability.

In his book *The arts of leadership*, Keith Grint concludes with a discussion headed, 'The end of leadership?'[96] He clarifies his question:

> I do not imply by this that we can do without leadership, but probably we could do without leaders. That is to say, that it may well be a requirement of all human organizations that some individual or group takes responsibility for ensuring its direction is one that secures the interests of the members. But this is a long way from saying that we need leaders – if that implies a group that is clearly and permanently distinguished from the rest.

His main argument is that all leaders inevitably make mistakes, so 'the most successful leaders appear to be those who cultivate the least compliant followers, for when leaders err – and they always do – the leader with compliant followers will fail'. From this perspective, members of the G8 and others who are now being called to account by a global civil society should, in principle, welcome the trend towards less compliant followers as it should ultimately assist their survival. Grint continues that the problem for leadership in the modern world is

> to develop an organizational culture that prevents the leader from believing that his or her position of responsibility is a reason for omnipotence.[97]

The global accountability movement represents a global 'organizational culture' that may be moving the concept of leadership into a new era.

But paradoxically perhaps the most significant outcome of leadership accountability will be local – a greater support for law enforcement and administrative justice generally. Public cynicism about the rule of law stems mainly from knowing that throughout history power elites have evaded accountability. As mentioned in the Introduction, the view at the start of the twentieth century was that leaders could never be made accountable in the long term. Until now, there has always been 'one law for the rich and one law for the poor'. If global leadership accountability can redress this, it could bring about a significant change in the support for and the democratic functioning of justice, administrative and governance systems, locally and globally.

Implications

- **Journalists** and **historians** influence future challenges.
  - Journalists look backwards in history, while historians look forwards, which closes the **time gap** through which miscreant leaders have escaped identification.
  - **The Western construction** of leadership history is revised, and heroes become despots.
  - **American leadership** is the main focus of challenge.

- Leadership **integrity** ('moral capital') is more significant in a globalizing world, because it is the only basis for the relationship between leaders, 'distant others' and global populations.

- **Leadership deceit** has been hard to redress because:

  (i) laws address harm caused by **interpersonal, not public, deceit**
  (ii) **cheating** must entail clear losses and gains, but leadership cheating usually entails intangible losses and gains
  (iii) the outcome of **incitement** must be a crime, and leaders control criminal law.
    - Laws to redress '**Causing harm through deceiving a population**' emerge.

- **Moral authority moves from West to East**, as the post-Second World War/Cold War claim to authority by the West erodes.
  - The perception of deceitful leadership in the West creates a '**push**' of moral authority.

- East Asian leaders broaden their emphasis on economic development to include moral development which creates a '**pull**'.

- A **Global Leadership Responsibility Index** (GLRI) can be created from other relevant indexes and the willingness to support international agreements and institutions.
  - **American leadership** responsibility has declined over forty years, and the ranking is now below China, Japan and South Korea.

- Democratic voting assumes less importance than **direct democratic accountablility**.
  - '**Managerial elites**' are favoured more and survive longer than traditional leadership and 'great men'.
  - Up-system accountability will increase **public respect for justice and administrative systems**, because the law will be seen to be equitable irrespective of power.

Changing Power Relations

The power of leaders changes in relation to the power of the population around them (Chapters 1, 5 and 6). In 1995, world leaders attended a special commemorative meeting of the General Assembly, to mark the 50th anniversary of the UN. Photos and extracts from their speeches record the images they presented at that time. Over the past ten years, many of those leaders have faced significant accountability challenges. Even since the 1999 General Assembly, the status of some world leaders has changed dramatically.

7

Prime Minister PV Narasimha Rao of India states that developing countries must be adequately represented in the Security Council (1995)

In 2000 Rao was convicted of bribing opposition MPs, and he became the first Indian prime minister to receive a prison sentence.

UN/DPI photo by E. Schneider

8

President Pasteur Bizimungu of Rwanda stresses that mankind must never again witness horrors of genocide or ethnic cleansing (1995)

Bizimungu became president following the 1994 genocide. In 2000, he resigned and was put under house arrest, and his privileges as a former head of state were removed. In 2004, he was sentenced to 15 years in prison for embezzlement, inciting violence and associating with criminals.

UN/DPI photo by G. Kinch

9

President Jean-Bertrand Aristide of Haiti says that the United Nations helped bring about a political miracle in restoring democracy to Haiti (1995)

Months after becoming President in 1990, Aristide was forced out by a military coup, and was helped by the US military to return in 1994. He was forced out into exile again in 2004, a day after Washington questioned 'his fitness to govern'.

UN/DPI photo by G. Kinch

10

President Jacques Chirac of France says that the United Nations affirms a universal conscience through legal instruments and programmes of action (1995)

In March 2001, amid allegations of corruption, Chirac became the first head of state of the French Fifth Republic to receive a formal witness summons by an investigating judge. A petition for his impeachment was then started. Chirac's daughter Claude was questioned, and his wife, Bernadette Chirac, became the first French first lady to be required to give evidence. Chirac's immunity was contested in the courts, and could be removed after he leaves office.

UN/DPI photo by G. Kinch

11

Prime Minister Benazir Bhutto of Pakistan says that the principles of equal rights and self-determination lie at the heart of the UN Charter (1995)

Bhutto was twice removed from office, accused of corruption. She then went into self-exile in Dubai, and in 2006 Interpol issued a warrant for her arrest.

UN/DPI photo by G. Kinch

12

Vice-President Taha Marouf of Iraq says that a unipolar world has left mechanisms of the United Nations at the service of narrow self-interest (1995)

Marouf was the only Kurd in the Baath Party. Following the US-led invasion and occupation of Iraq, he was put on the US Central Command's list of the 55 most-wanted Iraqis. He was taken into custody in 2003.

UN/DPI photo by G. Kinch

13

Alberto Fujimori, President of the Republic of Peru, addresses the General Assembly: 'The concepts of democracy and fairness must prevail ... the twentieth century has been deeply scarred by enduring human failures: by greed and lust for power, by hot blooded hatreds and stone-cold hearts' (UN General Assembly, September 1999)

In December 2000 Fujimori resigned and sought asylum in Japan, from where he could not be extradited. He was simultaneously sacked by Congress as 'morally unfit' for office. Three months later, charges of 'illicit enrichment' and inappropriate use of public funds were filed against him, and then in March 2001 legal proceedings were started in relation to the murder of 14 Marxist rebels in 1997. By August, the Peruvian Congress had removed Fujimori's immunity to permit his arrest for murder.

UN/DPI photo 201462C

14

Mohammad Nawaz Sharif, Prime Minister of Pakistan (UN General Assembly, September 1999)

In July 2000, Sharif was put in prison and tried by Pakistan's anti-terrorism courts. He was given several life sentences for corruption, hijacking, tax evasion, embezzlement and terrorism. The military government agreed to commute his sentence from life in prison to exile in Saudi Arabia.

UN/DPI photo by Eskinder Debebe

15

Frederick Chiluba, President of the Republic of Zambia (UN General Assembly, September 1999)

In 2002, the Zambian government removed Chiluba's presidential immunity, and he was then charged with 59 counts of 'theft by a public servant' – of stealing two million dollars of public money while in office.

UN/DPI photo 201565C

16

William Jefferson Clinton, President of the United States of America (UN General Assembly, September 1999)

In April 1999, Judge Susan Webber Wright ruled that Clinton gave 'false, misleading and evasive answers' in a 1998 deposition in which he denied having sexual relations with a member of his staff, Monica Lewinsky. He was fined $90,686, an unprecedented penalty against a serving US president. He also paid $850,000 to Paula Jones to settle a sexual harassment case. He was impeached, but acquitted by the Senate. The Arkansas Supreme Court Committee on Professional Conduct complained of 'willful professional misconduct by lying under oath in a court of law', the first time a serving president had received a formal legal ethics complaint. In October, the Supreme Court disbarred Clinton from practising law before the high court, his Arkansas law licence was suspended for five years and he was fined $25,000. He agreed to the fine and suspension on 19 January 2001. The next day he left the presidency.

UN/DPI photo 201463C

6
Conclusion: The Accountability Webs

The impetus driving global leadership accountability is evident at all levels of society. It is neither a centrally dictated top-down innovation nor entirely a bottom-up social movement, and it is not a clear class war between the masses and the elites. It is a diversity of unlinked formal and non-formal responses to a common problem, the personal abuse of power. It represents a new aspect of global ethics which populations and elites are starting to uphold on a case-by-case basis, depending on the merits of the issue and reflecting the multiple loyalties of the individual actors.

The elements of leadership accountability and the main arguments of this book are presented in Figure 6.1. Deceit and cheating are at the centre of abuses of power, because leaders *must* deceive to do harm on a significant scale. If not deliberate, leadership deceit arises because of the 'cumulative lock-in' that traps those who do not do U-turns when they realize they have made bad decisions. The 'social impetus' that challenges leadership wrongdoing is an instinctive evolutionary-based response to deceit, extended globally by modern ICT. This awakens the 'dormant precedents' of leadership accountability, some extending back many centuries. Joseph d'Oronzio talks of 'inexorable' and 'serendipitous' 'webs of accountability',[1] and global civil society movements are personalizing protest and building accountability webs on a framework provided by the formal international and national systems that aim to uphold 'international public order'. This conclusion summarizes the implications from the previous discussions and addresses the questions raised in the Introduction that framed the subsequent chapters. It ends with a vision of how a global senior citizenry may come to play a role in leadership accountability in the future. The lessons are for those learning to be or learning to question leaders.

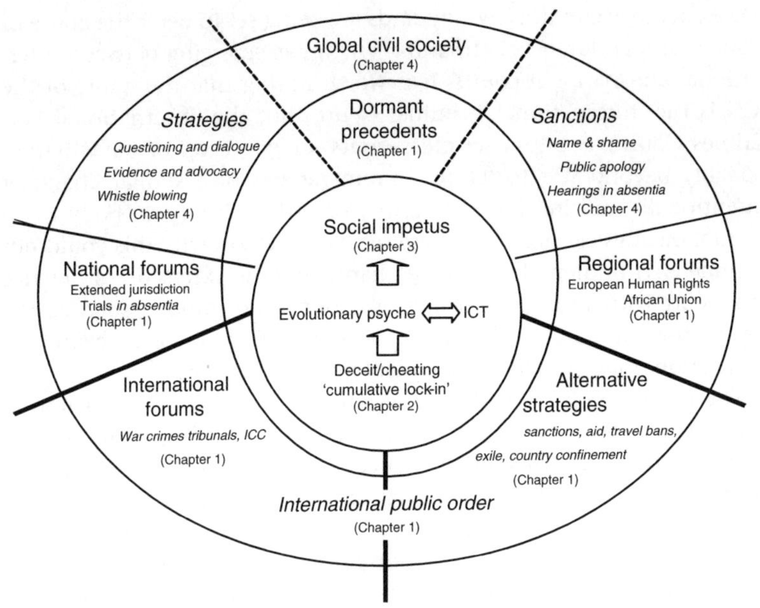

Figure 6.1   The webs of global leadership accountability

Personalized up-system accountability

Up-system leadership accountability has increased significantly in recent years, and in some instances there has been a clear domino effect around the world. This includes a 'second track' challenge to low-profile local power elites. Many new precedents are being set, and there is likely to be a fundamental change in the relationship between leaders and those they have traditionally viewed as followers.

There is certainly a new frame of reference for leadership accountability for political violence, stemming from the Nuremberg and Tokyo tribunals, and given a new life by the ending of the Cold War. Paradoxically, the fact that these post-war trials were essentially victors' justice probably gave a force to the challenge to wrongful leadership that would have taken many more years to evolve in other circumstances. Those who created the retrospective rules of accountability for these one-sided post-war trials did so with astonishing clarity and determinism. But they probably did not envisage that these principles would become 'dormant precedents' that could then be used to hold their successors to account. New standards are being set to deter the abuse of women and children in war, and a synergy is emerging between international and national courts. It is worth noting that the name of the ICC is the 'International Criminal Court', not the 'International War Crimes Court'. The ICC statute permits an extension of its activities, possibly beyond war to 'Other inhumane acts of a similar character intentionally causing great suffering, or serious injury to body or to mental or physical health'.[2] There seems no reason why this could not include environmentally mediated harm, and the extension of practice may start with cases concerning environmental impacts such as the destruction of water supplies or poisoning of crops, or to economic corruption, for example to engender 'ethnic cleansing'.

The turning point for addressing political and economic corruption was not so clear, but arguably it also stemmed from the end of the Cold War and the strengthened insistence on 'good governance' that has been associated with international aid and institutions such as the World Bank, IMF and OECD. As in the area of political violence, the original thrust of the anti-corruption initiatives was from the leaders of the powerful Western nations against less powerful and supposedly errant leaders in other countries. There was surprise that the accountability net has quickly swung round to catch those in the wealthy nations who were implicated with corruption in less developed countries or were equally corrupt in their own countries. Some of the strongest action has been within North East Asia, and like economic development in the tiger economies, economic accountability seems to be happening at astonishing speed and the West seems slow to grasp the significance of this.

In the area of environmental security, there were no clear turning points. Until recently, the mainstream environmental movements have sought to redress and prevent abuse of the environment, but have rarely tried to make specific powerful individuals answer for environmental harm. The action in response to the Chisso mercury poisoning at Minamata Bay in the 1950–60s brought senior leaders to account, albeit late and largely symbolically. This has had an ongoing influence throughout Japan, but post-war international dynamics prevented that example from having wider impact, because any form of solidarity with people in Japan was not fashionable at that time. The avoidance of personal accountability in relation to the Union Carbide poisoning in Bhopal and the nuclear power disaster in Chernobyl seemed setbacks in international ethics. This has reinforced the perception that powerful industrialists, often in collaboration with politicians, can evade responsibility.

Even so, there seems to be an increase in low-profile instances of personal accountability in response to environmental victimization, through domestic health and safety legislation, and this will probably set significant precedents that will later be used more widely. Again, North East Asia has been showing a lead, which is largely unnoticed in the West. It seems that within the Confucian ethic, the notion of 'responsibility' is more closely associated with 'blame'.[3] A responsible leader is automatically culpable and open to sanction, even if he or she is not tangibly at fault, and is duty-bound to resign and accept sanctions to protect institutions and companies from further shame.

Currently there seems to be an underestimation by power elites of the potential of an accountability movement to revitalize and extend 'dormant precedents'. In relation to violence, many political leaders ignored the latent longevity of the Second World War Nuremberg–Tokyo ethos. The US Alien Tort Claims Act of 1789 gave American courts international jurisdiction at a time before its contemporary implications could have been imagined, and was rediscovered in 1976 when it was used against Paraguayan despots.[4] It is now being used to challenge US and foreign power elites for a spectrum of misdeeds across the world. In 2005, Vietnamese war victims who claimed compensation for exposure to Agent Orange used precedents from 1984 when chemical companies had made payments to US war veterans who had also been exposed. Fraud and deceit laws framed to hold the mafia to account were used to charge US tobacco company executives with causing widespread health problems. Blair was challenged through his own vanguard Human Rights Act and Freedom of Information legislation which subsequently permitted journalists to discover the seemingly disingenuous way that he had presented legal advice about the Iraq war. In some circumstances, the dynamics of globalization are now activating dormant precedents so fast that they become boomerang precedents.

Precedents and jurisdiction are extending as national courts claim or are given international reach, international law is incorporated within national legislation, and the EC spreads its influence within and beyond the European Union. Precedents are also extending across sectors. In 2003, new British anti-terrorism legislation had the effect of making any bribes from British companies to politicians and industrialists in other countries illegal, even if the act was carried out wholly outside the UK. Human rights abuses by US security companies operating in Iraq were brought to court using US laws designed to redress mafia crime.[5] In 2005, a Dutchman, Frans van Anraat, was charged with genocide because he provided the Iraqi regime with Japanese and US chemicals that were used to poison 5,000 Kurds in Halabja. This was the first time a Dutch citizen had been tried for genocide, it implicated two countries that were claiming to have brought the Iraqi regime to account, and it entailed commercial dealings and environmental impacts in the context of war. Trials and other hearings *in absentia* represent another form of extending jurisdiction. These are likely to increase in legitimacy if powerful people continue to try to evade justice by refusing to attend democratically supported forums.

Traditional forms of immunity are being overturned or circumnavigated, and extradition is creating a world in which despots can 'hide but cannot run'. However, this will engender new forms of self-protection by power elites in the form of mutual sanctuary, media control, authoritarian laws, and distraction through challenging others or creating public fear of intangible enemies. There also needs to be recognition that occasionally the self-imposed exile of a despot, to a remote region of a country such as Nigeria, may be the most effective way to remove a problematic individual without causing collateral damage to whole nations.

The reemergence of dormant precedents, extension of precedents and jurisdiction, and removal of immunity create uncertainty and unpredictability. This might appear to be rough justice, but it means that powerful people can now never quite be sure that questionable deeds that seemed legal last year will be legal next year. They cannot predict if another nation or international forum will suddenly spread its jurisdiction to a country where they are operating improperly or are hiding. A chemical that industrialists have claimed is 'not shown to be dangerous' might suddenly be listed as a poison, and documents leaked that show that this was previously known. And they can never be certain that laws will not be made to act retrospectively. The director-general of the Association of the British Pharmaceutical Industry seemed aware of this when he told British MPs at the start of 2005, 'The aggressive programme of class-action suits which have emerged must be factored into a company's decisions-making.' He talked of 'A major shift of perception in risk and benefit.'[6]

The concept of 'international public order' provides an appropriate framework for the future accountability movement. This extends the principle of local public order legislation to prevent and redress harmful force and violence, the creation of fear, and deliberate provocation on a global scale. The maintenance of justice can deter feuding at a global level, just as it can at a village level. But whatever the next steps in global accountability, they must be based on mutually agreed ethics and rules, not the self-interested power of the global bully.

The retributive aspect

The challenge to the Western leaders responsible for invading and occupying Iraq was unprecedented, and seemingly hard to explain because they had presented themselves as upholding rather than transgressing the new norms of global accountability. The challenge against them was largely intra-group and did not represent traditional sides, nationalistic sentiments or loyalties. A better understanding of the post-9/11 events is likely to come from viewing Bush, bin Laden, Blair, al-Qaida and their supporters as all trying to do the same thing – bring leaders to account.

The challenges against the American and British leaders were fuelled by the new digitalized global media, which also set new standards for the publication of hitherto secret documentation. Leaders had tried to distance themselves from challenge by using next step agencies, but these opened the possibility for other novel legal approaches to redress wrongdoing. The emergent public realization was, as Margaret Mead had pointed out sixty years ago, that wars are made by leaders, and populations on all sides usually suffer from, rather than being a party to, international political violence. The main public perception was of the seemingly deceitful nature of many of their leaders – that the rationale for the conflict had been based on misleading information. As a result it is likely to become increasingly difficult for political leaders to construct the means for war based on contrived images of good and bad sides, or on unverifiable information.

The invasion of Iraq, like many wars, seemed to happen because of a coincidence of interests among allied parties *and* among adversaries, rather than from a single issue. But 'cumulative lock-in' seemed to play a significant part. From overhasty intuitive and belief-based decisions, British and American leaders trapped themselves in a spiral of events within which deceit built on deceit and turning back and seeking verifiable evidence became a vanishing possibility. The lesson both for leaders and public is to value U-turns, if they reflect better evidence or understandings.

The weaker parties in retributive accountability will resort to 'instruments of mass effect' to achieve their ends, including the precipitation of own goals by their enemies, and the 'winners' will be those with the least to lose, not those with most power. But 'instruments of mass effect' may come to be seen as a progressive form of conflict because, compared with traditional military force, they 'de-link war from violence'.

Dialogue with 'terrorists' will become inevitable, as it always has been. International agreement about the rules of leadership accountability and intervention, following the example set by the African Union (AU), could reduce 'terrorism' because 'terrorists' would lose their moral high ground. If a vision of George W. Bush sitting around a table negotiating with Osama bin Laden seems fanciful, consider the potential of new ICT to facilitate meetings like this. There is no reason why in the future such negotiations cannot be held through a sophisticated form of videoconferencing with security systems to ensure the immunity of all parties. We could even have a UN communications department with its own satellite – 'Mediator 1' – dedicated to this process. And around the world, we could all participate, creating a truly global democratic process, much as the contributors to BBC web discussions are already doing.

If the trend towards internationally legitimate global accountability is repressed by power elites, retributive aspects will continue, and the outcome is likely to be more attacks like those of 9/11 or like those against other symbols of Western domination such as McDonald's. This new non-state violence is distinct from traditional freedom-fighting or protest, which has direct messages and goals – such as those of the IRA, PLO, Eta or animal rights activists. And the punitive and authoritarian state responses are far from upholding the modern view of a just war or maintaining public order. In this new global feuding the target is the message and the goal is the at-any-cost humbling of an enemy constructed through characterizations such as 'capitalists', 'terrorists', 'imperialists' or 'fundamentalists'.

An extreme development of this new retributive ethos could see more attacks like that on the United Nations headquarters in Baghdad in August 2003, in which one of the most effective and popular UN leaders, Sergio Viera de Mello, was killed. Within traditional logic, in this instance the target was seemingly not the message. Those responsible did not seem to acknowledge the difference between the US and the UN, and other extremists might not see the difference between McDonald's and an Oxfam coffee shop. Similarly, the suicide bomber and terrorist leader do not now seem to see the difference between an armed enemy soldier and a one-month-old baby, but then neither apparently do the pilots of the high-altitude B52 bombers and their Western politico-military leaders. Global feuding does not function in terms of traditional retributive logic, and that is the distinct and worrying aspect of its threat.

The evolutionary–technology synergy

The perception of deceit was central to the challenge to American and British leaders over the invasion of Iraq. Almost all harm done by leaders employs deceit in some form, because that is the only way to use carrot-and-stick means to get others to implement questionable leadership goals. But why do 'disinterested others' respond to deceit done by 'distant others' in other countries which may never have the potential to affect them? Why would a barber in a remote fishing village in Japan be concerned about what American leaders do in the Middle East?

Much of the motivation underpinning leadership harm stems from our evolutionary psyche – favouring kin, mating (sex), territoriality, and breaking contracts and cheating. Psychological studies find that the same traits that make a good liar also make a good leader. But human beings are programmed to detect and respond to cheating as this was a key evolutionary survival skill. The new contemporary aspect is that ICT can expand this personal 'cheater-detector' skill into a global intelligence network. ICT compresses time and space, constructs a perception that everyone can be part of an accountability system, shifts immunity from the powerful to the people, and creates a massive feedback loop within a newly networked 'global brain'. One outcome of this new global dynamic is that it will be harder for belief-based leadership to achieve moral authority on a global scale because, rightly or wrongly, any form of belief will inevitably be perceived as deceitful somewhere in the world.

A simple 'social impetus–trends theory', reflecting the synergy between our evolutionary psyche and technological change, can explain and predict social change on a global level. This is likely to provide very reliable perspectives on global change, because the basic mental characteristics of human beings are common across the world, and so too is the nature of new technology which is reasonably predictable by the time it is used globally.

The personalization of protest

Civil society organizations are increasingly directing their energies at identifiable power elites. But there is no unified global accountability movement, and the nature of the challenge is not a simple people versus the powerful dynamic. The different islands of civil society endeavour may fuel one another through global information networks which create a unifying context but, taken on a world scale, planned cooperation is rare. The common sense of purpose arises, as argued in Chapter 3, more from a common human evolutionary history, our innate 'cheater-detector' and the dislike of deceit, within a common technological context which amplifies the dynamics globally.

Civil society strategies include questioning and dialogue, evidence-gathering and advocacy, and whistle-blowing; the sanctions include naming and shaming, public apology, and non-formal hearings *in absentia*. Increasingly, these strategies and sanctions are coordinated. Organizations also unify traditionally polarized social groups. The actors are not driven by nationalist interests, political parties, social class or other group alliances. They have multiple loyalties and operate and judge on a case-by-case basis.

Ensuring the legitimacy of civil society action is crucial, and this is likely to mean a shift from direct action towards the 'accountability of accountability'. This could entail encouraging 'smart accountability' – well-focused action against the most significant wrongdoing – 'policing the police' – ensuring that force is not used politically or retributively by any power elites – and commending good acts of leadership, particularly sensible U-turns.

A more accountable world will not be achieved by indiscriminate witch-hunts, scapegoating or the mass removal of 'regimes', because the potential collateral damage will be too great. The general conclusion by political analysts over past decades, which was exemplified again in Iraq, is that killing or even arresting many thousands of people is not a viable means to achieve leadership accountability. It does not permit the asking of good questions and achievement of good answers in a manner that permits a society to move forward from despotic leadership, as in South Africa.

'Smart accountability' will come about through identifying those who are most powerful and most culpable in relation to agreed local or global standards, requiring them to answer for their conduct and take responsibility for their actions, and surgically removing those who are most to blame from the possibility of doing further harm. This needs to be done in the way that is most effective and appropriate in the context of the events. That may range from the high-profile justice of a UN court, to lowly back-door exile in a remote land. It may be achieved by creating social isolation, by humbling as in traditional Japanese *dogeza*, or by 'country arrest' through court summonses which preclude a despot travelling to the jet-set countries. It may happen through a truth and reconciliation process, or by naming and shaming on a state-of-the-art website or in a school history textbook.

Changing power relations

The accountability movement is being fuelled by journalists looking back and historians looking forward, which is closing the 'time gap' through which despots have often evaded identification. The Western construction of recent leadership history will inevitably be revised, heroes will become despots and American leaders will probably come under the greatest scrutiny. Global leadership accountability will become a significant new determinant of the legitimacy, integrity, moral authority and therefore of the power of leadership of all types, because accountability and integrity are the only way to build relationships between world leaders and distant global followers.

As the awareness of the centrality of deceit to leadership harm increases, so too will the awareness that laws honed by centuries of leadership self-interest rarely preclude harmful deceit by power elites. Laws are currently framed in such a way that deceit only has legal meaning on a localized interpersonal level, not if it involves the use of power to deceive a population to cause harm to third parties. Laws about cheating require proof of tangible losses and gains as a result of the deceit, but the gains to power elites and losses to a population are usually intangible. In parallel, law on incitement is hard to apply because the outcome must be a criminal act, and political leaders control how crime is defined. To improve up-system accountability in law, we may see legislation to address 'Causing harm by deceiving a population'. Such legislation could also cover misuse of the internet and other media, faith-based crime, religious extremism and harmful cults. Precedents for such legislation are already emerging from the international tribunals, and in relation to education systems.

There is growing evidence that the moral authority claimed by the West may move to the East, as conduct such as that over Iraq lowers respect for Western leaders and 'pushes' authority away, and up-system moral development in the East catches up with economic development and 'pulls' authority towards the region. As a measure of leadership responsibility more generally a Global Leadership Responsibility Index can be constructed, based on relevant existing indexes and measures of support for international codes and institutions. Although US leaders set up these institutions and therefore should appear in a good light, this proposed index indicates that leaders from North East Asia are now showing more responsibility than those from America.

It seems likely that future generations will become increasingly indifferent to the apparent political hue of a government or ideology of a chief executive, and not very concerned which forms of proto-global governments, transnational corporations or NGOs are in the ascendancy. Allegiances will increasingly be framed in terms of preventing and redressing particular wrongdoings, and less in relation to nationalist and other group identities. With a few exceptions, future generations will probably be little more than entertained by the personalities and qualities of individual leaders as they come and go. They will favour honest, efficient 'managerial elites' over charismatic 'great man' leadership, and voting systems may become secondary to 'direct democratic accountability'.

As populations become aware that justice systems are at last putting everyone beneath the law, even the most powerful, the respect and support for the principles and practice of the law generally will probably increase. If the historical legacy of 'one law for the rich and one law for the poor' is overcome, global leadership accountability has the potential to rewrite history for future generations.

A global senior citizenry

Unless the world again becomes polarized and frozen by another superpower stand-off, the next fifty years will probably see more rapid developments to uphold international public order than the past half-century. It is very unlikely that powerful people will be able to evade the dormant precedents, rule only through deceit, and time out justice as they have in the past. The trend is that those who have abused their power will now live with the expectation of being called to account at some point in their life, even when they are in their nineties.

The striking aspect of high-profile court cases of the past decade is not just that the defendants are senior in terms of position, but that so many are also senior in terms of their age. This change, combined with the trend for longer healthy lifespans and ageing populations, will mean that increasingly cases will be brought when the main protagonists are out of power, perhaps decades after the misdeeds were committed. This represents a novel dynamic because protest and challenge have usually been associated with younger people.

In the future, many of the challenges may be among a global senior citizenry who are no longer protected by, and also no longer constrained by, their positions. Former peers will settle old scores, as Pinochet discovered, or try to demonstrate their revised views of international morality like Robert McNamara. There will also be a retired cadre of civil society activists with time to pursue fully the goals that eluded them during their careers, using the ever increasing power of ICT across the world. And there will be a retired cadre of civil servants and commercial administrators who will know where to look for incriminating evidence.

One curious example embraces this dynamic, and many other elements of leadership accountability that have been identified throughout this book. In 2005, the conviction for manslaughter of the Ku Klux Klan leader ('Kleagle'), Edgar Ray Killen, occurred 41 years after the killings. The media had maintained a global awareness of the issue through newspaper interviews with Klan members and the film *Mississippi burning*, made in 1988. Killen was not the murderer, but was found responsible through what was essentially 'command control', for recruiting and motivating the actual killers. His actions were belief-based, a perverted Christian ideology of racial hatred. He had been a religious leader, a Baptist minister, and a sign with the Ten Commandments was in his front garden. He appeared in court at the age of 80 in orange prison dress, in a wheelchair and attached to an oxygen supply, and was given a 60-year prison sentence. Witnesses, many of them civil rights activists, were from a similar generation, and the case is likely to fuel further investigations of former police chiefs and public officials. In the same week another 80-year old, John Rigas, was given a 15-year prison sentence for corporate crimes in the US.

Imagine a future when international leaders of the present era – such as Kofi Annan, George W. Bush, Hans Blix, Tony Blair and Clare Short – are retired. And so too are the soldiers sent to Iraq and the civil servants who had to implement the US and British policies. By that time the present-day 'terrorists' may be seen in a different light as it is argued that their 'instruments of mass effect' caused less harm than the military means of retributive accountability employed by the *circa* 9/11 Western leaders. Consider this in the context of a strengthened international jurisdiction, such as is being created by the Alien Tort Claims Act and Belgian courts, and fully affirmed Nuremberg–Tokyo principles which clearly outlaw the use of war to implement policy.

Envisage a new world order where China has ethically annexed Korea, Japan and Taiwan, is using Australia and New Zealand as a source of cheap skilled labour, and has embraced international law within its own justice system like European countries. This morally developed North East Asia may well be playing a central role in the international courts, and some or all of the UN HQ may have moved to Beijing.

This will be within an era when the 'axis of evil' has become, in Kofi Annan's words, 'a new Silk Road' of transport routes created by the recent UN Asian Highway Agreement.[7] This will facilitate a mutually dependent relationship between North East Asia and the Muslim world, based on an oil-for-technology trade, and perhaps also a string of Chinese universities across the region.[8] At the western end of the route will be an indigenous Iraqi government that may have amended the remit of its own courts to turn the dormant precedents created by the Iraq Tribunal in the 2000s against the American and British leaders who set them, and to include extradition agreements with North East Asia. Place all this in the context of an America that may be losing its moral authority through a perception of a leadership that demonstrates diminishing global responsibility.

The weakness of those who abuse their power – the bullies and the cheats, village or global – is that they usually fail to see that their power changes in relation to the changing power and ethics of the population around them. And in a fast-changing global world this self-deception will increasingly bring about their downfall.

Notes

Introduction

1. Hall, M.N. (1997) *International law*. Cambridge University Press: Cambridge, p491.
2. Michels, R. (1915) *Political parties*. Free Press: Glencoe, p423.
3. Williams, Christopher (2001) *Leaders of integrity: ethics and a code for global leadership*. UN University Leadership Academy: Amman.
4. Bortin, Meg (2004) Poll finds little faith in politicians worldwide, *International Herald Tribune*, 19 November, p1.
5. Ciulla, Joanne B. (1998) *Ethics: the heart of leadership*. Praeger: London.
6. Williams, Christopher (2001) *Leaders of integrity: ethics and a code for global leadership*. UN University Leadership Academy: Amman, p154.

1 An Era of Accountability

1. Falk, Richard (2001) *War crimes and collective wrongdoing*. Blackwell: Oxford, p115.
2. Hain, Peter (2001) *The end of foreign policy?* Fabian Society/RIIA: London, p25.
3. Howell, David (2002) Britain faces constitutional earthquake, *International Herald Tribune*, 15 January, p7.
4. Vulliamy, Ed (1999) 'Neutrality' and the absence of reckoning: a journalist's account, *Journal of International Affairs*, 52(2), pp15–33.
5. Keane, Fergal (2001) Two arrests, one message to human rights abusers, *The Independent (Review)*, 30 June, p3.
6. O'Neill, Onora (2002) *A question of trust*, BBC Reith Lectures – www.bbc.co.uk/radio4/reith2002/lecture_text.shtml
7. Unpublished comment at '2005: make or break for global governance', lecture, London School of Economics, 18 February 2005.
8. Jackson, Robert L. (1945) Statement by Justice Jackson on War Trials Agreement, *Department of State Bulletin*, US Government: Washington, 12 August.
9. Williams, Christopher (2001) *Leaders of integrity: ethics and a code for global leadership*. UN University Leadership Academy: Amman, pp65–74.
10. Thompson, Mark (2000) *Forging war: the media in Serbia, Croatia, Bosnia and Herzegovina*. University of Luton Press: Luton, pv.
11. Bush, George (2004) The driving force behind America's foreign policy, *The Independent*, 26 February, p35.
12. Carr, Simon (2004) Blair takes the Mel Gibson approach to conflict in Iraq, *The Independent*, 4 March, p10.
13. Berkeley, Bill (2001) *The graves are not yet full: race, tribe and power in the heart of Africa*. Basic Books: New York, p263.
14. Drakulic, Slavenka (2004) *They would never hurt a fly: war criminals on trial in the Hague*. Viking Press.

15. BIICL (2001) Khmer Rouge – legislation to investigate and prosecute leaders, *Bulletin of Legal Developments*, 1, 15–22 January, p7 (British Institute of International and Comparative Law: London).
16. Robertson, G. (1999) *Crimes against humanity*. Allen Lane: London.
17. *The Economist* (2001) Can sanctions be smarter?, 26 May, pp29–31.
18. Somavia, Juan (1996) *Civil society and the security council* (Remarks to the NGO working group on the Security Council) – http://www.globalpolicy.org/security/docs/somavia.htm
19. UN (1985) *UN Declaration on … Victims of Crime and Abuse of Power*, Article A.11.
20. ECCHR, Article 13.
21. International Conversation Civil and Political Rights, Article 3a.
22. BBC (2002) US renounces world court treaty, *BBC News Online*, 6 May.
23. Annan, K. (1999) *The question of intervention: statements by the Secretary General*. UN: New York, p31.
24. Black, Ian (2003) International criminal court comes to life, *The Guardian*, 11 March, p14.
25. Roth, Ken (2004) *War in Iraq: not a humanitarian intervention, World Report 2004* – http://hrw.org/wr2k4/3.htm
26. Stephen, Chris (2004) *Judgement day: the trial of Slobodan Milosevic*. Atlantic: New York.
27. *The Economist* (2001) Can sanctions be smarter?, 26 May, pp29–31.
28. HRW (2001) Yugoslavia – link EU aid to co-operation with international tribunal, *Human Rights Watch News*, 7 February.
29. HRW (2001) Yugoslavia: link US aid to co-operation with tribunal, *Human Rights Watch News*, 1 May.
30. Mydans, Seth (2004) Khmer Rouge leader offers an ignorance defense, *International Herald Tribune*, 5 January, p3.
31. Pyongyang Tribunal indicts U.S. for crimes against Koreans – www.korea-np.co.jp/pk/194th_issue/2003072603.htm
32. Keane, Fergal (2001) Two arrests, one message to human rights abusers, *The Independent (Review)*, 30 June, p3.
33. Coughlan, Sean (2003) Do human rights stand a chance post-9/11?, *Times Higher Education Supplement*, 29 August, pp18–19.
34. Oh, John Kie-Chiang (1999) *Korean politics*. Cornell University Press: Ithaca, NY, p164.
35. Becker, Jasper (2005) 'Down with Kim': dissenters in North Korea find their voice, *The Independent*, 19 January, p27.
36. Robertson, G. (1999) *Crimes against humanity: the struggle for global justice*. Allen Lane: London, p248.
37. Rubin, A.P. (1997) *Ethics and authority in international law*. Cambridge University Press: Cambridge, p173.
38. Robertson, G. (1999) *Crimes against humanity: the struggle for global justice*. Allen Lane: London, p248.
39. Barkun, M. (1968) *Law without sanctions*. Yale University Press: New Haven, CT.
40. Barkun, M. (1968) *Law without sanctions*. Yale University Press: New Haven, CT.
41. Braithwaite, J. (1994) Resolving crime in the community: restorative justice reforms in New Zealand and Australia, in K. van Eden, The way of Inkundla, *Child & Youth Care*, January 1997, p10.

42. Tutu, Desmond (2000) *No future without forgiveness*. Rider: London.

43. Wilson, R.A. (2001) *The politics of truth and reconciliation in South Africa: legitimising the post-apartheid state*. Cambridge University Press: Cambridge.

44. Campbell, Duncan (2001) Past masters, *The Guardian*, 20 June, p16.

45. Gray, Kevin (2001) Menem indicted over arms dealing, *The Independent*, 5 July, p15.

46. Popham, Peter (2004) A conspiracy of silence is broken, *The Independent*, 2 July, p28.

47. BBC (2004) Japan awards WWII damages, *BBC News Online*, 9 July.

48. Williams, C. & Lee, Y.-J. (2005) The minds of leaders: de-linking war from violence, in Brian Walker (ed.), *Preparing for peace – by asking the experts to analyse war*. Westmoreland General Meeting: Kendal.

49. Tzu, Sun (1981) *The art of war*. Hodder & Stoughton: London, p17.

50. HRW (2000) *The Pinochet precedent: how victims can pursue human rights criminals abroad*. Human Rights Watch: New York, pp9–10.

51. Robertson, Geoffrey (1999) *Crimes against humanity*. Allen Lane: London, p371.

52. Steinhardt, R.G. & D'Amato, A. (eds) (1999) *The Alien Tort Claims Act: an annalistical anthology*. Transnational Publishers: New York, p3.

53. Castle, S. (2001) Nuns convicted of mass slaughter in Rwandan convent, *The Independent*, 9 June, p18.

54. *The Jordan Times* (2001) Massacre survivors open proceedings against Sharon, 19 June, p4.

55. Mead, M. (1940) Warfare is only an invention – not a biological necessity, *Asia*, 40(8), pp402–5.

56. Williams, C. & Lee, Y.-J. (2003) *The minds of leaders: de-linking war and violence*, Preparing for Peace – www.preparingforpeace.org/lectures.htm

57. Pinker, Steven (1997) *How the mind works*. Allen Lane: London, p511.

58. World Bank (1989) *Sub-Saharan Africa: from crisis to sustainable growth*. World Bank: Washington.

59. Actionaid (1995) Multilaterals and accountability, in *The reality of aid*. Earthscan: London, pp19–23.

60. World Bank – www1.worldbank.org/publicsector

61. Central Vigilance Commission (India) – http://cvc.nic.in

62. Kenya ITSA – http://www.cddc.vt.edu/knownet/articles/kenya-case.html

63. Bardacke, T. (2000) Thai minister guilty on assets claim, *Financial Times*, 29 March, p12.

64. BBC (2000) Nigeria's senate president impeached, *BBC News Online*, 8 August, www.news.bbc.co.uk

65. BBC (2000) Burma sacks forty corrupt officials, *BBC News Online*, 16 November.

66. BBC (2000) Azerbaijan corruption verdict: 16 officials jailed, *BBC News Online*, 21 November.

67. BBC (2000) Lebanese official jailed for corruption, *BBC News Online*, 21 December.

68. BBC (2000) Top Russian general charged with corruption, *BBC News Online*, 13 December.

69. BBC (1998) Imelda Marcos acquitted, *BBC News Online*, 6 October.

70. *The Japan Times* (2000) Ill Suharto charged with graft during presidency, 4 August, p4.

71. McKinnon, Ian (2000) Former Indian premier jailed for corruption, *The Independent*, 13 October, p18.
72. Popham, P. (2001) Revenue boss's downfall exposes India's corrupt customs, *The Independent on Sunday*, 15 April, p18.
73. Bedhi, R. (2001) India in turmoil over internet bribes sting, *Daily Telegraph*, 15 March, p20.
74. National Accountability Bureau (NAB) – www.nab.gov.pk
75. Lee, Yun-Joo (2003) Perceptions of leadership and development in South Korea and Egypt, unpublished PhD thesis, School of Oriental and African Studies, University of London.
76. Lee, Yun-Joo (2003) Perceptions of leadership and development in South Korea and Egypt, unpublished PhD thesis, School of Oriental and African Studies, University of London.
77. BBC (2004) Raking over S Korea's colonial past, *BBC News Online*, 26 August.
78. OPEN – www1.worldbank.org/publicsector/egov/seoulcs.htm
79. Hutzler, C. (2000) Chinese execute deputy governor in sleaze scandal, *The Independent*, 9 March, p17.
80. BBC (2001) China steps up war on corruption, *BBC News Online*, 5 January.
81. Lloyd, John (2001) How the rich rule politics again, *New Statesman*, 26 March, p10.
82. Gittings, John (2000) China's graft net scares little fishes, *The Guardian*, 23 August, p13.
83. Editorial (2000) The French old guard must now accept new rules, *The Independent*, 20 December, p3.
84. Ramonet, Ignacio (2001) Presidents under pressure, *Le Monde diplomatique*, August, leader.
85. Lichfield, John (2001) Has France become a banana republic?, *The Independent*, 26 January, p5.
86. Lichfield, John (2004) Judge who convicted Juppé complains of intimidation, *The Independent*, 2 February, p19.
87. BBC (2001) Dumas corruption trial to start, *BBC News Online*, 22 January, http://news.bbc.co.uk
88. *The Economist* (2001) Liberty, equality, impunity?, 21 July, p9.
89. BBC (2001) French corruption suspect seized, *BBC News Online*, 2 February.
90. Lichfield, John (2001) French presidents condoned bribery, says ex-Elf boss, *The Independent*, 19 May, p16.
91. Pacitti, Domenico (2001) Running on a clean-up ticket, *Times Higher Education Supplement*, 11 May, pp19–20.
92. Popham, Peter (2004) Berlusconi to face bribery charges as court withdraws his immunity, *The Independent*, 14 January, p27.
93. Lane, David (2004) *Berlusconi's shadow: crime, justice and the pursuit of power*. Allen Lane: London.
94. Griffiths, Katherine (2004) Lies, cover-ups, fat cats and an oil giant in crisis, *The Independent*, 20 April, pp1,4,5.
95. BBC (2002) Corporate bribery verdict in Lesotho, *BBC News Online*, 20 May.
96. *The Economist* (2002) Small place, big wave, 21 September, p89.
97. O'Shaughnessy, Hugh (2004) Tax havens to face new UN code on corruption, *The Independent on Sunday*, 19 December, p3.

98. Cray, Charles (2000) U.S. undermines POPs Treaty, *Rachel's Environment & Health Weekly*, 703, 13 July – www.rachel.org

99. Blix, Hans (2004) Comment on MTV interview, 'Caught between Iraq and a hard place' (transcript) – www.mtv.com/bands/i/iraq/news_feature_031203/index5.jhtml

100. BBC (2004) Global warming 'biggest threat', *BBC News Online*, 9 January.

101. BBC (2004) Shell boss 'fears for the planet', *BBC News Online*, 17 July.

102. Connor, S. (2005) Bush accused of 'fiddling while world burns' by ignoring climate change, *The Independent*, 7 March, pp4–5.

103. Williams, C. (ed.) (1998) *Environmental victims: new risks, new injustice.* Earthscan: London.

104. Global Witness – http://www.oneworld.org/globalwitness/

105. California Global Corporate Accountability Project – wysiwyg://9/ http://www.nautilus.org/cap/

106. Dinham, B. (1998) Introduction to the Charter of Rights Against Industrial Hazards: for communities, workers and the protection of the environment, in C. Williams (ed.), *Environmental victims: new risks, new injustice.* Earthscan: London, pp151,181.

107. Williams, C. (1997) *Terminus brain: the environmental threats to human intelligence.* Cassell: London, p198.

108. Minamata Forum (1999) *Minamata exhibition.* Minamata Forum: Tokyo.

109. See Williams, Christopher (1998) *Environmental victims: new risks, new injustice.* Earthscan: London.

110. Fedorychyk, Serghiy (1994) Experiences of Chernobyl, unpublished paper presented to the Permanent People's Tribunal, London.

111. Sarangi, Satinath (1998) The movement in Bhopal and its lessons, in C. Williams (ed.), *Environmental victims: new risks, new injustice.* Earthscan: London.

112. Shah, Saeed (2004) US giant's defence on Bhopal could be undermined by company papers, *The Independent*, 6 December, p23.

113. Shah, Saeed (2005) Dow ordered to appear in court to answer for deadly Bhopal gas leak, *The Independent*, 8 January, p52.

114. Kahn, Joseph (2004) Gas producer blamed for deaths, *International Herald Tribune*, 5 January, p3.

115. Allison, R. (2000) Director guilty in landmark toxic waste dumping case, *The Independent*, 26 February, p5.

116. Carrell, Severin (2001) Porton Down scientists face prosecution, *The Independent on Sunday*, 8 July, p4. And Carrell, Severin (2004) MoD to be sued over Porton Down tests, *The Independent on Sunday*, 2 May, p. 7.

117. Arthur, Charles (2004) Revealed: UK's worst polluting companies, *The Independent*, 27 July, p19.

118. Usborne, D. (2005) Mining executives 'won't pay with their lives for asbestos poisoning', *The Independent*, 9 February, p23.

119. Friends of the Earth (2004) Study assesses ExxonMobil's contribution to global warming (press release) – www.foe.org/new/releases/104exmob.html

120. Stevenson, Rachel (2004) Big tobacco in the dock as America prepares for biggest ever lawsuit, *The Independent*, 13 August, p41.

121. Williams, C. (1997) *Terminus brain: the environmental threats to human intelligence.* Cassell: London, Chapter 11, 'Law and regulation', pp189–206.

122. Connor, S. (2005) The end for GM crops, *The Independent*, 22 March, p1.

123. HRW (2000) *The Pinochet precedent: how victims can pursue human rights criminals abroad*. Human Rights Watch: New York.

124. HRW (2000) Paraguay: Stroessner extradition effort hailed, *Human Rights Watch News*, 11 December.

125. HRW (2001) Mexican foreign minister's decision to extradite Argentine torturer hailed, *Human Rights Watch News*, 5 February.

126. BBC (2001) Arrest warrant for war crimes suspect, *BBC NewsOnline*, 19 February.

127. Cormier, B. (2001) Argentinean 'dirty war' officers to face justice, *The Independent*, 7 March, p13.

128. The National Commission to Review the Working of the Constitution of India – consultation papers – http://ncrwc.nic.in

129. Gumbel, Andrew (2004) Former president faces genocide charges, *The Independent*, 24 July, p32.

130. OECD (2000) *Trust in government: ethics measures in OECD countries*. OECD: Paris.

131. BBC (2000) Court removes bar to Gaddafi trial, *BBC News Online*, 20 October, www.bbc.co.uk.

132. Lichfield, J. (2000) Jacques' house starts to crumble, *The Independent on Sunday*, 1 October, p23.

133. Henley, Jon (2001) French MPs move to impeach Chirac, *The Guardian*, 22 May, p10.

134. Lichfield, John (2001) Chirac kickbacks case may be sent to appeal court, *The Independent*, 19 July, p14.

135. Haphen, E. (2002) Nixon quit for less, *International Herald Tribune*, 15 January, pp1,2.

136. Popham, Peter (2004) Berlusconi to face bribery charges as court withdraws his immunity, *The Independent*, 14 January, p27.

137. Moore, Mike (1998) *A brief history of the future: citizenship of the millennium*. Shoal Bay Press: Christchurch, p76.

138. BBC (2000) Peru congress sacks Fujimori, *BBC News Online*, 22 November, http://news.bbc.co.uk

139. Parry, R.L. (2000) Fujimori turns Japanese to evade Peruvian justice, *The Independent*, 13 December, p13.

140. Traynor, Ian (2000) Vote gives Putin chance of life-long criminal immunity, *The Guardian*, 30 November, p17.

141. Williams, C. (1998) *Environmental victims: new risk, new injustice*. Earthscan: London, pp8–9.

142. Carrel, Severin (2004) UK troops in Iraq face new court threat, *The Independent on Sunday*, 28 November, p2.

143. Robertson, Geoffrey (1999) *Crimes against humanity: the struggle for global justice*. Allen Lane: London, p261.

144. *BBC News*, 14 April 2000 – http://news2.thls.bbc.co.uk/hi/english/world/europe/newsid%5F713000/713547.stm

145. Sandford, G. (2000) Milosevic puts Nato leaders on trial, *The Guardian*, 19 September, p17.

146. Boyes, R. (2000) Nazi doctor 'killed 772 children', *The Times*, 21 March, p21.

147. HRW (2000) Chile: Pinochet to undergo questioning, *Human Rights Watch News*, 21 December.
148. BBC (2000) Iran arrests judges, *BBC News Online*, 31 December.
149. InterAction Council – www.asiawide.or.jp/iac/intro/EngIntro.htm
150. McGirk, Jan (2001) Elephant reveals size of Mexico's problem with corrupt customs, *The Independent on Sunday*, 4 February, p20.
151. Keane, Fergal (2004) Africans are now taking responsibility for the failings of their own leadership, *The Independent*, 28 February, p43.
152. BBC (2002) Pope condemns US church sex abuse, *BBC News Online*, 23 April.
153. Cornwell, Rupert (2004) Church reveals 4,400 priests were accused of child sex abuse, *The Independent*, 28 February, p39.
154. Howden, D. (2005) Bribery scandal engulfs Greek church, *The Independent*, 4 February, p2.
155. Williams, C. (1995) *Invisible victims: crime and abuse against people with learning difficulties.* Jessica Kingsley Publishers: London.
156. O'Neill, Onora (2002) *A question of trust*, BBC Reith Lectures – www.bbc.co.uk/radio4/reith2002/lecture1_text.shtml
157. Kuper, J. (2005) We have finally begun to care about child soldiers, *The Independent*, 29 March, p31.
158. House of Lords (1999) Judgment – *Regina v. Bartle and the Commissioner of Police for the Metropolis and other Ex Parte Pinochet. Regina v. Evans and another and the Commissioner of Police for the Metropolis and others Ex Parte Pinochet (On appeal from a Divisional court of the Queen's Bench Division)*, 24 March.
159. Shaw, M. (1997) *International law.* Cambridge University Press: Cambridge, p782.
160. Williams, C. (1996) Environmental victimisation and violence, *Aggression and Violent Behaviour*, 1(3), pp191–204.

2   Global Feuding: Regime Change and Retribution

1. BBC (2004) W Africa war crimes court to open, *BBC News Online*, 10 March.
2. Chomsky, Noam (2004) *Hegemony or survival: America's quest for global dominance.* Penguin: London, pp38–9.
3. CIS (2004) Instruments of mass effect, in *A new security paradigm, The Cambridge Security Seminar, 30–1 July 2003.* The Cambridge Programme for Security and International Society: Cambridge University, pp46–50.
4. *Independent Record* (2004) Bush defends taking US to war in Iraq, 27 January – http://66.102.9.104/search?q=cache:3EQ9PNoWGXcJ:www.helenair.com/articles/2004/01/27/ap/Headlines/d80biba80.txt+Independent+grave+and+gathering+threat+to+America+and+the+world%E2%80%99.&hl=en&ie=UTF-8
5. CIA (2002) *Iraq's mass destruction weapons programs* – http://www.cia.gov/cia/reports/iraq_wmd/Iraq_Oct_2002.htm
6. US (2003) Letter from the United States government to the UN Security Council President, S/2003/351, 21 March.
7. Cook, Robin (2004) It will be a gross injustice if the intelligence services get the blame, *The Independent*, 4 February, p31.

8. 10 Downing Street (2002) *Iraq's weapons of mass destruction. The assessment of the British Government* – http://www.number-10.gov.uk/output/page271.asp

9. *Daily News* (2003) Right as reign Blair declares – http://www.nydailynews.com/news/story/101824p-92178c.html

10. Cornwell, Rupert (2003) Is the search for weapons over?, *The Independent*, 19 December, p1.

11. BBC (2004) Iraq 'ended nuclear aims in 1991', *BBC News Online*, 12 August.

12. BBC (2004) In quotes: Blair and Iraq weapons, *BBC News Online*, 6 October.

13. *The Independent* (2004) Iraq: the final verdict, 7 October, p5.

14. BBC (2005) *Panorama*, 20 March.

15. BBC (2005) Bush pledge over intelligence, *BBC News Online*, 31 March.

16. Richards, Steve (2005) Reinvigorated, Blair sets out his stall for historic third term, *The Independent*, 21 April, p2.

17. Hills, Sarah (2005) We were wrong about Iraq, admits Blunkett, *Metro*, 14 March, p15.

18. *The Mail* (2004) Iraq casualties, 26 July, p19.

19. Roberts, L. *et al.* (2004) Mortality before and after the 2003 invasion of Iraq: cluster sample surveys, *The Lancet*, 29 October – http://image.thelancet.com/extras/04art10342web.pdf

20. Randall, David (2004) 10,433 and rising: the non-combatant body count, *The Independent on Sunday*, 15 February, p20.

21. Sengupta, Kim (2004) 777 Americans and 67 Britons … , *The Independent*, 17 May, p1.

22. Buncombe, A. (2005) Aid worker uncovered America's secret tally of Iraqi civilian deaths, *The Independent*, 20 April, p22.

23. Gumbel, A. (2005) Americans turn against Bush and a war on Iraq that is getting nowhere, *The Independent*, 9 June, p32.

24. Brown, C. (2005) US lied to Britain over use of napalm in Iraq war, *The Independent*, 17 June, p10.

25. Vidal, Gore (2004) The war against lies, *The Independent on Sunday*, 18 January, p25.

26. Vidal, Gore (2004) The war against lies, *The Independent on Sunday*, 18 January, p25.

27. BBC (2004) In quotes: Iraq–al-Qaida links, *BBC News Online*, 18 June.

28. BBC (2004) Iraq WMD threat 'misrepresented', *BBC News Online*, 8 January.

29. Whitaker, Raymond (2004) More trouble for Blair as another claim against Saddam falls apart, *The Independent*, 11 January, p16.

30. BBC (2004) Rumsfeld questions Saddam–Bin Laden link, *BBC News Online*, 5 October.

31. Buncombe, Andrew (2004) Saddam's WMD never existed, says chief American arms inspector, *The Independent*, 24 January, p1.

32. Borger, Julian (2004) The inspector's final report, *The Guardian 2*, 3 March, pp2–3.

33. BBC (2004) US expert slams WMD 'delusions', *BBC News Online*, 5 June.

34. *Metro* (2004) Powell in U-turn on Iraq weapons, 26 January, p2.

35. Cornwell, Rupert, (2004) Belligerent Bush takes campaign to American heartland, *The Independent*, 22 January, p31.

36. BBC (2004) George Bush defends Iraq invasion, *BBC News Online*, 27 January.

37. Buncombe, Andrew (2004) CIA deny 'imminent threat' claim, *The Independent*, 6 February, p9.
38. BBC (2004) Iraq: mindset behind intelligence failures, *BBC News Online*, 6 February.
39. BBC (2004) Powell admits evidence mistake, *BBC News Online*, 2 April.
40. BBC (2004) Lawyers hail Guantanamo ruling, *BBC News Online*, 29 June.
41. Buncombe, Andrew (2004) US torture at Guantanamo 'increasingly repressive', *The Independent*, 1 December, p27.
42. Russell, Ben (2003) Exposed: Blair, Iraq and the great deception, *The Independent*, 18 June, p1.
43. Rangwala, Glen (2003) The lies that led us into war, *The Independent on Sunday*, 1 June, p2.
44. Dejevsky, Mary (2004) Libya decided 10 years ago against developing WMD without pressure, Foreign Minister says, *The Independent*, 11 February, p6.
45. Cornwell, Rupert (2004) White House 'exaggerated extent of WMD breakthrough', *The Independent*, 26 March, p6.
46. Marks, Kathy (2003) Australian case for Iraq war was 'fabricated', *The Independent*, 23 August, p8.
47. Cornwell, Rupert (2004) Powell might not have pushed for war had he known of lack of evidence, *The Independent*, 4 February, p8.
48. *The Independent* (2004) George W Bush and the real state of the Union, 20 January, p1.
49. Waugh, Paul (2004) Intelligence chief's bombshell: 'We *were* overruled on dossier', *The Independent*, 4 February, pp1,2,6,7.
50. Wilson, Graeme (2004) Sacked: the intelligence chief who dared to criticise Blair over war claims, *The Mail*, 26 July, p8.
51. BBC (2004) Transcript of Clare Short interview, *BBC News Online*, 26 February.
52. Waugh, Paul (2004) I quit because the war against Iraq was illegal ... , *The Independent*, 28 February, p7.
53. Sengupta, Kim (2004) US terror laws 'damage human rights', *The Independent*, 17 February, p6 (describing the IISS report – *Human rights and counter-terrorism in America's Asia policy*).
54. Woodcock, Andrew (2004) Scarlett asked for 'lies' in WMD report, *The Independent*, 1 August, p15.
55. Brown, Colin (2004) No 10 fails to deny Scarlett's influence on survey group, *The Independent*, 3 August, p2.
56. Russell, Ben (2004) A war of words, *The Independent*, 20 August, pp1,4–5.
57. Mueller, A. (2005) After the storm, *The Independent on Sunday Magazine*, 20 March, p25.
58. Morris, Nigel (2004) No 10 employs extra staff to open post, *The Independent*, 8 May, p2.
59. Grice, A. (2005) Labour MPs to fight on anit-war ticket, *The Independent*, 30 March, p2.
60. BBC (2005) Blair appeals for voters' trust, *BBC News Online*, 4 May.
61. Buncombe, Andrew & Huggler, Justin (2004) The torture victim, *The Independent*, 6 May, p1.
62. BBC (2004) Rumsfeld to testify on Iraq abuse, *BBC News Online*, 7 May.

63. Watt, N. (2004) UK troops broke the law, admits Hoon, *The Guardian*, 14 May, p3.

64. Russell, Ben (2004) Government 'misled MPs' over inquiries into abuse in Iraq, *The Independent*, 9 June, p5.

65. BBC (2004) UK accused of major rights abuses, *BBC News Online*, 26 May.

66. BBC (2004) ICRC still concerned on Iraq jail, *BBC News Online*, 19 May.

67. Sengupta, Kim (2004) Officer who rallied UK troops condemns 'cynical' Iraq war, *The Independent*, 17 September, p8.

68. BBC (2004) Abuse row woman 'followed orders', *BBC News Online*, 12 May.

69. BBC (2004) Iraq abuse 'ordered from the top', *BBC News Online*, 15 June.

70. Buncombe, Andrew (2004) General tells Congress army leadership was to blame for mistreatment of Iraqis, *The Independent*, 12 May, p6.

71. Cornwell, Rupert (2004) Rumsfeld implicated in Abu Ghraib abuse by damning report, *The Independent*, 25 August, p22.

72. *The Independent* (2005) 'We were only following orders'. But whose orders?, 20 January, pp1,5–9,38.

73. Gray, John (2004) Power and vain glory, *The Independent Review*, 19 May, p3.

74. Gumbel, Andrew (2004) Prisoners sue Abu Ghraib security firms, *The Independent*, 12 June, p36.

75. Williams, Christopher (2001) *Leaders of integrity: ethics and a code for global leadership*. UN University Leadership Academy: Amman, p69.

76. Cornwell, Rupert & Russell, Ben (2004) Bush backtracks over case for war against Saddam, *The Independent*, 9 February, p1.

77. Penketh, Anne (2004) Bush and Blair behaved as if they were on a 'witch-hunt' over Iraqi weapons, says Blix, *The Independent*, 8 March, p29.

78. Morris, Nigel (2004) Tutu tells Blair: apologise for 'immoral' war, *The Independent*, 16 February, p1.

79. Ekklesia (2004) http://www.ekklesia.co.uk/content/news_syndication/article_2004_03_22_carter.shtml

80. Peta, Basildon (2004) Mandela marks 10-year anniversary with speech criticising Britain and US, *The Independent*, 11 May, p25.

81. BBC (2004) Spain 'to withdraw Iraq troops', *BBC News Online*, 15 March.

82. Nash, E. & Russell, B. (2004) Spain's PM ups pressure on Blair: 'You can't organise a war with lies', *The Independent*, 16 March, p1.

83. Barder, Sir Brian *et al.* (2004) A letter to Blair: your Middle East policy is doomed, say diplomats, *The Independent*, 27 April, p1.

84. Barder, Sir Brian *et al.* (2004) A letter to Blair: your Middle East policy is doomed, say diplomats, *The Independent*, 27 April, p5.

85. Buncombe, Andrew (2004) Former diplomats say Bush is a failure, *The Independent*, 16 June, p24.

86. BBC (2004) Howard dismissed critics of war, *BBC News Online*, 9 August.

87. Whitaker, R. (2005) This UK diplomat says Britain is part of a worldwide torture plot. Is he telling the truth?, *The Independent on Sunday*, 20 February, p20.

88. Morris, Nigel (2001) Allies demand new tactics to win propaganda war, *The Independent*, 1 November, p1.

89. *The Independent* (2004) The Butler Report (Insert), 15 July, p1.

90. McSmith, Andy, Buncombe, A. & Whitaker, R. (2004) It comes down to this: what did Blair know?, *The Independent on Sunday*, 8 February, p8.

91. Bull, John (2004) Letters, *The Independent on Sunday*, 14 March, p28.
92. Carr, Simon (2005) Richard and Judy bring out the Hugh Grant in chat-show Tony, *The Independent*, 11 February, p25.
93. 10 Downing Street (2002) *Iraq's weapons of mass destruction. The assessment of the British Government* – http://www.number-10.gov.uk/output/page271.asp
94. Reported on the BBC *Today* programme, Radio 4, 16 January 2004.
95. BBC (2004) Blair says WMD 'may never be found', *BBC News Online*, 6 July.
96. Cornwell, Rupert (2004) Bush ignored threat from al-Qa'ida prior to 11 September, *The Independent*, 22 March, p13.
97. Anonymous (2004) *Imperial hubris*. Brassey's Inc: New York.
98. Hodgson, Godfrey (2004) The sect that captured the United States, *The Independent*, 14 August, p19.
99. Rai, Milan (2004) *Regime unchanged*. Pluto Press: London, pp185–6.
100. Buncombe, Andrew (2004) White House braced for latest assault by hardback, *The Independent*, 29 April, p26.
101. BBC (2004) Moore embarrasses new CIA chief, *BBC News Online*, 13 August.
102. BBC (2004) CIA slammed for Iraq intelligence, *BBC News Online*, 9 July.
103. Buncombe, Andrew (2004) 'A global intelligence failure': report damns pretext for war, *The Independent*, 10 July, pp4–5.
104. *The Independent on Sunday* (2004) Quotes of the week, 11 July, p26.
105. Buncombe, Andrew (2004) Rice to testify in public as White House backs down, *The Independent*, 31 March, p25.
106. Buncombe, Andrew (2004) Bin laden memo puts Bush on back foot, *The Independent*, 12 April, p18.
107. Buncombe, Andrew (2004) 'I saw papers that show US knew al-Qa-ida would attack city with aeroplanes', *The Independent*, 2 April, p1.
108. BBC (2004) 9/11 inquiry blames government 'failures', *BBC News Online*, 22 July.
109. 9/11 Commission (2004) *The 9/11 Commission*. National Commission on Terrorist Attacks upon the US: Washington, pp14,23.
110. *New Scientist* (2004) Truth and consequences, 7 February, p5.
111. Fisk, Robert (2005) How Arabic text of WMD dossier was massaged by Downing St, *The Independent on Sunday*, 24 April, p21.
112. 10 Downing Street (2002) *Iraq's weapons of mass destruction. The assessment of the British Government* – http://www.number-10.gov.uk/output/ page271.asp
113. Sengupta, Kim (2003) Spy chief undermines key plank of case for war, *The Independent*, 27 August, p1.
114. Fazackerly, Anna (2004) Kelly's last paper: WMD threat real, *Times Higher Education Supplement*, 23 January, p1.
115. Hutton Report (2004) Summary of conclusions – http://news.bbc.co.uk/1/ shared/spl/hi/uk/03/hutton_inquiry/hutton_report/html/chapter12.stm
116. Brown, C. (2005) WMD expert reopens row about 'sexed-up' dossier, *The Independent*, 16 February, p2.
117. Scrivener, Anthony (2004) Hutton's demand for hard proof is a stroke of luck for Blair, *The Independent*, 29 January, p35.
118. *The Independent* (2004) Whitewash?, 29 January, p1.
119. Hencke, David & White, Michael (2004) Top BBC resignations astonished Hutton, *The Guardian*, 4 March, p1.

120. Morris, Nigel (2004) Blair admits he did not know 45-minute claim referred to battlefield weapons, *The Independent*, 5 February, p6.
121. BBC (2004) Hoon faces grilling on Iraq war, *BBC News Online*, 5 February.
122. Brown, C. (2005) Blair finally admits leaking Kelly's name, *The Independent*, 22 April, p5.
123. *The Economist* (2003) In the dock (Leader), 30 August, p9.
124. Jackson, Glenda (2004) Letter to the editor, *The Independent on Sunday*, 15 February, p27.
125. BBC (2004) WMD committee to press on, *BBC News online*, 2 March.
126. Grice, Andrew (2004) Now Blair cites regime change as a basis for war, *The Independent*, 15 July, p5.
127. BBC (2004) Analysis: devil in the detail, *BBC News Online*, 14 July.
128. Sengupta, Kim & Morris, Nigel (2004) Blair: the attacks mount up, *The Independent*, 19 July, p1.
129. Brown, Colin (2004) Lord Butler lambasts Blair over 'bad government', *The Independent*, 10 December, p2.
130. Brown, Colin & Grice, Andrew (2004) No respite for Blair as MPs reopen intelligence inquiry, *The Independent*, 22 July, p4.
131. Brown, Colin (2004) No 10 admits: Hutton was hoodwinked, *The Independent*, 17 July, p1.
132. BBC (2004) Australia's Iraq war case damned, *BBC News Online*, 23 July.
133. Chandler, G. (2004) Letter to the editor, *The Independent*, 24 July, p37.
134. Russell, Ben (2004) Butler renews attack on weapons dossier, *The Independent*, 8 September, p7.
135. Wright, Patrick (2004) The PM thinks the debate is over: he is wrong, *The Independent*, 15 July, p21.
136. *The Economist* (2003) Got him, but what now, 20 December, p54.
137. Baldry, Tony (2003) Iraq needs a special court for prosecution of war crimes (letter), *The Independent*, 17 April, p21. (The author is an English MP.)
138. Dejevsky, Mary (2003) Straw shrugs off concerns about death penalty, *The Independent*, 18 December, p15.
139. Statute – http://www.cpa-iraq.org/audio/20031210_Dec10_Special_Tribunal.htm
140. Statute of the Yugoslavia Tribunal – http://www.un.org/icty/basic/statut/stat2000.htm#1
141. Sierra Leone Special Court – http://www.specialcourt.org/documents/Statute.html
142. *The Independent* (2003) US leaders named in war crimes charge, 19 March, p19.
143. Fisk, Robert (2004) Revealed: the female victims of Saddam's secret police, *The Independent*, 23 January, p30.
144. BBC (2004) Wedding video clouds US denials, *BBC News Online*, 24 May.
145. Sengupta, Kim (2004) This is Hana Matrud … , *The Independent*, 11 May, p1.
146. Fisk, Robert (2004) 'Can't Blair see that this country is about to explode? Can't Bush?', *The Independent on Sunday*, 1 August, p11.
147. Woolf, Marie (2004) Lawyer who quit over war questions immunity deal, *The Independent*, 5 July, p6.
148. Smith, Helena (2003) Greeks accuse Blair of war crimes in Iraq, *The Guardian*, 29 July, p11.

149. Carrell, Severin (2003) Blair waged war illegally, says panel of lawyers, *The Independent on Sunday*, 2 November, p2.
150. Carrell, Severin (2004) Blair faces new 'war crimes' accusation, *The Independent on Sunday*, 18 January, p6.
151. Verkaik, Robert (2004) Court studies Blair 'war crimes' claim, *The Independent*, 21 January, p8.
152. Chalmers, Robert (2004) Trials and tribulations, *The Independent on Sunday* (*Magazine*), 9 May, pp9–12.
153. Price, Adam (2004) A case to answer – http://image.guardian.co.uk/ sys-files/Politics/documents/2004/08/26/impeach.pdf
154. Paterson, Tony (2004) Rumsfeld sued for war crimes over Abu Ghraib, *The Independent*, 1 December, p27.
155. Judd, Terri & Carrell, Severin (2004) On trial, *The Independent*, 1 March, p10.
156. Carrell, Severin (2004) UK troops in Iraq face new court threat, *The Independent on Sunday*, 28 November, p2.
157. Verkaik, Robert & Morris, Nigel (2004) Judges back inquiry Blair did not want, *The Independent*, 15 December, p4.
158. Verkaik, Robert (2004) MoD faces hefty compensation claims after Kosovo ruling, *The Independent*. 8 April, p6.
159. Berkeley, Bill (2001) *The graves are not yet full: race, tribe and power in the heart of Africa*. Basic Books: New York, p263.
160. BBC (2004) Analysis: President's private testimony, *BBC News Online*, 29 April.
161. BBC (2005) Global poll slams Bush leadership, *BBC News Online*, 19 January.
162. *The Observer* (2004) The credibility gap, 15 February, p18.
163. Morris, Nigel (2004) Opinion polls show backlash against Blair after 'whitewash' of report, *The Independent*, 2 February, p4.
164. Waugh, Paul (2004) After Hutton, the verdict: 51% say Blair should go, *The Independent*, 7 February, p1.
165. Grice, Andrew (2004) Why Short row may yet be good news for PM, *The Independent*, 28 February, p5.
166. BBC (2004) Public 'don't trust politicians', *BBC News Online*, 8 September.
167. Morris, N. (2005) Women warn Blair that he has lost their respect and votes, *The Independent*, 14 March, p8.
168. Russell, Ben (2005) PM has 'lost the authority to persuade voters', *The Independent*, 23 May, p4.
169. Campbell, Anne (2004) Blair 'failed to stand up to Bush over Iraq', *Metro*, 14 January, p16.
170. Waugh, Paul & Penketh, Anne (2004) US weapons expert: Iraqi threat distorted, *The Independent*, 30 January, p13.
171. BBC (2004) Interview, *Today* programme, BBC Radio 4, 28 July.
172. Ellsberg, Daniel (2004) Comment on 'Taking a stand', BBC Radio 4, 20 January.
173. Cornwell, Rupert (2004) Kennedy evokes the Vietnam 'quagmire' fears of Americans, *The Independent*, 7 April, pp5,29.
174. Ekklesia (2004) http://www.ekklesia.co.uk/content/news_syndication/article_ 2004_03_22_carter.shtml
175. BBC (2004) *Today* programme (interview), BBC Radio 4, 5 March.
176. Fisk, Robert (2004) Column, *The Independent*, 10 April, p8.

177. Kampfner, John (2004) The five deceptions of Tony Blair, *The Guardian*, 20 October, p27.

178. Jenkins, Simon (2004) Democracy in Iraq: the dodgiest deception of all, *The Times*, 3 March, p7.

179. Anderson, Bruce (2005) Once I defended Tony Blair against charges of lying. But I now realise that I was wrong, *The Independent*, 27 April, p29.

180. BBC (2003) Full text: 'Bin Laden tape', *BBC News Online*, 15 April.

181. Gledhill, Ruth & Charter, David (2004) Archbishop accuses Labour of damaging democracy, *The Times*, 21 April, pp1,2.

182. Ramonet, Ignacio (2004) Spanish lies, *Le Monde diplomatique*, April, p1.

183. *The Independent* (2004) Words that will haunt PM, 4 July, p13.

184. *The Independent* (2004) Words that will haunt PM, 4 July, p13.

185. CIA (2002) *Iraq's mass destruction weapons programs* – http://www.cia.gov/cia/reports/iraq_wmd/Iraq_Oct_2002.htm

186. 10 Downing Street (2002) *Iraq's weapons of mass destruction. The assessment of the British Government* – http://www.number-10.gov.uk/output/page271.asp

187. Kerry, J. (2004) Full text: John Kerry speech, *BBC News Online*, 30 July.

188. Cook, Robin (2004) Reporting for duty – and now he can rescue America, *The Independent*, 31 July, p1.

189. Grice, Andrew (2004) Howard accuses PM of lying about Iraqi weapons, *The Independent*, 30 September, pp4,5.

190. Tzu, Sun (1981) *The art of war.* Hodder & Stoughton: London.

191. 10 Downing Street (2002) *Prime Minister's Iraq Statement to Parliament 24 September 2002* – www.number-10.gov.uk/output/Page1727.asp

192. Baldwin, Tom (2004) Bloodshot but unbowed, Hoon admits one regret, *The Times*, 7 February, p16.

193. 10 Downing Street (2002) *Iraq's weapons of mass destruction. The assessment of the British Government*, introduction – http://www.number-10.gov.uk/output/page271.asp

194. Richards, Steve (2005) Reinvigorated, Blair sets out his stall for historic third term, *The Independent*, 21 April, p2.

195. BBC (2004) W Africa war crimes court to open, *BBC News Online*, 10 March.

196. Penketh, Anne (2004) West's backing of Putin policies leads to terrorism, *The Independent*, 7 September, p7.

197. Whiteley, P. (2005) Commands don't work. Blair needs legitimacy, *The Independent*, 23 May, p4.

198. Prins, Gwyn (2002) The man is a tyrant whose time has come – This war must be fought, *The Independent*, 29 September, p15.

199. Hobsbawm, Eric (2003) United States: wider still and wider, *Le Monde diplomatique*, June, pp1,2.

200. Chomsky, Noam (2003) *Hegemony or survival: America's quest for global dominance.* Penguin: London, p22.

201. Roth, Ken (2004) *War in Iraq: not a humanitarian intervention, World Report 2004* – http://hrw.org/wr2k4/3.htm

202. Said, Yahai (2004) Thriving right under Saddam's nose, *Times Higher Education Supplement*, 6 August, p16.

203. BBC (2005) Key quotes: the President's speech, *BBC News Online*, 20 January.

204. Penketh, Anne (2002) Fudge expected as Bush and Blair seek international backing for war, *The Independent*, 13 September, p5.

205. Thring, James B. (2004) Illegal attack, *The Independent on Sunday* (Letters), 11 January, p26. (The author is the president of Legal Action Against War.)
206. US Department of State – http://usinfo.state.gov/topical/pol/terror/02110803.htm
207. Carrell, Severin (2003) Blair waged war illegally, says panel of lawyers, *The Independent on Sunday*, 2 November, p2.
208. Tickell, Crispin (2004) *The UN and the future of global governance*, Preparing for Peace lecture – www.preparingforpeace.org/tickell.htm
209. Mansfield, Michael (2004) Lord Hutton got it wrong, *The Independent on Sunday*, 1 February, p27.
210 Waugh, Paul (2004) I quit because the war against Iraq was illegal … , *The Independent*, 28 February, p7.
211. Waugh, Paul (2004) Attorney General conceded doubts over legality of war, *The Independent*, 4 March, p4.
212. Brown, Colin (2004) Blair has departed from the rule of law, says former advisor, *The Independent*, 9 November, p5.
213. BBC (2004) Transcript of Clare Short interview, *BBC News Online*, 26 February.
214. Penketh, Anne (2004) Blix: Iraq war was illegal, *The Independent*, 5 March, p1.
215. BBC (2004) Iraq war illegal, says Annan, *BBC News Online*, 16 September.
216. Strawson, John (2005) Letter: Why a sordid war in Iraq may still have been legal, *The Independent*, 29 March, p32. Prins, G. (2005) Lord Castlereagh's return, *International Affairs*, 81(2), pp1–14.
217. Woolf, M. (2005) Blair broke code to keep war advice from Cabinet, *The Independent*, 9 March, p1, 8.
218. Woolf, M. (2005) MPs urge Bar Council to investigate advice on war, *The Independent*, 12 March, p2.
219. Woolf, M. (2005) Goldsmith 'failed duty to MPs' by withholding advice on war, *The Independent*, 26 March, p2.
220. Brown, C. (2005) The smoking gun?, *The Independent*, 24 March, p1.
221. Anderson, B. (2005) It is now beyond doubt that Tony Blair lied to the country and to the Butler Inquiry, *The Independent*, 2 May, p23.
222. Bunting, Chris (2005) Attorney General 'distanced himself from war advice', *The Independent*, 14 February, p6.
223. 10 Downing Street (2005) *Secret – Iraq: resolution 1441* – http://www.number-10.gov.uk/files/pdf/Iraq%20Resolution%201441.pdf (downloaded 28 April 2005).
224. Whitaker, R. & Elliott, F. (2005) The damning new documents that told Blair war was illegal, *The Independent on Sunday*, 1 May, p1.
225. Whitaker, R. (2005) The leaked Foreign Office paper that proves Blair saw caveats a year before the war, *The Independent on Sunday*, 1 May, p24.
226. Woolf, M. (2005) Regime change is no basis for war, *The Independent*, 29 April, p8.
227. *The Independent on Sunday* (2005) From eve of war to the release of Goldsmith's advice, 1 May, p13.
228. Heller, R. (2005) Letter, *The Independent*, 26 March, p40.
229. Meacher, Michael (2003) Plan now for a world without oil, *The Financial Times*, 5 January, p11.

230. Ward, Ibrahim (2004) Iraq: a licence to loot the land, *Le Monde diplomatique*, May, pp1,2.
231. Gumbel, Andrew (2004) How the war machine is driving the US economy, *The Independent*, 6 January, p17.
232. *Patent industrial design, undisclosed information, integrated circuits and plant variety law*, CPA Order No 81, 26 April 2004.
233. Popham, Peter (2004) Blair flies to Rome to soothe Berlusconi, *The Independent*, 5 March, p21.
234. Sterne, L. (1996) *Tristram Shandy*, Wordsworth Editions: London, p105.
235. Harris, Jack (2004) Planet primed for hair-trigger alert, *Times Higher Education Supplement*, 15 October, p24.
236. McNamara, R.S. (1995) *In retrospect: the tragedy and lessons of Vietnam*. Times Books: London.
237. Walker, Brian (2005) The anatomy of war: a study guide. Society of Friends Preparing for Peace project. Westmorland General Meeting: Kendal.
238. Davies, Lynn (2004) *Education and conflict: complexity and chaos*. Routledge/Falmer: London.
239. Beck, Ulrich (1992) *Risk society: towards a new modernity*. Sage: London.
240. Williams, C. (2002) 'New security' risks and public educating: the significance of recent evolutionary brain science, *Journal of Risk Research*, 5(3), pp225–48.
241. George, Alan *et al.* (2004) Revealed: the meeting that could have changed the history of Iraq, *The Independent on Sunday*, 17 October, pp10,11.
242. Libet, Benjamin (1985) Unconscious cerebral initiative and the role of conscious will in voluntary action, *Behavioural and Brain Sciences*, 8(4), pp529–66.
243. Ree, J. (2005) *Blink: the power of thinking without thinking*. Allen Lane: London.
244. George, Alan *et al.* (2004) Revealed: the meeting that could have changed the history of Iraq, *The Independent on Sunday*, 17 October, pp10,11.
245. Morris, Nigel (2005) Iraq war 'will haunt Blair's legacy like Suez', *The Independent*, 2 May, p6.
246. Elliott (2004) Blair told Bush he 'would not budge' in support for war, *The Independent on Sunday*, 19 September, p12.
247. Webster, Chris (2004) Letter: Fear and hopes that drove Blair to war, *The Independent*, 2 October, p42.
248. *Daily News* (2003) Right as reign Blair declares – http://www.nydailynews.com/news/story/101824p-92178c.html
249. George, Alan *et al.* (2004) Revealed: the meeting that could have changed the history of Iraq, *The Independent on Sunday*, 17 October, pp10,11.
250. Bush, George (2004) The driving force behind America's foreign policy, *The Independent*, 26 February, p35.
251. Kaplan, E. (2004) *With God on their side*. The New Press: New York, p9.
252. BBC (2004) Mugabe slams 'political God Bush', *BBC News Online*, 23 September.
253. Buncombe, Andrew (2004) 'A global intelligence failure': report damns pretext for war, *The Independent*, 10 July, pp4–5.
254. Williams, Christopher (2003) Global leadership, education and human survival, in P. Seidel (ed.), *World Futures*, 59(3–4), pp301–13.

255. BBC (2004) Blix details his 'mission impossible', *BBC News Online*, 9 March.
256. Peta, Basildon (2004) Mandela marks 10-year anniversary with speech criticising Britain and US, *The Independent*, 11 May, p25.
257. Park, R. (2000) *Voodoo science: the road from foolishness to fraud.* Oxford University Press: Oxford.
258. Phillips, Lawrence (2004) There's a high probability we'll end up certain, *The Independent*, 7 February, p43.
259. Davies, Philip (2004) 'Cherrypicking' a fight with Saddam, *Times Higher Education Supplement*, 20 February, p20.
260. Johnson, Dominic (2005) *Overconfidence and war: the havoc and glory of positive illusions.* Harvard University Press: Cambridge (Mass.).
261. Gray, John (2005) Mimic, missionary and a master of spin, *Times Higher Education Supplement*, 8 April, p18.
262. BBC (2005) *Newsnight*, 24 March.
263. Belsky, Gary & Gilovich, Thomas (2000) *Why smart people make big money mistakes – and how to correct them: lessons from the new science of behavioural economics.* Fireside Books: New York.
264. Smith, P.M. (1996) Leadership, in A.S.R. Manstead & M. Hewstone (eds), *Encyclopaedia of social psychology*, Blackwell: Oxford, p358.
265. King, John (2002) Bush calls Saddam 'the guy who tried to kill my dad', CNN.com, 27 September.
266. BBC (2004) *BBC World Service News*, 13 April.
267. Johnson, Chalmers (2001) Terrorism: a crisis in U.S. foreign policy, *The Japan Times*, 27 December, p19.
268. Fisk, Robert (2003) We are paying the price of an infantile attempt to reshape the Middle East, *The Independent*, 21 November, p37.
269. Straw, Jack (2003) Straw denies Turkey is about Iraq, *The Independent*, 22 November, p1.
270. Sengupta, Kim (2004) Occupation made world less safe, pro-war institute says, *The Independent*, 26 May, p5.
271. *New Scientist* (2004) The attacks Bush forgot, 19 June, p5.
272. BBC (2004) Full text: 'Al-Qaeda Madrid claim', *BBC News Online*, 14 March.
273. BBC (2004) Full text: 'Bin Laden tape', *BBC News Online*, 15 April.
274. BBC (2004) Spain 'to withdraw Iraq troops', *BBC News Online*, 15 March.
275. BBC (2004) Excerpts: Bin Laden video, *BBC News*, 5 November.
276. Malik, Shiv (2005) 'It's our beef because it's our people. I've never been to Iraq but it makes me angry', *The Independent on Sunday*, 24 July, p18.
277. Verkaik, Robert (2004) Ruling puts brake on attempts to weaken Human Rights Acts, *The Independent*, 17 December, p2.
278. Grey, John (2002) *Al Qaeda and what it means to be modern.* New Press: London.
279. Roy, Oliver (2004) Al-Qaida brand name ready for franchise, *Le Monde diplomatique*, September, pp1–2.
280. Ruthven, Malise (1997) *Islam: a very short introduction.* Oxford University Press: Oxford, pp8–9.
281. BBC (2004) Bin Laden 'topped Clinton agenda', *BBC News Online*, 23 March.
282. Sparrow, Andrew (2004) Cook attacks 'American warriors', *Daily Telegraph*, 9 April, p15.
283. Roy, Oliver (2004) Al-Qaida brand name ready for franchise, *Le Monde diplomatique*, September, pp1–2.

284. Williams, C. & Lee, Y.-J (2005) 'The minds of leaders: de-linking war from violence', in B. Walker (ed.), *Preparing for peace – by asking the experts to analyse war*. Westmorland General Meeting: Kendal – http://www. preparingforpeace.org/williamsjoo.htm
285. CIS (2004) Instruments of mass effect, in *A new security paradigm, The Cambridge Security Seminar, 30–1 July 2003*, The Cambridge Programme for Security and International Society: Cambridge University, p49.

3 Social Impetus: Deceit, Evolution and ICT

1. Greenfield, S. (1997) *The human brain: a guided tour*. Phoenix: London.
2. Williams, C. (2002) 'New security' risks and public educating: the significance of recent evolutionary brain science, *Journal of Risk Research*, 5(3), pp225–48.
3. Wilson, E.O. (1998) *Consilience: the unity of knowledge*. Little, Brown: London, p188.
4. Byrne, D. & Whiten, A. (1988) *Machiavellian intelligence: social expertise and the evolution of intelligence in monkeys, apes and humans*. Clarendon Press: Oxford.
5. Keating, C.F. & Heltman, K.R. (1994) Dominance and deception in children and adults: are leaders the best misleaders? *Personality and social psychology bulletin*, 20, pp312–21.
6. Lee, Yun-Joo (2005) Perceptions of leadership and development in South Korea and Egypt, PhD thesis in progress, School of Oriental and African Studies, University of London.
7. Nye, J.S. (2004) *Power in the global information age*. Routledge: London.
8. Wooley, Benjamin (2004) *The herbalist: Nicholas Culpeper and the fight for freedom*. HarperCollins: London.
9. Curzon, L.B. (1998) *Dictionary of law*. Pitman: London.
10. Curzon, L.B. (1998) *Dictionary of law*. Pitman: London.
11. Green, Stuart (2004) Cheating, *Law and Philosophy*, 23, pp137–85,174.
12. BBC (2004) Interview on the *Today* programme, BBC Radio 4, 12 March.
13. Rawls, John (1999) *The law of peoples*. Harvard University Press: Cambridge, Mass., p100.
14. Cockburn, Patrick (2004) Apocalypse now?, *The Independent on Sunday*, 11 April, p10.
15. Cosmides, L. & Tooby, J. (1992) Cognitive adaptations for social exchange, in J.H. Barkow, L. Cosmides & J. Tooby (eds), *The adapted mind: evolutionary psychology and the generation of culture*. Oxford University Press: New York.
16. Wilson, Edward O. (2002) *The future of life*. Little, Brown: London.
17. Wilson, Edward O. (2002) *The future of life*. Little, Brown: London.
18. Fletcher, T. (1997) Risk and risk assessment: the importance of getting everyone involved, *Environment and Health*, 2, pp5–6.
19. Laurance, J. (1998) Best smoking ads are those that knock industry, *The Independent*, 11 March, p7.
20. Williams, C. (2002) 'New security' risks and public educating: the significance of recent evolutionary brain science, *Journal of Risk Research*, 5(3), pp225–48.

21. Fukuyama, Francis (1995) *The social virtues and the creation of prosperity.* Penguin: London.
22. Giddens, Anthony (1990) *The consequences of modernity.* Polity Press: Cambridge.
23. Mackie, J.L. (1980) *The cement of the universe: a study of causation.* Oxford University Press: Oxford.
24. Hajnal, Peter. I. (2002) *Civil society in the information age.* Ashgate: Aldershot.
25. McMillan, John (2004) How democracy was subverted in Peru, *Stanford Graduate School of Business Research News* – http://www.gsb.stanford.edu/news/research/polecon_peru.shtml
26. Parry, Lloyd (2001) THE TXT MSG REVOLUTION, *The Independent* (*Review*), 23 January, pp1,7.
27. Ramonet, Ignacio (2004) Spanish lies, *Le Monde diplomatique*, April, p1.
28. Weiner, N. (1949) *Cybernetics: or control and communication in man and machine.* MIT Press: Cambridge, Mass.
29. Foucault, Michel (trans. Sheridan, A.) (1995) *Discipline and punish: the birth of prison.* Vintage Books: New York.
30. Taylor, Jane (2000) Citizens century, *Positive News* (UK), 26, p1.
31. *Independent Media Centre* – www.idymedia.org
32. McLuhan, Marshall (1994) *Understanding media: the extensions of man.* MIT Press: Cambridge, Mass., pp302–3.
33. *Digital Governance* – www.cddc.vt.edu/digitalgov/gov-menu.html
34. Lee, Yun-Joo (2003) Realities and perceptions of leadership and development in South Korea and Egypt, unpublished PhD thesis, School of Oriental and African Studies, University of London.
35. Bem, D.J. (1972) Self-perception theory, in L. Berkowitz (ed.), *Advances in experimental social psychology*, Vol. 6. Academic Press: New York, p5.
36. Reber, Arthur S. (1995) *Dictionary of psychology.* Penguin: London, p703.
37. Weiner, N. (1949) *Cybernetics: or control and communication in man and machine.* MIT Press: Cambridge, Mass.
38. Lyman, P. & Varian, H.R. (2003) How much information? – http://www.sims.berkeley.edu/research/projects/how-much-info-2003/
39. Surowiecki, James (2004) *The wisdom of crowds: why the many are smarter than the few.* Little, Brown: New York.
40. Fletcher, W. (2004) Delusions of the masses, *Times Higher Education Supplement*, 23 July, p30.
41. Parry, Geraint (1969) *Political elites.* George Allen & Unwin: London, p37.
42. Bloom, Howard (2000) *Global brain: the evolution of mass mind from the big bang to the 21st century.* John Wiley: New York.
43. Jolly, A. (1999) *Lucy's legacy: sex and intelligence in human evolution.* Harvard University Press: Cambridge, Mass.
44. Leslie, M. (2001) Tales of the sea, *New Scientist*, 2275, pp32–5.

4 Personalizing Protest: Global Civil Society

1. Hain, Peter (2001) *The end of foreign policy?* Fabian Society: London, p60.
2. O'Keefe, Ken (2004) Bush the deserter and traitor, private email circulation uksociety@hotmail.com, 13 February.

3. Lindisfarne, Nancy (2004) The paradigms of people power, *Times Higher Education Supplement*, 8 October, p23.
4. Keane, J. (1988) *Civil society and the state*. Polity: Cambridge.
5. Edwards, Michael (2004) *Civil society*. Polity: Cambridge.
6. Kaldor, M. (2003) *Global civil society*. Polity: Cambridge.
7. Kaldor, M. (2004) *Global civil society in an uncertain world*, 2004/5 yearbook. Sage: London.
8. Suri, Jeremi (2003) *Power and protest*. Harvard University Press: Cambridge, Mass., pp261–2,88.
9. Rittberger, Volker & Bruhl, Tanja (1999) Global governance: civil society and the UN, *Work in Progress: A Review of Research Activities of the United Nations University*, 15(3), p7.
10. Cohen, R. & Rai, R. (2000) *Global social movements*. Athlone Press: London.
11. Edwards, M. & Gaventa, J. (2001) *Global citizen action*. Earthscan: London.
12. Judicial Watch (2003) www.revue-politique.com
13. www.nobribes.org
14. HRW (2001) *The Pinochet precedent: how victims can pursue human rights criminals abroad*. Human Rights Watch: New York.
15. Roulet, Florencia (1999) *Human rights and indigenous peoples*. IWGIA: Copenhagen.
16. Giffard, Camille (2001) *The torture reporting handbook*. The Human Rights Centre, University of Essex – www.essex.ac.uk/torturehandbook
17. Lindelow, Magnus (2002) *Holding governments to account: public expenditure analysis for advocacy*. Save the Children: London.
18. AFP (2002) Seoul firms to chime in on candidates, *International Herald Tribune*, 5 March, p13.
19. Yuen, Eddie *et al.* (eds.) (2002) *The battle of Seattle: the new challenge to capitalist globalization*. Soft Skull Press: New York.
20. Graham, K. & Williams, C. (eds) (2002) *Freedom is a universal value: an interview with Mike Moore*. UN University Leadership Academy (Leaders Interviews Series No. 2): Amman, p24.
21. Moore, Mike (1998) *A brief history of the future: citizenship of the millennium*. Shoal Bay Press: Christchurch, p83.
22. Taylor, Jane (2000) Citizens century, *Positive News* (UK), 26, p1.
23. BBC (2005) India and Pakistan build trade, *BBC News Online*, 17 April.
24. Foley, Stephen (2003) How the cat lost the cream at Britain's biggest drugs firm, *The Independent*, 20 May, p4.
25. Dillon, Jo (2003) TUC threatens global drive against corporate 'fat cats', *The Independent on Sunday*, 25 May, p6.
26. Macleod, C. & Macleod, L. (2000) The desperate search for justice by Chinese peasants is Peking's worst nightmare, *The Independent on Sunday*, 17 September, p25.
27. Smith, Alex-Duval (2000) How Milosevic's defeat is inspiring the repressed, *The Independent*, 26 October, p15.
28. Parry, R.L. (2000) Estrada under pressure to resign, *The Independent*, 19 October, p19.
29. Hell, Irene (2004) He makes markets move. Now can he bring down Bush? *The Independent on Sunday* (*Business*), 1 February, p7.
30. Fine, P. (2001) Inquiry criticises police action at student protest, *Times Higher Education Supplement*, 10 August, p48.

31. Edwards, Michael & Gaventa, John (2001) *Global citizen action*. Earthscan: London.
32. Fahamu (2000) *Writing for change*. International Development Research Centre: Ottawa.
33. FoE (1999) The world trade system: an activists guide (Policy and Research Unit) – www.foe.co.uk/resource/reports/qatar_activists_guide.pdf
34. ORG (2000) *Everyone's guide to achieving change: a step-by-step approach to dialogue with decision-makers*. Oxford Research Group: Oxford (51 Plantation Road, Oxford OX2 6JE, UK).
35. Centre for Public Integrity – www.publicintegrity.org
36. Williams, P. & Cigar, N. (2001) *War crimes and individual responsibility: a prima facie case for the indictment of Slobodan Milosevic*, The Balkan Institute – www.nesl.edu/centre/balkan1.htm
37. Public Concern at Work: 42 Kingsway, London, WC2B 6EN UK.
38. Woolf, M. (2000) New whistleblower hotline to stop NHS prescription fraud, *The Independent*, 14 December, p10.
39. National Whistleblower Centre – www.whistleblowers.org/inex.html
40. Williams, Christopher (1995) *Invisible victims: crime and abuse against people with learning disabilities*. Jessica Kingsley Publishers: London, p66.
41. Kohn, M. (2001) *Concepts and procedures in whistleblower law*. Quoran Books: Westport, Conn.; Lewis, David (2000) *Whistleblowing at work*. Athlone Press: London; Miceli, M.P. & Near, J.P. (1992) *Blowing the whistle: the organizational and legal implications for companies and employees*. Lexington Books: New York.
42. VCAP, Article 4.5.
43. UK Civil Service Code, Article 11.
44. Private correspondence to the author from Mr F. Jaeger, Office of the Civil Service Commissioners (UK), 6 June 2000.
45. Harding, Luke (2003) Website pays price for Indian bribery exposé, *The Guardian*, 6 January, p11.
46. Commission for Racial Equality (2001) *Election Compact* 2001 – see: http://www.guardian.co.uk/racism/Story/0,2763,477539,00.html#article_continue
47. Mutsuko, M. (2000) A gift from Korea, *Asiaweek.com* – www.asiaweek.com/asiaweek/foc/2000/06/09/
48. Parry, Lloyd (2001) THE TXT MSG REVOLUTION, *The Independent* (Review), 23 January, pp1,7.
49. Dillon, J. (2000) MPs plot against sleaze watchdog, *The Independent on Sunday*, 10 December, p13.
50. Kennedy, F. (2000) Pope confesses 2,000 years of church sins (but makes no mention of the Inquisition), *The Independent*, 13 March, p3.
51. McGirk, Jan (2000) Guatemalan leader admits civil war atrocities, *The Independent*, 11 August, p12.
52. BBC (2001) Megawati says sorry for rights abuses, BBC *News Online*, 16 August.
53. Comment made by Lord Douglas Hurd at the Ethics and Foreign Policy conference, 22 March 2001, London School of Economics.
54. Lazare, Aaron (2004) *On apology*. Oxford University Press: Oxford.
55. Lelio Basso International Foundation for the Rights and Liberation of Peoples, via della Dogma Vecchia 5, 00186 Rome, Italy.

56. Connolly, K. (2000) Europe's gypsies lobby for nation status, *The Guardian*, 31 July, p7; www.romnews.com

57. Dinham, B. (1998) Introduction to the Charter of Rights Against Industrial Hazards: for communities, workers and the protection of the environment. In Williams, C. (1998) *Environmental victims: new risks, new injustice.* Earthscan: London, pp151,181.

58. Nayar, Jayan (2000) Doing law differently, *New Internationalist*, 330, pp20–1.

59. *The Independent* (2004) Budapest strips 'criminal' Stalin of city honour, 1 May, p28.

60. Donegan, Lawrence (2004) Bringing it all back home, *The Observer (Review)*, 8 February, pp1,2.

61. Edwards, Michael (2000) Civil society and global governance, in Ramesh Thakur & Edward Newman (eds), *New millennium, new perspectives: the United Nations, security and governance.* UN University Press: Tokyo, pp205–19.

62. BBC (2001) WTO chief blasts 'dot.com types', *BBC News Online*, 6 July.

63. Wintour, P. (2000) Down to the last drop (and other articles), *The Guardian*, 13 September, p1.

64. Amnesty (2001) China's execution frenzy, *Amnesty*, 109, p9.

65. BBC (2002) French fury at Le Pen intensifies, *BBC News Online*, 23 April.

66. MacLeod, Calum (2000) Justice minister held in Chinese corruption purge, *The Independent*, 1 December, p18.

67. Amnesty (2001) Worldwide appeal, *Amnesty*, September/October, p22.

68. Monbiot, G. (2002) A war against the peacemaker, *The Guardian*, 16 April, p15.

69. Pincus, W. & Lynch, C. (2002) U.S. probed record of UN arms inspector, *International Herald Tribune*, 16 April, p1.

70. BBC (2002) Climate scientist ousted, *BBC News Online*, 19 April.

71. Roehrig, Terence (2002) *The prosecution of former military leaders in newly democratic nations.* McFarland: London, pp196–8.

72. Rai, Milan (2003) *Regime unchanged.* Pluto Press: London, pp8,xix,128,190.

73. Unpublished presentation at the 'Advancing Global Citizenship' conference, Royal Society of Arts, London, 13 July 2004.

74. Crocker, David A. (1999) Reckoning with past wrongs: a normative framework, *Ethics & International Affairs*, pp43–64.

5   Prognoses: Changing Relationships

1. Howell, David (2002) Britain faces constitutional earthquake, *International Herald Tribune*, 15 January, p7.

2. Pilger, John (2004) Comment during an interview, BBC Radio 4 *Night Waves*, 9 October.

3. Fisk, Robert (2001) Why don't we try to collar all the war criminals?, *The Independent*, 25 August, p9.

4. Fisk, Robert (2001) We are the war criminals now, *The Independent (Review)*, 29 November, p5.

5. BBC (2003) Profile: Kim Jong-IL, *BBC News Online*, 31 July.

6. Osborn, Andrew (2004) Dictator orders ice palace to be built in central Asian desert, *The Independent on Sunday*, 15 August, p21.

7. Chomsky, Noam (2003) *Hegemony or survival: America's quest for global dominance*. Penguin: London, pp112,114.

8. Meo, Nick (2004) Afghan warlords poised to take up power, *The Independent*, 14 October, p30.

9. Berkeley, Bill (2001) *The graves are not yet full: race, tribe and power in the heart of Africa*. Basic Books: New York, p78.

10. Palaima, Tom (2001) The world did not change, *Times Higher Education Supplement*, 26 October, p13.

11. Kifner, John (2003) Ex-GI's confirm tales of Vietnam brutality, *International Herald Tribune*, 29 December, p1.

12. Trounson, Alan (2003) A crime against humanity, *New Scientist*, 22 November, p23.

13. Albala, Nuri (2003) International law: justice as a commodity, *Le Monde diplomatique*, 12 December, pp2,3.

14. Tickell, Crispin (2003) *The UN and the future of global governance*, Preparing for Peace project – www.preparingforpeace.org/tickell.htm

15. Gumbel, Andrew (2003) Bush gives American industry a green light to pollute, *The Independent*, 23 August, p16.

16. Cornwell, Rupert (2001) Employees sue CIA for 'abuse of power', *The Independent*, 4 December, p14.

17. Chomsky, Noam (2003) *Hegemony or survival: America's quest for global dominance*. Penguin: London.

18. Chelala, Cesar (2003) Shedding light on Kissinger's dark legacy, *The Japan Times*, 27 December, p16.

19. Hitchens, Christopher (2001) Why has he got away with it?, *The Guardian Weekend*, 24 February, p25.

20. Hitchens, Christopher (2001) *The trial of Henry Kissinger*. Verso: London, px.

21. Kissinger, H.A. (2001) The pitfalls of universal jurisdiction, *Foreign Affairs*, July/August, 80(4), p86.

22. Prospect (2001) Pinochet, Milosevic…Henry Kissinger?, *Prospect*, 66, pp16–20.

23. Hitchens, Christopher (2001) *The trial of Henry Kissinger*. Verso: London, ppx,68.

24. *The Independent* (2001) Judge seeks to quiz Kissinger, 6 July, p13.

25. McGirk, Jan (2001) Kissinger sued over CIA-backed kidnap, *The Independent*, 12 September, p16.

26. Reuters (2002) U.K. court rejects Kissinger warrant, *International Herald Tribune*, 23 April, p3.

27. Williamson, Murray (1999) *War in the air*. Cassell: London, p124.

28. Beevor, Anthony (2002) *Berlin: the downfall*. Viking Penguin: London.

29. Lichfield, John (2001) General 'does not regret' murdering prisoners, *The Independent*, 27 November, p13.

30. Cumings, Bruce (2004) Korea: forgotten nuclear threats, *Le Monde diplomatique*, December, pp6–7.

31. Chomsky, Noam (2003) *Hegemony or survival: America's quest for global dominance*. Penguin: London, p182.

32. Halliday, J. & Chang, J. (2005) *Mao: the forgotten story*. Jonathan Cape: London.

33. Rauch, Jonathan (2002) Firebombs over Tokyo, *The Atlantic Online* – www.theatlantic.com

34. *The Independent* (2004) The Island idyll and US occupation, 12 August, p26.
35. Kane, John (2001) *The politics of moral capital.* Oxford University Press: Oxford, p27.
36. Bass, B.M. & Steidlmeier, P. (1999) Ethics, character, and authentic transformational leadership behaviour, *Leadership Quarterly*, 10(2), pp181–217.
37. Confucius (ed. D.C. Lau) (1979) *The analects.* Penguin: London, Book XII, para. 17.
38. Lee, Yun-Joo (2003) Perceptions of leadership and development in South Korea and Egypt, unpublished PhD thesis, School of Oriental and African Studies, University of London.
39. Thucydides, *History of the Peloponnesian war*, Chapter 2.65, p8.
40. Wills, G. (1994) *Certain trumpets: the call of leaders.* Simon & Schuster: New York, p12.
41. Kane, John (2001) *The politics of moral capital.* Cambridge University Press: Cambridge.
42. Fisher, L. (1950) *The life of Mahatma Gandhi.* Harper & Brothers: New York, p10.
43. Waslekar, Sundeep (2000) *Dharma Rajya: path-breaking reforms for India's governance.* Konark Publishers: Delhi, p48.
44. Morgenthau, Hans J. (1963) *Politics among nations: the struggle for power and peace.* Alfred A. Knopf: New York, p248.
45. House of Lords (1999) Judgment – *Regina* v. *Bartle and the Commissioner of Police for the Metropolis and other Ex Parte Pinochet. Regina* v. *Evans and another and the Commissioner of Police for the Metropolis and others Ex Parte Pinochet (On appeal from a Divisional court of the Queen's Bench Division*, 24 March.
46. BBC (2002) S Korean president's second son arrested, *BBC News Online*, 21 June.
47. Smith, A.D. & Griffiths, K. (2003) Fat cat, *moi?*, *The Independent*, 19 August, p3.
48. Berkeley, Bill (2001) *The graves are not yet full: race, tribe, and power in the heart of Africa.* Basic Books: New York, p80.
49. BBC (2001) Mugabe: 'Excellent meeting' in Paris, *BBC News Online*, 7 March.
50. Brauman, Rony (2001) Unpublished paper at the 'Ethics and Foreign Policy' conference, LSE, London, 22 March.
51. *The Japan Times* (2000) Kid's Diet discusses range of issues, 4 August, p3.
52. *Institute of Business Ethics* (2001) www.ibe.org.uk (January).
53. Williams, C. (1998) *Environmental victims: new risks, new injustice.* Earthscan: London, pxviv.
54. Tumim, Stephen (2001) A passionate look at low self-esteem, *Times Higher Education Supplement*, 5 October, p27.
55. Thompson, Mark (2000) *Forging war: the media in Serbia, Croatia, Bosnia and Herzegovina.* University of Luton Press: Luton, pv.
56. Michels, R. (1915) *Political parties.* Free Press: Glencoe, p423.
57. Curzon, L.B. (1998) *Dictionary of law.* Pitman Publishing: London.
58. Williams, C. (1998) *Environmental victims: new risks, new injustice.* Earthscan: London, p8.
59. Williams, Christopher (2001) *Leaders of integrity: ethics and a code for global leadership.* UN University Leadership Academy: Amman, p118.
60. DfES (2004) *Making sense of citizenship: a CPD handbook.* Department for Education and Skills: London.

61. Reuters (2005) Woman charged with Blair powder hoax, 27 May.
62. Cornwell, Rupert (2004) Church reveals 4,400 priests were accused of child sex abuse, *The Independent*, 28 February, p39.
63. Bush, George (2004) The driving force behind America's foreign policy, *The Independent*, 26 February, p35.
64. Taylor, Laurie (2004) Ear for the death rattle of an empire, *Times Higher Education Supplement*, 16 April, pp14–15.
65. Sengupta, Kim (2004) US terror laws 'damage human rights', *The Independent*, 17 February, p6 (describing the IISS report *Human rights and counter-terrorism in America's Asia policy*).
66. Russell, Ben (2004) Support for Bush 'has harmed UK's reputation', *The Independent*, 14 April, p6.
67. BBC (2004) Blix details his 'mission impossible', *BBC News Online*, 9 March.
68. Kennedy, Charles (2004) Flawed judgement, double standards, *The Independent on Sunday*, 22 February, p23.
69. Buncombe, Andrew (2004) A global intelligence failure, *The Independent*, 10 July, p4.
70. Grimes, C. (2004) Universities in US hit by tighter visa demands, *Financial Times*, pp29,7.
71. Cornwell, Rupert (2004) Americans worry about their image in the world, *The Independent*, 9 September, p35.
72. WEF (2003) *Survey of Trust* – www.weforum.org
73. Ramonet, Ignatio (2004) China wakes up and alarms the world, *Le Monde diplomatique*, August 2004, p1.
74. BBC (2004) China's parliament: power to the people?, *BBC News Online*, 5 March.
75. BBC (2004) China's new middle class revolution, *BBC News Online*, 11 October.
76. Private conversation: Yun-Joo Lee, fellow, United Nations University International Leadership Academy, 2002.
77. TI (2004) *Corruption Perceptions Index, overview* – www.user.gwdg.de/~uwvw/corruption.cpi_olderindices_overview.html
78. Guardian Human Rights Index – http://www.guardian.co.uk/rightsindex/Story/0,2763,201762,00.html
79. *People's Daily* (2004) Full text of human rights record of the US in 2003 – http://english.peopledaily.com.cn/200403/01/eng20040301_136190.shtml
80. *People's Daily* (2004) Full text of human rights record of the US in 2003 – http://english.peopledaily.com.cn/200403/01/eng20040301_136190.shtml, p11.
81. *People's Daily* (2004) Full text of human rights record of the US in 2003 – http://english.peopledaily.com.cn/200403/01/eng20040301_136190.shtml, p13.
82. Williams. C. & Lee, Y.-J. (2002) *The minds of leaders: de-linking war from violence* (Preparing for Peace Lectures, Society of Friends) – http://www.preparingforpeace.org/williamsjoo.htm
83. Marden, Peter (2003) *The decline of politics: governance, globalisation and the public sphere*. Ashgate: Aldershot.
84. IDEA (2005) *Turnout over time: advances and retreat in electoral participation*, International Institute for Democracy and Electoral Assistance – www.idea.int

85. Mann, J. & Woolas, P. (1986) *Labour and youth: the missing generation*. Fabian Society: London.
86. Unpublished comment at 'How will history judge Tony Blair?' debate, National Portrait Gallery, 10 March 2005.
87. Howell, David (2002) Britain faces constitutional earthquake, *International Herald Tribune*, 15 January, p7.
88. Wolfensohn, James (2004) The missing ethical values in economic development, *The Independent*, 19 May, p29.
89. Parry, Geraint (1969) *Political elites*. George Allen & Unwin: London, p31.
90. Williams, Christopher (2002) New security risks and public educating: the significance of recent evolutionary brain science, *Journal of Risk Research*, 5(3), pp225–48.
91. Burnham, James (1942) *The managerial revolution*. Putnam: London.
92. Usborne, David (2004) Haiti's despot Aristide stirs up revolution, *The Independent*, 13 January, p33.
93. Lenczowski, George (ed.) (1975) *Political elites in the Middle East*, American Enterprise Institute: Washington, p5.
94. Welsh, William A. (1979) *Leaders and elites*. Holt, Rinehart & Winston: New York, p143.
95. Blum, W. (2001) *Rogue state: a guide to the world's only superpower*. Zed Books: London.
96. Grint, Keith (2000) *The arts of leadership*. Oxford University Press: Oxford, pp419–20.
97. Grint, Keith (2000) *The arts of leadership*. Oxford University Press: Oxford, p420.

6   Conclusion: The Accountability Webs

1. d'Oronzio, J. (2002) Practicing accountability in professional ethics, *Journal of Clinical Ethics*, 13(4), pp359–66.
2. ICC Statute, Article 7(k).
3. Williams, C. (2001) *Leaders of integrity: ethics and a code for global leadership*. UN University Leadership Academy: Amman, p77–78.
4. Alan, R. (2004) *Breaking the silence: the case that changed the face of human rights*. Georgetown University Press: Georgetown.
5. Gumbel, Andrew (2004) Prisoners sue Abu Ghraib security firms, *The Independent*, 12 June, p36.
6. Webb, Tim (2005) Litigation culture threatens future of drugs industry, MPs warned, *The Independent on Sunday*, 9 January, p17.
7. Lee, Y.-J. (2004) *Leadership and international understanding: linking Korea and the Arab Middle-East*. United Nations International Leadership Academy: Amman.
8. Delaney, M. (2005) China goes fishing for more undergraduates – in Egypt, *Times Higher Education Supplement*, 17 June, p10.

Index